The publisher and the University of California Press Foundation gratefully acknowledge the generous support of the Joan Palevsky Endowment Fund in Literature in Translation.

Sensitive Reading

Sensitive Reading

The Pleasures of South Asian Literature in Translation

———

Edited by

Yigal Bronner and Charles Hallisey

Translations by

David Shulman

UNIVERSITY OF CALIFORNIA PRESS

University of California Press
Oakland, California

© 2022 by The Regents of the University of California

Suggested citation: Bronner, Y. and Hallisey, C. *Sensitive Reading: The Pleasures of South Asian Literature in Translation*. Oakland: University of California Press, 2022. DOI: https://doi.org/10.1525/luminos.114

Library of Congress Cataloging-in-Publication Data

Names: Bronner, Yigal, 1966– editor. | Hallisey, Charles, 1953– editor. |
    Shulman, David Dean, 1949– translator, writer of added commentary.
Title: Sensitive reading : the pleasures of South Asian literature in translation /
    edited by Yigal Bronner and Charles Hallisey ; with translations
    by David Shulman.
Description: Oakland, California : University of California Press, [2021] |
    Includes bibliographical references and index.
Identifiers: LCCN 2021029647 (print) | LCCN 2021029648 (ebook) |
    ISBN 9780520384477 (paperback) | ISBN 9780520384484 (epub)
Subjects: LCSH: South Asian literature—Translations into English. |
    South Asian literature—History and criticism. | BISAC: LITERARY
    COLLECTIONS / Asian / Indic | LANGUAGE ARTS & DISCIPLINES /
    Translating & Interpreting
Classification: LCC PK85 .S46 2021 (print) | LCC PK85 (ebook) |
    DDC 891/.1—dc23
LC record available at https://lccn.loc.gov/2021029647
LC ebook record available at https://lccn.loc.gov/2021029648

31 30 29 28 27 26 25 24 23 22
10 9 8 7 6 5 4 3 2 1

CONTENTS

Introduction

Yigal Bronner and Charles Hallisey

ALLOW US TO RESTATE THE PROBLEM

So you find yourself with a translation in your hands. This one, for instance:

> The king stares, unblinking, at your portrait
> on the wall, drinking you in
> with eyes red from tears
> or maybe it's from the fire
> you've lit inside him.

The questions start. Who is this crying king? Who is the speaker? Who is the "you" being addressed? More questions follow, but of a different kind. Where does this come from? What is the text's name? In what language? Who wrote it? When? These are all good questions, and there are good answers to be had for them. But notice how your mind is off and running. Running away from the text.

What comes next in the translation may make you stop in your tracks:

> Allow me to restate this problem:
> 1) He's studying that painting of you
> 2) Unblinking
> 3) With deep attention and affection.
> 4) There are tears in his eyes.
> 5) Those tears are mine, says the eye. That's what happens
> if you don't blink.
> 6) No way, says Love. They're all mine.
> 7) This dispute remains
> unsolved.

Note that this second verse does what it says: it restates the first. It stays with it, closely, but it also adds something. It asks what it means to "stare, unblinking." What it means to have a fire lit "inside you." These, too, are good questions, but where are answers to be found for them? Actually, nowhere but here. Answers

1

present themselves when the act of looking and crying is redescribed as an unsolved dispute between the eye and Love. Did you see this coming?

We didn't.

This volume shares what we discovered after our initial surprise. It is all about the pleasures of reading and rereading translations with unblinking eyes.

It's common knowledge that we live in a boomtime for translations. There are publishers dedicated to making literatures of one culture available to readers from another; universities teach courses like "Japanese Literature in Translation" and "Introduction to World Literature"; there are literary prizes given to translators. Good translations are there, but less available is help in reading them. Ezra Pound published his *ABC of Reading* a century ago, but there is still no *ABC of Reading Translations*.

The situation is particularly dire for English translations of texts from South Asia: there is finally a growing body of such works, from masterpieces brought out by the Murty Classical Library of India to contemporary poetry and prose, but hardly any guidance on how to read them and especially how to enjoy them.

This volume is offered as a first step in that direction, although even this first step makes it clear that there are many good ways of reading translations. Let us turn again to the translation at hand, which, by the way, is from *Life of Naishadha*, a Sanskrit poem composed in the twelfth century by a celebrated poet, Shriharsha. As a whole, *Life of Naishadha* narrates a story that was already famous when it was written, the love story of Nala and Damayanti with its many twists and turns. But let's not be too quick to go away from the text again. Let's stay with Shriharsha and go to his next verse, which again revisits the scenario of the previous two. Nala is still gazing at a painting of her, Damayanti is told. We, however, also hear some suggestions about what we should expect of ourselves when we read a translation of a text like this:

> You, lady, live in his heart,
> but you're also somehow outside him,
> in fact you're his very life's breath
> moving through nose and mouth.
> His mind, too, being utterly absorbed
> in you, never budges from that wondrous
> painting, and this, too,
> is a wonder.

We know that when we are utterly absorbed in reading, something from the outside comes to life in our heart too. The object of such rapt attention is wondrous, but so is what happens to us.

We are among the first to admit that what happens to us when we read translations, however, is often less than wondrous. This may be more about us than about the translations themselves. We are suspicious, and we justify our suspicions with the old saw about what is lost in translation. We, in fact, worry about being deprived of the "authentic experience" of the original, instead receiving a "kiss through a veil," as the Hebrew poet Bialik once dubbed translation. Or it may be that our awareness of how much we don't know gets in the way. Then our good intention to learn more about another culture may overshadow the text to such an extent that we deny ourselves any of the usual pleasures of reading and prevent ourselves from imagining that it might have something to say to us.

Finally, we may worry about what the translator has added. Translators do add things, of course, just as much as they leave things out. What they add may be more valuable to us readers than we might assume, especially when what they add opens up the original text to us, sharing with us its pleasures and its possibilities.

Some might say that in the second verse of the poem quoted here, the opening line, "Allow me to restate this problem," is an addition. Those exact words are not in the original Sanskrit text, that's for sure. At the same time, the translation only makes explicit what is tacit in the original; namely, that the poet Shriharsha recasts in this second verse all the key players of the first one, using the very same lexical items but in a different key. As one of Shriharsha's most sensitive readers, the fourteenth-to-fifteenth-century Sanskrit commentator Mallinatha noted: "he repeats the very same thing with a different twist." Something is learned in the restatement, and there is also pleasure when the elegance of the "different twist" is highlighted. By adding the line "Allow me to restate this problem," the translator, David Shulman, who did all the translations for this volume, has shared with us his own pleasure in seeing this twist, which, in fact, is a pleasure given by the text itself with its own habits of self-translation and reiterations. Shulman's translation thus allows us to appreciate the text through his appreciating eyes; to read following the mind of a sensitive reader.

Rather than worrying over whether this line is an addition, we might better ask who the "me" in "Allow me to restate the problem" might be. There is more than one answer, and they get better as they go on. On the most basic narrative level, that "me" belongs, well, to a goose. This winged creature happens to be the go-between in this story, depicting Nala's love to Damayanti. On another, deeper level, it belongs to the poet himself, who is restating his words from the previous verse. The "me" in question may also be the translator, literally showing us what he is doing in making Shriharsha accessible. But as an indexical word, the "me" refers to every reader of this poem who rethinks the text's words in her own mind. When we see that anyone who voices this verse—ourselves just as much as the speaking goose—must "restate the problem" for themselves, we begin to feel that the text anticipates its readers, even the readers of its translations. We can, of course, only restate the problem if we mentally follow the lead of the text, to take up the metaphor in Toni Morrison's apt description of reading as experiencing "one's own mind dancing with another's," and especially when such active reading is experienced as possibly leading to something unfamiliar, something new, indeed something surprising.[1]

Let us restate the problem to see what is being asked of us. When we read a translation, we are asked to suspend our objections and suspicions in a leap of faith. Can a goose speak? Let's not worry about this now. How do Nala and Damayanti fall in love without even meeting? We'll find out as we read along, partly because reading a translation is like falling in love without meeting in person. Aspects of another culture seem foreign and incomprehensible? So what! That's part of the fun. A good translation is a heightened act of reading, one that uniquely embodies and boldly invites coimagination. Let us conclude this brief prologue with one more lesson from Shriharsha—the verse that immediately follows the same section:

> You are continually climbing up
> the tall ladder of his imagination
> as he showers a rain of sighs.
> From thinking only about you
> he's *become* you.

It is we, the readers, who have to provide "the tall ladder of imagination," and we have to get better at using it, setting it up in ways that the contents of the texts we read, even in translation, can climb higher and higher. To put this another way, how do we get better at reading translations, and what will we become when we do?

GETTING BETTER AT READING TRANSLATIONS

We can make a start by giving some thought to ourselves and to how we read. This includes reminding ourselves that we read in different ways for different purposes. Sometimes we read to get something that we can use, other times our reading is an end in itself. This means that when we read translations, sometimes we read to learn more about a culture in a different time or place, while sometimes we read translations just for the pleasure that the text in translation will hopefully give us. We can also remind ourselves that we approach a text in different ways. We can try to get nearer by gathering knowledge about the context and about the other texts that the original assumed its readers would know. We can also read while remaining afar, unfazed by our lack of such knowledge. For instance, we can read the translated selection from Shriharsha's text while seeking information about the characters of Nala and Damayanti and then formulate educated guesses about what may or may not happen to them, or we may approach it pretty much for the first time, aware that we lack not only expertise but also preconceptions, anticipating discovery but ever unsure about "the way in."

We can keep on adding such dichotomies, but what already seems more important is the question of how we use them: whether we see them as "either/ or" options or as possibilities for taking a "both/and" approach. By habit, we tend to see these different ways of reading in an "either/or" way, and quite frequently a value judgment comes with that perception. That is, we see one way of reading the text as preferable to the other.

In this volume, the "both/and" approach is embraced as a way forward to our becoming better readers. The translated texts that follow—and we will say more about the process of their selection later—are coupled with short "near" and "far" essays. In our original conception, this meant that for each piece, there would be two responses. One would be written by someone who knows quite a lot about the text and its cultural and linguistic contexts, the other by someone who does not. The initial idea was that for the readers of this volume, the translations—and, in two cases, a work of visual art and two musical pieces—would be made accessible and enjoyable precisely because they are mediated by the responses of two very different readers.

We asked the writers of "near" responses to supplement the translation with knowledge and skills that the original likely assumed. This would include background information, of course, but also some insights into the protocols of reading that would inform a reader from the more immediate audience of that text. If we stick to the Shriharsha piece with which we began, we can take the essay by Gary Tubb as an example of this approach. Tubb places *Life of Naishadha* in the broad context of Sanskrit literary culture, speaking of both its accomplishments and its deserved fame. He also shares with us some of the knowledge that Shriharsha assumed in his readers, including the literary conventions that would have been familiar to them. For instance, Tubb shows us that the selection from which we sampled forms a playful meditation on a canonical list of the "ten stages of love," beginning with the visualization of the beloved. In effect, the essay moves away from the translation to the world of its intended readers and then back to the translation in order to help us read a little bit more like they might have. Other near essays, for instance those by Archana Venkatesan and Anna Lise Seastrand (to mention but two), employ similar strategies to enable us to read an ancient Tamil poem and a work of sculptural art, respectively, closer to home.

We initially asked the writers of the "far" essays to provide a reading that would be directed toward more general insights and sensibilities with the expectation that this would help someone totally new to South Asian texts to read them in translation. We invited contributors who we admired as readers but who were at least once-removed from these texts to share their responses to the translations. In doing so, we were guided by the truth expressed by Robert Scholes, following Derrida, that "a written text can survive the absence of its author, the absence of its addressee, the absence of its object, the absence of its context, the absence of its code—and still be read."[2] South Asian texts are no exception to this truth.

But we were, at first, surprised to discover how difficult the writing of such a far response proved to be. This happened for two reasons. All of the texts translated here come from South Asia, and for some far-readers who had no familiarity whatsoever with such works—for us, the ideal far-readers—they felt completely inaccessible. Others, who had considerable knowledge about South Asia generally but little familiarity with the specific text at hand, sometimes found it very difficult not to try to read as "experts." The varied difficulties that the writers of the far essays faced or articulated taught us something about the challenges of reading translations in general, and South Asian texts in particular.

The resulting far essays illuminated something critical about the different ways we can read translations, something that becomes obvious when they are compared with the near essays: the far essays are far more diverse than the near ones. Some far readers opted for a comparative approach. For instance, Meir Shahar compares a translation of the Malayalam-language version of the earlier-mentioned Nala-Damayanti story to the Chinese *Peony Pavilion*, and Yehoshua Granat reads the translation of the Tamil Ramayana with the Song of Songs in mind. Muzaffar Alam's approach is to grab ready-at-hand comparisons, and he reads the Telugu version of *Story of the Four Dervishes* in the light of versions he already knew in other languages. Other readers go personal, allowing the translation to resonate with aspects of their own life story. For example, Sanjay Subrahmanyam brings his childhood memories into his reading of a translation of a modern Telugu short story, and R. Cheran reads some selections from Tamil texts that are nearly two millennia old as a witness and victim of the recent genocidal war against Tamils in Sri Lanka.

Then there is the reflexive approach, also seen in Cheran's essay, where he reflects on his reading as that of a survivor. Other far readers try to bracket their own personal identity. A striking example is Sheldon Pollock's response to the Tamil-language version of, yet again, the Nala-Damayanti story, in which he imagines how he would have read the text had he been totally unfamiliar with it and its conventions (framing, of course, his imagined unfamiliarity with his intimate knowledge of South Asia). The result is a pointed meditation on the topic of sensitively reading a translation or even reading more generally. In turning their attention to the act of reading itself, these far readers model how to become sensitive to our own sensitivities when reading translation. Finally, a far-reading can result in a literary piece in its own right, a poem that responds to a poem, as in the case of Peter Cole's reaction to translations of Ghalib and Hafez.

The authors of some near essays are super near, in the sense that there is hardly a degree of separation between them and their subject matter. For example, Afsar Mohammad personally knew his fellow Telugu poet Ismail, and refers in his essay to conversations they had. An even more extreme example is T.M. Krishna, one of the world's most acclaimed Carnatic vocalists, who writes on a piece he himself performs regularly. This is, of course, a privilege that the far readers did not have, and they sometimes compensate for its lack by establishing some kind of kinship with the translator, David Shulman. One example is Gabriel Levin's reading of the same poems by Ismail, with the help of Shulman's published diary from his time in

Andhra. Another is Donald Davis's sense of affinity with and admiration for Shulman as a scholar that emboldens him to approach Carnatic music sympathetically.

Our comparison of the near essays with the far ones revealed something else important. The near essays often seem to aim at a certainty about their resulting interpretation and to provide reassurance that it is correct. Indeed, they do give us good reasons to feel confident about what they say about the meanings of the text. By contrast, the far essays, in all their variety, relish the new possibilities of understanding and insight that become present, once the initial obstacles on the way into the texts are overcome. In the near essays, definite interpretations hold our attention; in the far ones, the new possibilities of meaning invite us to go further, even if they come with considerable uncertainty, such as is expressed in the title of Thibaut d'Hubert's essay, "If I Am Reading You Right." In a crucial way, it may be that the practices of translation themselves create the conditions for encountering and engaging exciting new possibilities of meaning, so much so that we can talk about, to use the words of the title of Sonam Kachru's far essay, "What's Gained in Translation."

The contrasts that we have been making between the near and far essays are not the last thing to be said, though, since the comparison reveals important similarities as well. Taken together, it is obvious that every author in this volume refers to additional works other than the translated. This is a simple observation but an important one. It reminds us of that basic truth that reading is inherently an intertextual activity. We cannot help but connect whatever we are reading at the moment with what we have read before, and our understanding of any literary work depends on how we read it in the light of others. Of course, choices are made, but the fundamental point that reading translations, too, is always an intertextual activity needs to be highlighted.

Some of the near essays subsist on a somewhat more ascetic diet of texts that are deemed intertextually relevant. In some cases, the restriction is primarily to very intimate intertexts, as in Ilanit Loewy Shacham's study of Bhattumurti's Telugu *Vasu's Life*: she compares the section translated here with other portions from the same work and with a passage from the *Mahabharata* epic that serves as a source to Bhattumurti. In others, an entire literary corpus comes to the fore, as when Jennifer Clare states, speaking of ancient Tamil poetry, that "the poems' deep connection with other poems in the tradition generates an intertextual web of signification from which an individual verse cannot be extricated." Ironically, as Clare helps us to see, it is only by first seeing a text as representative of a received tradition that we can also appreciate it as a unique work, by appreciating the ways in which it departs from the conventional system to which it belongs.

The realization about the intertextual nature of all acts of reading helps us understand the limits of the far-near dichotomy without undermining its usefulness. Many of the near essays also invoke remote texts in their reading of the translations, just as they employ personal resources and reflexive practices, whereas many far essays claw their way back to stay near the original and its reception history. In fact, we should be careful not to essentialize South Asian literature in this (or any other) context. Thus when Thibaut d'Hubert frames his reading of the translation of the Sanskrit *Life of Naishadha* by citing Shriharsha's European contemporary, the Occitan troubadour Jaufré Rudel, this is not essentially different from his turning to another intertext, the Prakrit-language anthology ascribed to King Hala, who lived in a different part of South Asia roughly a millennium earlier, or his citation of a verse from a different part of the same text by Shriharsha. In fact, it could even be said that the use of the frame from Rudel's notions of *amor de lonh* (love from afar) to read *Life of Naishadha* is a generative condition for d'Hubert's subsequently turning to other examinations of love in separation. A turn to one intertext, far or near, thus opens up the possibility of other intertexts that might not have been considered otherwise.

So how do we become better readers of translations of South Asian texts? Our experience with this volume has taught us a key lesson, one that surprisingly came from reflecting on the far essays offered here. We never had a doubt that the patient and careful learning of the protocols of reading from other times and places can enhance our understanding and appreciation of texts that were loved in those contexts. Now we are equally sure that the more improvisatory reading that inevitably happens whenever we engage a translation, independent of the original text and the contexts that it assumes, is indispensable to discovering the potentials of a text, as new audiences climb further rungs on "the tall ladder of imagination."

Moreover, following Robert Scholes, we have been emphasizing that reading is an intertextual activity, and the translations that are increasingly available to us create new opportunities for it. Scholes also says that "reading, though it may be a kind of action, is not the whole of action but a part of it, remaining incomplete unless and until it is absorbed and transformed in the thoughts and deeds of readers."[3] To us, this makes clear that translations are not condemned to remaining incomplete because they are somehow removed from their original. Translations, like all texts, are incomplete until they are absorbed and transformed in the thoughts and deeds of new readers. But in a way that would have delighted Borges, it is the originals that are incomplete until they are translated. In the end, it does not really matter which came first, as reading is always an intersubjective activity, a meeting of minds. This is an insight that Shriharsha knew firsthand, as we see if we take the goose's words to Damayanti as instructing us on how to read the translations in this volume:

> [I]n fact you're his very life's breath
> moving through nose and mouth. . . .
> he's *become* you.

THE TRANSLATIONS IN THIS VOLUME

This volume does not offer a representative selection of South Asian literatures, past or present. Nor is it a presentation of a canon of the greatest works in any of the languages of South Asia, let alone all of them. Rather, it is the personal choice of one reader, David Shulman, the translator. We will say more about him later in this introduction. But first, we want to talk about the selection itself and its significance. We often take up something to read because someone else has recommended it to us: "I like this, and I think you will like it too." The translations found in this volume are the choices of one person who has selected them from the works that he himself has found pleasure in. These, then, are his recommendations.

The vast swath of the world that we refer to as "South Asia" has a long history of literature in dozens of languages, not to mention its many traditions of sculpting, painting, theater, and music. There are cosmopolitan languages that claimed prestige and crossed regional boundaries, such as Sanskrit, Persian, and English. Then there are more local literary cultures, many of which are very old and claim equal prestige, such as Tamil, Sinhala, Hindi, and Urdu. As we speak, there is also a large number of modern expressive media, which include those mentioned earlier and many more, and the literary-linguistic situation is and has always been complex and layered, in the sense that many texts participate in conversations across linguistic lines (as we have already begun to see with the Nala and Damayanti story). This volume is not meant to be a methodical entrance into this intricate and large literary world, using the selections as if they could be gates. It is not a list of the "Great Books" of South Asian literatures.

Rather, it offers us a chance to share in someone else's pleasures of reading, and to learn to read on the basis of the perceptions and understanding that pleasure affords. Let us formulate two principles of reading here, the principle of pleasure and the principle of sharing. What these principles actually look like in the act of reading translations can be seen in the manner in which the twentieth-century Sri Lankan novelist, Martin Wickramasinghe, introduced his translation of the poems of the first Buddhist women, the *Therigatha*. Wickramasinghe does not begin with any statement of the significance of these poems or their status as great literature. Rather, he begins with a reference to a Sinhala-language classic of poetry, the *Guttila Kāvyaya*, with which he was more at home. "Whenever I was troubled or distressed," he says, "the poetry in *Guttila* eased my mind; whenever my mind shined with happiness, *Guttila* increased the happiness. On the many occasions that I was happy just being lazy, it was usually to *Guttila* that my hand reached out, and I would read whatever caught my eye wherever I happened to open the book." He then goes on to speak about his motivation to translate poetry written in the cosmopolitan Buddhist language of Pali into Sinhala: "That satisfaction and comfort that I used to get from *Guttila*, I now get from some of the verses of the Buddhist nuns. . . . Because of the pleasure that my mind received from reading them, I wanted to share those songs by translating a few of them into Sinhala. There was pleasure for me even in translating these few verses into Sinhala."[4]

Note that in articulating the rationale for his translation, Wickramasinghe begins with pleasure. As we understand it, the principle of pleasure is not at all a simple desire to feel good. Rather, it is an imaginative process of opening yourself up to comfort, to happiness, to being surprised, or even to becoming someone different. Key to this process is not approaching reading as a task to be done; on the contrary, reading might best be done when feeling lazy, even if other moods also recommend themselves.

The second principle is that of sharing. Or you might think of it as a second type of pleasure, the pleasure of sharing. For the translator, sharing entails the pleasure of imagining the pleasure of the reader. Sharing for the reader involves the pleasure of receiving a gift. David Shulman shared these selections with us in response to our request for him to translate from texts that he liked, texts that continue to give him pleasure.

None of the translations in this volume have been published before. And, as already noted, they were not selected to represent any canon. In fact, they are not even particularly representative of the work for which Shulman is known. Rather, they are translations that resulted from our request to "translate what you love, whatever you like." Shulman's response surprised us. It included not only texts, but also visual art and music. The textual selections went beyond what we anticipated and included texts in Malayalam and Persian (and, in the case of some stanzas, Arabic), languages from which we did not expect to receive translations. Even in translations from languages in which Shulman has done a lot of work, such as Telugu, his choices were often surprising, as in the example of *The Story of the Four Dervishes*. Shulman provided us with an "English translation of the Telugu version of the Urdu rendering of this Persian" storybook, as Muzaffar Alam insightfully portrays this layered text. The selections can be seen as a display of particularly beloved items that Shulman personally curated. We invite you to engage them as instances of our two principles of pleasure and sharing.

Let us look now at what Shulman has put into this gallery, which we have arranged in six "display rooms," or units.

The volume begins with a unit consisting of three tellings of the Nala and Damayanti story written in three different languages: Sanskrit, Tamil, and Malayalam. None of the three is the "original" version, if there ever was one. Shulman is not alone in loving this story. It is one of the formative narratives of South Asia, just like those of Rama, Krishna, and the Buddha, and has been told numerous times. The texts Shulman translated for this unit engage not only with this vast received tradition but also with one another: the Malayalam and Tamil authors, Malamangala Kavi and Ativirarama Pantiyan, are clearly familiar with Shriharsha's Sanskrit work. There is thus an added value in reading the three translations together, especially the Sanskrit and Malayalam poems, which deal with the very same mission of the go-between goose. Nonetheless, the texts stand alone in important ways. For one thing, they are written in different languages; for another, they reflect and participate in shaping the aesthetic horizons associated with these languages.

Something of these larger received traditions is present in Shulman's translations, and the near essays help us to see this. This aid may come by drawing attention to the language resources available to the poet or to his thematic resources. For the first, consider Sivan Goren-Arzony's essay, where she contextualizes Shulman's translation in the linguistic reality of "Rubies and Coral," the name given to the particular combination of Sanskrit and Malayalam in which Malamangala Kavi composed his Nala and Damayanti story, all the while making us aware of the pleasures to be had when a skilled author tells an old story in fresh and appealing ways. For the second, look at N. Govindarajan's essay, where he contextualizes Ativirarama's telling of the same story in Tamil Tantric culture, where religious practices of meditative visualization are key. We have already alluded to the other essays in this unit—Tubb's close reading of Shriharsha's Sanskrit poem, d'Hubert's reading of it (among other things) in the light of Occitan poetry, and Shahar's comparison of the Malayalam telling to the Chinese *Peony Pavilion*. The unit concludes with Pollock's meditation on sensitive reading.

The second room of this gallery brings together translations of more recent works written in Telugu. The first is the aforementioned anonymous *The Story of the Four Dervishes*. The second is a twentieth-century short story by Abburi Chayadevi (1933–2019) that tells of a daughter visiting her aging father. Finally, there are six short poems by Mohammad Ismail (1928–2003). Taken together, they prompt the question that Gabriel Levin quotes from Shulman himself, "What does it mean to be 'modern' in Telugu?" They also share another significant quality that actually distinguishes them from each other: their use of styles and genres that have crossed linguistic, cultural, and geographical boundaries to become deeply rooted in new places. This is particularly apparent in Ismail's poems, written in free verse and a Modernist style that Levin compares to that of T. S. Eliot. One of them, "Rembrandt," depicts a painting by the Dutch artist, and another, "Left Bank, Paris," places its writing along the Seine. *Touch* is a concise short story in the tradition of Guy de Maupassant and Edith Wharton that, as Sanjay Subrahmanyam highlights, very elegantly illuminates current social issues in middle-class India (he also offers another comparison: Kafka). Afsar Mohammad, writing a near essay about Mohammad Ismail, and Gautham Reddy, writing a near essay about Abburi Chayadevi, both remind us that in order for styles and genres to cross the linguistic, cultural, and geographical boundaries that they do, individual authors have to challenge various conventions dominant in the worlds in which and about which they write. It is in a complementary vein that Muzaffar Alam, in his far essay, helps us to see that even as the fable of "Khwaja the Dog-Worshiper" from *The Story of the Four Dervishes* has a shared Islamic frame of references, the narrative and its figures are also thoroughly grounded in locales that have their own concrete particularities; indeed these particularities sometimes remind us that this story moves beyond the confines of familiar Islamic geographies. The near essay by Jamal Jones on the same fable helps us enjoy the vast potentials of the technique of embedding inherent in it and in the larger corpus of which it is part.

You will need your media player and headphones when entering the next room. The works here also cross boundaries, this time expressive boundaries. There is a text about a performance of music, from *Chivakan's Gem that Fulfills All Wishes*, and there are recordings of two performances of vocal music in which the performers sing lyrics, as texts are called when they come with music. In short, the selections here raise questions for us about text and performance. Please bear in mind that, at least in South Asia, the literary and the performative arts are closely connected, even if some current habits dispose us to engage them separately. This separation may come at the cost of understanding, appreciating, and enjoying.

Chivakan's Gem, the first item here, is an eighth-century Tamil poem written in south India by a Jain monk, Tiruttakkatevar. Like *The Story of the Four Dervishes*, the contents of *Chivakan's Gem* involve travels to exotic lands in search of love and adventure. The selection here is about a music contest between Chivakan and a woman he meets on his travels. It tells us much about the performance of music, but it is also about love, since the contest is part of their courtship. It thus invites us to think about the similarities between music and love, and the three essays responding to this piece guide us through different ways of exploring what this similarity entails. The near essay, by Talia Ariav, lays out Tamil-specific protocols of reading that go back centuries to the oldest extant canon of love poetry in this language, which we visit again in unit 5. Kesavan Veluthat creates a middle position for us between a near and far perspective: he places the selection in a context of Sanskrit conventions and intertexts that were also in conversation with those of Tamil. Finally, Sonam Kachru meditates on the act of listening itself: listening to music, to poetry, and to oneself when reading. Kachru's essay should also be read together with Pollock's as a general reflection on how to read translations.

The recordings in this unit are of two pieces by Muttusvami Dikshitar (1775–1835), a south Indian poet and composer, performed by two musicians: one a world-famous professional, the other a talented amateur. The songs are addressed to Hindu deities, and the closeness of art and religion is felt here, just as it is in the Jain *Chivakan's Gem* and in the Islamic *Story of the Four Dervishes*. If *Chivakan's Gem* makes us see what music can look like, these recordings enable us to hear how poetry can sound. The first recording is by T.M. Krishna, and he also provides his own essay about the two performances. His essay guides us from looking at music from the inside—that is, how it feels when he performs—to looking at it from the outside—that is, what happens when he listens to someone else singing. Donald Davis's essay reverses this movement of engagement and appreciation, starting from a standpoint of distance and even dislike and looking for a way in. Davis reminds us that not everything we encounter presents itself to us as something we want to "get inside." Sensitive reading can lead to discomfort and disapproval as well as to the satisfaction, comfort, and pleasure that Wickramasinghe found in his reading of the poems of the first Buddhist women.

The selections in the fourth unit give us a chance to consider this contrast between pleasure and disapproval in the context of a tacit concern of this volume, namely, the many contours and vagaries of love. The first item here is a sculpture of a loving couple, embodiments of love and desire, found in a Hindu temple in the south Indian city of Kanchipuram; another reminder of the expressive closeness of art and religion in this world. Anna Lise Seastrand, a specialist on south Indian art, and Tawfiq Da'adli, a specialist on West Asian Islamic art, share with us how they look at sculptures. They do so as if they were taking us by the hand through the temple and to the sculpture, all the while directing our attention to various details that caught their attention, each from her or his own perspective. What they show us is that reading sculptures is not all that different from reading translations.

The sculpted figures sit atop their mounts, armed and ready for battle, reminding us of the complex power dynamics that love and desire can entail. These are the focus of the next two selections in this unit. The first is from Kamban's Tamil version of the Rama story, which, as we noted, is one of the formative narratives of South Asia, told again and again, like the story of Nala and Damayanti. The selection here focuses on a key moment in the story. It is a scene of threat, seduction, and resistance, when Ravana, king of demons, thinks he can win the heart of Sita, Rama's wife, whom he has abducted and keeps as his prisoner. The entire scene is witnessed by Rama's trusted deputy, the monkey Hanuman, sitting atop a tree. The two readers, for their part, come to this ambiguous, indeed troubling, scene from very different directions. Yehoshua Granat approaches it with comparisons from afar, including the Bible's primordial temptation scene in the Garden of Eden, while Whitney Cox uses comparisons that are nearer at hand in Sanskrit. Their comparisons help us to see that what Cox said about the transcendent and the everyday is also true about the comforting and the discomforting: they are "found side by side: they join up, blur into one another, and come away transformed."

Discomfort and comfort are to the fore in the last item in this unit, from *Vasu's Life* by the sixteenth-century Telugu poet Bhattumurti. The selection consists of two separate scenes: one between a mountain (male) and river (female) that ends in rape; the other, which ends very differently, features Vasu, the hero of the work, and Girika, the daughter born as a result of that earlier rape. Ilanit Loewy Shacham and Deven Patel focus our attention on how Bhattumurti shapes his version of this complex and disturbing story, known in other versions too, and voice for us some of the doubts and questions to which the story can give rise. For example, Loewy Shacham focuses on the river's desperate attempts to talk her way out from the encounter with the aggressive mountain, whereas Patel highlights, among other things, the mountain's words as "a coarse, craggy finger brushing against her moist cheek." Bhattumurti's accomplishment is that he takes us, in language, to the very limits of language; here what can be said and what can't be said are, to quote Cox again, "found side by side: they join up, blur into one another, and come away transformed."

The selections in the penultimate unit five are from the earliest extant Tamil anthologies, dating to the first centuries CE and collectively known as "Sangam poetry." The intricate system of conventions that permeates this corpus continued to play an important role for many centuries and informs all of the Tamil works in this volume: from *Chivakan's Gem* and Kamban's *Ramayana* to Nammalvar's *A Hundred Measures of Time*, featured in the next and final unit. Here we offer two selections from Sangam poetry. The first is a series of ten poems, "Ten on the Wild Boar," from what is probably the earliest anthology of love poetry in Tamil. A woman is speaking to a confidante about the man she loves, but "a boar with small eyes / and big rage" is repeatedly alluded to in her words. Archana Venkatesan places this decad in the context of the ancient system of Tamil poetics and helps us see that it presents a picture of love that is, once again, uncomfortable: "savage, capricious, and disruptive"; a love that is "both nourishment and illness, and . . . that needs to be both tamed and contained." The second selection consists of three more love poems from three additional anthologies: in the first, a man berates his heart, compared to a wingless heron, for falling for a faraway woman; in the second, a separation from a man whose heart was "still thinking about money" is averted at the last minute in a sudden moment of softness; in the third, a complex love triangle, involving a man, his wife, and his lover, gradually unfolds through a seemingly innocent street-encounter between the lover and a child whose mother turns out to be the wife. Jennifer Clare gives these three vignettes a slow, careful reading that compares them to one another and that places them in the system of Tamil "interior landscapes." She also uses the poems to reflect on the experience of reading them. She notes, for instance, apropos of the third poem, that we readers "realize, along with the faithless husband, that we too have been subjected to a sleight of hand, in which what appeared simple and innocent is in fact full of deceptions." R. Cheran then gives the entire section a broad overview from his multiple perspectives as a reader, as a poet in both Tamil and English, and as a refugee from Sri Lanka now living in the Tamil diaspora in Canada. He thus places them within a new "interior landscape" of the twenty-first century.

The last unit in this volume brings together poetry by three authors: a selection from *A Hundred Measures of Time* (to use the title Archana Venkatesan has given this poem in her own translation of it) by the eighth or ninth century Hindu saint, Nammalvar; a poem by the fourteenth-century Persian poet, Hafez; and a poem by Ghalib, who wrote in Urdu and Persian in the nineteenth century.[5] These three will strike many as poles apart: one Hindu, the others Muslim; one writing in Tamil, the others in Persian and Urdu; each distant from the others by about half a millennium; two cherished across north India and Pakistan, the third in south India and Sri Lanka. Taken together, however, the three authors teach us about reading as an intertextual activity: it pays to be experimental. The texts brought together in this unit also highlight that an ever-present question in sensitive reading is *who am I when I am reading you?* In fact, they articulate the question for us. A couplet from Ghalib's ghazal in this unit puts it this way:

> Don't ask what state I'm in after you.
> Ask yourself what you're feeling when you're around me.

We see the presence of this question acknowledged directly in Andrew Ollett's far essay on *A Hundred Measures of Time*, where he describes how it was only when his initial frustrating efforts to make sense of the poem gave way to the command in the poem itself to "look to your own lives inside this world" that he could sense what the work brought into being. In a complementary way, Anand Venkatkrishnan's near essay brings into relief how "the puzzles in Nammalvar's . . . jagged, searching poems" disorient readers and prepare us for possibilities for living that as yet remain hidden to us. The selections by Hafez, a Persian poet whose works came to be loved in South Asia, and Ghalib, a nineteenth-century poet who wrote in both Urdu and Persian, also thematize this question, as the couplet quoted above suggests. Rajeev Kinra's meditative essay traces the resonances between the intertextual and the intersubjective in these two poets. What Kinra says about Ghazal poetry is true of sensitive reading generally: its pleasures lie "precisely in the jostling of . . . multiple interpretations—as well as other potential readings—bouncing off one another, always in a state of suspended animation."

We end this unit with Peter Cole's own poetic and intersubjective response to Hafez and Ghalib, but especially to David Shulman himself, showing us that the implicit question "Who am I?" is really asking "Who are you?"

> *I imagine, therefore you*
>
> *are.* Therefore, imagine, so that I might be
> with you, wandering friend, when these debts come due.

ABOUT THE TRANSLATOR

David Shulman has translated many South Asian literary works into English (as well as Hebrew), on his own and in collaboration with others. These translations span a remarkable rainbow of South Asian languages—Sanskrit, Tamil, and Telugu—and include works that were composed at different times and places, in a whole spectrum of genres. Together with his teacher and friend Velcheru Narayana Rao, he produced a unique library of works from the Telugu literary tradition that had been inaccessible to English readers. This library includes poetry and prose, premodern and modern works, and also representative works as well as singular texts. Moreover, this rich output from Telugu is coupled with introductory essays and contextual scholarship that make the individual works and the tradition from which they come accessible to their new audiences.

Shulman's translations are not only to be found between the covers of individual publications. Translations of a wider range of texts and from an even wider range of languages are to be found in his scholarly monographs and articles, beginning with his first monograph, *Tamil Temple Myths*, and continuing through to his most recent publications, such as *More than Real*, his monograph on the history of imagination in south India. We can expect to see more of such *muktaka*s (independent pearls) in his scholarship to come, including his ongoing work on south Indian classical music and the living tradition of Sanskrit drama, Kudiyattam. We had a glimpse of these broader horizons of scholarship whenever we had a chance to listen to him think out loud about possible choices to include in this volume, and there were many that did not end up here: from the Vedas, the Sanskrit grammarians Panini and Patanjali, and the Persian poet Bedil, to name just a few.

Shulman's deserved recognition as a translator is not only due to the scale and scope of his corpus, but also its quality. This quality stems first from his outstanding philological skills and from the sheer expressive beauty of his English. This beauty is a function of his freedom and pleasure as a translator, and as a scholar he is unusually consistent about articulating his pleasure as a reader of South Asian texts; this quality of his scholarship is very visible in his *Tamil: A Biography*. But this pleasure and this freedom both originate in his deep respect for the original in all its levels: from the morphology to the lexical choices and from the musicality to the overall meaning. The beauty of the English in his translations is no surprise either, given that Shulman is a poet in his own right, and that his nonacademic writing is also stunningly poetic. The title of Whitney Cox's essay in this volume, "Tamil as a Kind of Sanskrit," applies, mutatis mutandis, to Shulman's translations: they are English as a kind of Telugu, Tamil, and so on.

In addition to his standard-setting translations, Shulman has helped to set new expectations from translations of South Asian texts in his efforts as an editor and a member of the editorial board of the Murty Classical Library of India and other venues and projects. Many have benefited from his generosity privately, as he has so often been willing to go over and make suggestions to a plethora of translations; the two of us can certainly testify to this wonderful generosity firsthand. This is also the experience of many of the contributors of this volume, a number of whom are either colleagues or students of Shulman.

We have emphasized the translations from Sanskrit and the languages of south India, primarily Tamil and Telugu, where Shulman is most at home, and on which he has published a great deal. But another aspect that enriches his abilities as a writer and a translator is his formidable command of other languages and literatures. His literary expertise includes Ancient Greek and Latin, Persian and Arabic, French and German, Russian and Yiddish, and, more recently, Malayalam, Kannada, and Old Javanese. This rare range partly makes him the sensitive reader and translator that he is.

Shulman's range as a scholar and as a translator overlaps with his lifelong willingness to put himself in the position of a student and to allow himself the pleasures of learning from someone else. It is thus fitting that this volume ends with an afterword by Wendy Doniger, Shulman's teacher at the University of London, who reminds us that David Shulman's persona as student and teacher cannot be separated. Doniger describes some of the things that she has learned from Shulman, and also describes his sharing of his generosity as a student, colleague, and friend.

As Shulman has taught all of us, in literature as in life, the principle of sharing and the principle of pleasure go hand in hand. The present volume is evidence of this lesson, and it is our hope that through it, the combination of both principles extends itself into new lives and new worlds.

Retelling Nala

EDITORS' NOTE

NALA AND DAMAYANTI ARE A MATCH MADE IN HEAVEN. They have not yet met, but with the help of a talking goose who acts as a go-between, they can envision one another and fall madly in love. This is just the beginning of a long saga: the gods conspire to take Nala's place in Damayanti's life, but she manages to choose him as her husband nonetheless; the two marry but then separate in a tragic twist of fate when Nala is overcome by his demons; and after many adventures and miseries, they reunite. This profoundly human story was and still is one of the most popular in all of South Asia, told and retold in numerous versions, genres, languages, and media. The translations here are from three very famous poetic versions of the story, each holding a unique place of honor in its own literary tradition (Sanskrit, Tamil, and Malayalam). All the selections are from the early part of the story, when the couple falls in love, and the overlap between them is intentional.

The first selection is from Shriharsha's *Life of Naishadha* (Naishadha is another name for Nala). It is the earliest of the three versions, although it is an heir to a long tradition of Nala stories in Sanskrit beginning at least with the *Mahabharata* epic. Shriharsha's work made such a name for itself that the two later works in Tamil and Malayalam can no longer tell the well-known narrative without acknowledging and engaging it.

Shriharsha's Sanskrit *Life of Naishadha*

TRANSLATOR'S NOTE AND TEXT

Shriharsha's twelfth-century masterpiece is the last of the classic Sanskrit Grand Poems (Mahākāvya). It tells the famous love story of Nala and Damayanti, with an emphasis on the dissonant innerness of the main protagonists and with a pronounced Tantric overlay: tradition has it that Shriharsha achieved his poetic prowess by reciting the famous mantra of the "philosopher's stone" (*cintāmaṇi*), which is then imparted to the protagonist, Nala. A tour de force on every level (including syntax, vocabulary, and complexity of thought and imagination), *Life of Naishadha* defies translation but was, perhaps for this very reason, adapted into Telugu, Tamil, and Malayalam (in each case, the vernacular versions themselves became classic works). In the passage selected here, a goose is a messenger mediating between Nala and Damayanti, who have yet to meet. The goose describes to the anxious Damayanti King Nala's hopeless love-madness, which is progressing remorselessly through the ten normative stages of infatuation toward the tenth stage, death.

SHRIHARSHA'S *LIFE OF NAISHADHA* (3.99–114)

The bird could see with total clarity
that Damayanti was already in love
with the Nishadha king, so with a smile
it unlocked the lock on its beak. (3.99)

"Princess," said the goose, "if I'm reading
you right, there's nothing left for me
to do. The god of love with his five arrows
has turned up the heat on both of you,
and by now you're already
welded together. (3.100)

His mind is entirely absorbed
in you, and that means his other
sense organs—eyes ears
nose tongue touch—are fasting, and this state
of severe self-abnegation has inevitably
produced the deathless state of reveling in
you, so they have fulfilled their destiny and truly turned
into gods.[1] (3.101)

Bodiless Desire must be thinking: 'Once
our two bodies were equal. Mine
got burnt, but his was never even
slightly boiled.' On fire with envy, seizing on the fact
that *you* are far away, Desire
is now scorching
his skin.[2] (3.102)

The king stares, unblinking, at your portrait
on the wall, drinking you in
with eyes red from tears
or maybe it's from the fire
you've lit inside him. (3.103)

Allow me to restate this problem:
1) He's studying that painting of you
2) Unblinking
3) With deep attention and affection.
4) There are tears in his eyes.
5) Those tears are mine, says the eye. That's what happens
if you don't blink.
6) No way, says Love. They're all mine.
7) This dispute remains
unsolved. (3.104)

You, lady, live in his heart,
but you're also somehow outside him,
in fact you're his very life's breath
moving through nose and mouth.
His mind, too, being utterly absorbed
in you, never budges from that wondrous
painting, and this, too,
is a wonder. (3.105)

You are continually climbing up
the tall ladder of his imagination
as he showers a rain of sighs.

From thinking only about you
he's *become* you. (3.106)

What his heart says to you—
his deepest secret—
his face openly reveals
by its pallor, as is only fitting
for a friend of the moon
who happens to be a friend
of his enemy, Desire. (3.107)

He lies at night on his bed.
Sleep no longer comes to embrace him,
to kiss his eyes, to drive him mad,
nor does any other woman
but you. (3.108)

He's grown thin, pierced in vain
by the arrows of Desire.
Only his beauty remains intact.
Yet even now, after losing almost
all his body, he's still competing with,
and defeating, that bodiless god. (3.109)

He's no longer afraid of sin, if sin
can bring you to him, and he's not ashamed
to be your slave. It seems that the sharp arrows
of Desire may have slightly punctured
his character. (3.110)

Speaking of shame, the expert physicians
who are treating him, shy as he is, for his high fever
have nothing whatever to say
about the etiology of his condition.
Embarrassment apparently
is contagious. (3.111)

He gets scared for no reason,
thinking you're angry. He laughs
inappropriately, certain he's won you.
He follows you everywhere, to no purpose.
When he thinks you're speaking to him,
he answers to no point. (3.112)

This king who holds up the earth is like a mighty
elephant stuck in the mud of a great blindness
on the Island of Unconsciousness in the middle

of the dark Yamuna River, flowing with an unbroken
stream of heartbreak because *you* are not there
beside him. Utterly helpless, he hollers:
'Ha! Ha!' (3.113)

He's in bad shape, this king: Desire has been shooting
his five arrows at him from both right and left hands,
which makes for ten sure hits. He's gone through all
the first nine stages of being in love. Let's hope that the tenth
will be like the flower unfolding
in the empty sky."[3] (3.114)

POINTS AND PROGRESSION: HOW TO READ
SHRIHARSHA'S *LIFE OF NAISHADHA*

Gary Tubb (Near Reader)

"The bird could see with total clarity" and opened its beak to speak. At the
beginning of our passage, the goose who will do the talking is presented in terms
traditionally applied to a Sanskrit poet, as someone who speaks after having
seen the realities of the world as clearly "as if they were a gooseberry in the
hand." And the world available to the vision of a poet working in the Sanskrit tradition is a distinctively well-endowed one, given its long history of poetic experimentation, bodies of convention, and familiarity with detailed mythologies and
highly developed scholarly disciplines, all of which enhance the possibilities both
for that vision and for the expressions of its fruits.

Shriharsha's *Life of Naishadha* is widely viewed as the richest example of the
Sanskrit Grand Poem, a genre with a recorded history reaching back a thousand
years before his time. The work's fame rests partly on his success in dealing with
the considerable burden of the past, especially in managing the genre's two apparently incompatible demands: an insistence on the independence of individual
verses, and the need to connect these verses within a larger whole.

The first task entails the expert use of what has been called a "pointed style,"
in which each verse, syntactically independent from those surrounding it, must
deliver to the reader's mind a single punch, resembling the point of a joke in that it
involves a combination of recognition (in the readers' discovery that the description or explanation offered is fitting in some way) and surprise (in their feeling of
hearing something newly formed). In Shriharsha's verses the power of this punch
is enhanced by his constantly shifting selection of elements brought into com-
pressed cooperation, drawn both from everyday life and from the many categories
of knowledge and practice accumulated throughout the Sanskrit language's centuries of continuous use.

The second task, that of providing these same verses some continuity within
the larger work, begins most broadly with the theme of the poem at hand. The

genre of the Grand Poem is in origin one dealing with the martial topic of a hero's military endeavor and success, but in *Life of Naishadha*, Shriharsha chose as his basic theme a marital one instead, imitating the choice made much earlier by Kalidasa in his *Origin of the Young God*, and using a royal love story taken from the old epic. He thus is able to deal throughout the poem with two of the favorite topics of Indian rulers (and therefore of Sanskrit court poets), that of royal power and its military and political components, and that of sex and the psychology of erotic love. Both topics provide their own frameworks of continuity. And underlying both of them here is a persistent interest in linguistic, philosophical, and spiritual matters.

The product of bringing together so many levels of meaning, through drawing on so many bodies of knowledge, will often be complex, and may rest on details both of the Sanskrit language and of its associated disciplines. Even so, a sensitive translation may convey much of its richness even in English, and an awareness of the dense combinations of meaning characteristic of Shriharsha's verses is useful even in places where only a portion of what the Sanskrit has to offer is reflected directly in the English translation.

I propose to focus on a single verse, occurring near the middle of our passage, in order to describe in some detail how the two tasks I have mentioned are addressed in the Sanskrit verse, and then to comment much more briefly on how the same tasks are approached in the verses leading up to it. Here, again, is the verse:

> What his heart says to you—
> his deepest secret—
> his face openly reveals
> by its pallor, as is only fitting
> for a friend of the moon
> who happens to be a friend
> of his enemy, Desire. (3.107)

Here the topic at hand, given that the goose is reporting on the symptoms of love in Nala, is that of the features of his face that indicate his lovesickness: its pallor and its growing thinness. Neither is mentioned explicitly in the original Sanskrit, but both will be obvious to an experienced reader as conventional elements at this point in a love story, and both are in fact clearly indicated through a standard poetic device, in which the description of Nala's face as being a "friend" of the moon is a way of referring to its similarity to the moon, which itself is pale in color and can repeatedly be seen growing thinner. What sets up the punch of the verse is the way in which Shriharsha uses this friendship, interpreting it in another way as well, as the basis for a poetic fancy operating not within the sphere of love but in that of politics.

The point made is one of treason, in which Nala's secret hopes are openly betrayed by his own face to the god of love, Kamadeva, who because he is torturing Nala in his separation from Damayanti is portrayed as Nala's enemy. The poetic fancy, a device that often rests on imagining some sentient explanation for the action of an insentient thing, works by justifying this treachery on the part of Nala's face by noting further that the moon is in turn a friend of the god of love; an experienced Sanskrit reader will understand that this is due to the moon's activity as a stimulant of love, and also that in political theory it is considered appropriate for the friend of a friend (of an enemy) to be useful in such a way, but anyone who knows Ella Fitzgerald's "Moonlight in Vermont" and the Beatles' "With a Little Help from My Friends" will understand the same point.

In terms of continuity, both the erotic and the political topics are fitting when viewed against the relevant conventional frameworks. For the love story, the preceding verses will have shown that Shriharsha is following a traditional list of the ten stages of love, and in this verse we have reached the stage of "intention," with its focus on internal hopes and planning. And on the martial side, the verse fits with the lists of topics to be described in a Great Poem as given in the earliest treatises on poetics, in which the first items listed are secret strategizing and the sending of an emissary or spy.

The invented political notion of the face's treachery not only provides the surprising and charming punch of this verse, but is also fitting both in providing a satisfying, albeit imaginary, explanation of the situation and in fitting, in its erotic context, perfectly into the sequence of stages being described. The verse is further enjoyable in that the erotic elements, which are actually the matter at hand, are understood without being explicitly described, while the invented political side is supported in the original Sanskrit by the use of martial terminology (such as naming the love god with reference to his weapon) and of technical terms from the discipline of statecraft (referring to enemies, allies, alliances, and appropriateness).

Other verbal devices in the Sanskrit could be pointed to as contributing to the punch of the verse, such as the fact that its first half, which gives the setup by stating the supposed situation matter-of-factly, is made up entirely of short uncompounded words (eleven in all), while the second half, delivering the punch line by providing the imaginary justification for the situation, is made up largely of two long compounds (and also has eleven words in all, but with most of them in compound).[4]

Here I can mention only a few of the ways in which the verses leading up to verse 107, each in its own way, reflect the two concerns of point and progression. Each verse offers in some form the same combination of a discrete punch, and a place in the larger structure, although not all of them involve to the same extent as this the collecting and compressing of diverse elements.

A principle of conservation of effort (of both poet and audience) is at work, in which if the required element of surprise can be achieved simply by an ingenious connection with something in the everyday world, reliance on conventional or technical material is not required. A clear example is in the first verse spoken by the goose (3.100), in which the poet speaks of Nala and Damayanti as having already been welded together by the love god, through his application of heat, a procedure familiar to everyone who has seen a blacksmith working at the forge (or the mixing of lac). This is enough to provide the expected punch, but also serves an important function in the parallel task of continuity, by initiating the theme of heat, which will run throughout this passage with the double relevance of being associated both with the fever of lovesickness and with the practice of austerities, referred to metaphorically as "heat" in Sanskrit.

This theme of heat is connected in turn with the mythological story of the goddess Parvati's love for Shiva and her resulting austerities, told earlier in Kalidasa's *The Origin of the Young God* and explicitly underlying Shriharsha's treatment of the love story in his own *Life of Naishadha*, thus providing another way in which individual verses find connections. Heat is prominent in a different way as well in Kalidasa's poem, in the episode in which the god of love is incinerated by the fire from Shiva's third eye, resulting in his being bodiless. This fact is referred to repeatedly in Shriharsha's poem, such as in our verse 102, "Bodiless Desire," one of many places where Kamadeva's lack of a body is contrasted to the wholeness and beauty of Nala's body, here treated somewhat more fully through the comparison and contrast between the ways in which both that god and Nala have been subjected to burning.

In the second of the verses spoken by the goose, "His mind is entirely absorbed" (101), we have once again a more complicated offering, drawing as it does on the technicalities of several bodies of knowledge and on double meanings in the Sanskrit. The verse once again attends to the larger contexts as well, by continuing the motif of yogic austerity and by touching on the theme of Nala's relationships to the gods, an important topic elsewhere in the poem (and in the epic tale on which it is based).

This verse also marks the beginning, according to the commentators, of connections with the sequential list of ten stages of love, the first of which is visual pleasure. The list promises to provide a straightforward framework for continuity, but it will turn out that Shriharsha partially abandons any strict attention to the list following the verse we first considered (107), although (as so often happens when a competent poet plays with the rules) he follows what is expected closely enough until then to make it clear that his later looseness is deliberate. His playful approach to the conventional list is also suggested by the several instances in which he uses the official name of one of the stages within the verse connected with it (something frowned upon in theory), and is probably also announced implicitly by the mention in the opening verse (99) that he began to speak "with a smile," and by his admission in the following verse (100) that his job was in fact already accomplished. In any case, it is necessary for the poet to have established a light approach to the ten stages by the time he reaches the last of them in verse

114 ("He's in bad shape"), since that stage is death, and it is far too soon for Nala to die.

In the verses that follow, many of the connections between adjacent verses will be obvious upon reading them in translation. Thus the topic of fire in verse 102 is continued in verse 103, "The king stares," where the punch is provided by a poetic fancy in which the redness of Nala's eyes, in itself a standard symptom caused by sleeplessness due to erotic attachment, is imagined as produced by the internal fire of his fever. Also continued from the previous verse is the attention to the first stage of love with its ocular preoccupation, and in the reference to Nala's rivalry with gods (since Nala here is called "unblinking," a traditional epithet of the gods).

Similar techniques for continuity are used in the verses that follow. Verse 104, "Allow me to restate," obviously contains numerous repetitions of ideas and even words from the verse that precedes it: red eyes, the first stage (mentioned again by name), the lack of blinking, paintings, tears, the action of drinking. The painting appears again in verse 105, which moves to the second stage of love, that of mental attachment, and appears to play with the official name of that stage, rereading it with a slight phonetic change to refer to attachment to a painting. And verse 106, dropping the visual theme while picking up on the theme of breathing introduced in verse 105, moves to the stage of intention or planning (Nala is imagining ways of getting Damayanti, although it is she who is climbing up stairs to reach him), imaginatively achieving its own punch through the poetic figure known as "apparent contradiction" (it is Damayanti who is climbing stairs, but Nala who is panting).

One could similarly trace the various repetitions and modes of continuation that bind the verses together in the remainder of our passage, and the various ways in which each of those verses makes its individual striking point. I hope that enough has already been said to provide some idea of the depth and complexity of meaning that Shriharsha achieves throughout the poem, and of the growing fullness that the accumulating force of that achievement might produce as the poem progresses.

Part of the pleasure in reading Shriharsha is in the growing awareness of the depth that underlies every verse and the knowledge that there are more depths to be plumbed. Such an experience has many parallels in the modern reception of the products of Sanskrit culture, especially the awareness of a depth that goes beyond each pointed moment of enjoyment. There is a traditional saying among learned devotees of Sanskrit literature that to really comprehend the meaning of *Life of Naishadha* is the work of a lifetime. Perhaps this means that the progression of a masterful work of literature continues as long as a life does, or that fully understanding it requires unblinking eyes. Or perhaps this is yet another sort of apparent contradiction. At any rate, Shriharsha teaches us that to enjoy a poem is to look both deeper and broader: there are always more points and further progression.

IF I'M READING YOU RIGHT: READING BODIES, MINDS, AND POETRY IN *LIFE OF NAISHADHA*

Thibaut d'Hubert (Far Reader)

These stanzas from Shriharsha's Sanskrit *Life of Naishadha* offer three "firsts": they depict a first moment of mutual recognition, which is a first union before the protagonists meet in person, and this is the first step in the gradual maturing of their relationship. After obtaining a vision of each other's charms, love awakens in their hearts. This vision is clearly not a direct encounter, nor is it mediated through a portrait, but it is a mental representation impelled by the oral praise of the lover's extraordinary attributes. The arousal of love in absentia—the *amor de lonh* (love from afar) of Shriharsha's close contemporary and Occitan troubadour Jaufré Rudel—may be seen as a *mise-en-abîme* of the very act of savoring poetry: it is the setting into motion of an imaginative process that eventually leads to the transformation of the perceiving subject. What this eventual transformation exactly is or should be is a matter of speculation that fueled some of the most elaborate debates on aesthetics over the centuries. In the domain of poetry, aesthetic experience per se depends on signifiers of the text but lies beyond them, even beyond the signified, and it is distinct from the mundane and psychological manifestation of emotions. A master of the poetic expression of speculative and didactic discourses, Shriharsha plays with the reader and strikes the perfect balance between challenging received knowledge about the symptoms of lovesickness and conveying the emotional density of his characters' experience.

A key figure in this passage is the goose that plays the role of the messenger between Nala and Damayanti. In addition to being equipped with wings that allow him to swiftly convey its message, the goose is itself closely associated with knowledge and speech as it is presented as Brahma's vehicle:

> Sarasvati dwells in our beaks
> among the Vedas, her neighbors;
> it is as if, timid, she didn't go astray from them,
> bound as she is
> by the fetter of good company.[5] (3.65)

The bird thus cultivates a special relationship with the craft of speech represented by Sarasvati, goddess of poetry and the arts, and the truthful, unfailing ritual speech of the Vedas. Its perceptive gaze and ability to read people's behaviors enables it to foresee the successful outcome of its mission:

> The bird could see with total clarity
> that Damayanti was already in love
> with the Nishadha king, so with a smile
> it unlocked the lock on its beak. (3.99)

The goose, then, finally lets Sarasvati out to perform her duty in sealing this love relationship:

> "Princess," said the goose, "if I'm reading
> you right, there's nothing left for me
> to do. The god of love with his five arrows
> has turned up the heat on both of you,
> and by now you're already
> welded together." (3.100)

The messenger opens his discourse with an eloquent confession regarding the irrelevance of his intervention in this particular case. His ability to read signs already brought him to the conclusion that Damayanti is as tormented by love as Nala. The bird is, of course, not entirely honest when it states that nothing is left for it to do: it must still obtain Damayanti's confession regarding the reciprocity of her feelings. The description of Nala's state and of the torments of separation is thus meant to extract these words of confession from Damayanti. Characterizing the goal as a fait accompli is part of the goose's strategy to achieve it.

That Shriharsha deliberately relies on the conventions regarding the various stages of parting's grief is evident from the last stanza of the passage under scrutiny:

> He's in bad shape, this king: Desire has been shooting
> his five arrows at him from both right and left hands,
> which makes for ten sure hits. He's gone through all
> the first nine stages of being in love. Let's hope that the tenth
> will be like the flower unfolding
> in the empty sky. (3.114)

With this verse, the poet turns the five-arrowed god of love into the concrete representation of the ten stages of love in separation of the Sanskrit tradition. These ten stages end with death, which, as this verse suggests, cannot actually occur when a poem is displaying erotic emotion. This is what is meant by the image of the last flower-arrow becoming "like the flower unfolding in the empty sky," an expression that stands for an impossible event. It is impossible in theory, and it is unlikely to happen in this particular context since the bird already knows that Damayanti will return Nala's love. The bird uses this idiom to formulate a threat that is meant, again, to precipitate the princess's confession, as if to say: we have read the relevant treatises, and we know how such things end, so please do not waste precious time and just admit that you love him.

In a way, by openly—and ironically—stating the irrelevance of his function as a messenger, the bird set the tone for the interpretation of the rest of his discourse. As we already saw, the concluding stanza also suggests the connivance between him and the reader regarding the fortunate outcome of his endeavor. More than the progression of Nala through various stages of love in separation, it is his state of constant contemplation of the mental image of Damayanti that the poet wants to convey. Whereas the term *lovesickness* and the description of its symptoms emphasize the external dimension of parting's grief, Shriharsha focuses on the character's inner states and describes them as a form of austerity: we are dealing with a lover turned ascetic.

In a stanza that describes Nala's anxiousness, the beloved becomes an ethereal entity that pervades her lover's meditative state:

> You, lady, live in his heart,
> but you're also somehow outside him,
> in fact you're his very life's breath
> moving through nose and mouth.
> His mind, too, being utterly absorbed
> in you, never budges from that wondrous
> painting, and this, too,
> is a wonder. (3.105)

This stanza shows the total absorption of the mind in the visualization of the still absent beloved. Shriharsha was operating within a paradigm of the stages of love in separation that foregrounds a contemplative approach to love. Separation becomes a means to foster both concentration and the inner heat with which the goose opened its description:

> Bodiless Desire must be thinking: "Once
> our two bodies were equal. Mine
> got burnt, but his was never even
> slightly boiled." On fire with envy, seizing on the fact
> that *you* are far away, Desire
> is now scorching
> his skin. (3.102)

> The king stares, unblinking, at your portrait
> on the wall, drinking you in
> with eyes red from tears
> or maybe it's from the fire
> you've lit inside him. (3.103)

Desire turns into its own antidote and the fire of passion is alleviated by the fire of austerities. The lover-ascetic is a very productive theme in South Asian literature and we find beautiful early examples of it in Prakrit literature, such as this stanza from Hala's *Seven Hundred Short Poems* (ca. second century CE, Deccan):

> Scorched by long, burning, repeated sighs,
> drenched by a stream of tears,
> away from you
> the woman's lower lip
> performs the austerity of water and fire.[6] (*Seven Hundred Short Poems* 2.85/185)

Nala is equally consumed by the love that burns within, which brings him closer to the figure of his tormentor, Desire, who became bodiless after being burnt by Shiva's third eye for attempting to disturb the god's meditation:

> He's grown thin, pierced in vain
> by the arrows of Desire.
> Only his beauty remains intact.
> Yet even now, after losing almost
> all his body, he's still competing with,
> and defeating the bodiless god. (3.109)

In the goose's speech, the lovers are already united because the heat of desire welded them together, because Damayanti is the vital breaths of Nala the meditating yogi, and because of the constant reminiscence of his beloved, the object of his contemplation with whom he eventually becomes one:

> You are continually climbing up
> the tall ladder of his imagination
> as he showers a rain of sighs.
> From thinking only about you
> he's *become you*. (3.106)

The beauty of the stages of love is not the logic that governs them, which countless theoreticians have described, discussed, and debated, from Andreas Capellanus in medieval Europe to Ibn Hazm and Ibn ʿArabi in the Islamicate world to scores of South Asian literary theorists. Rather, it is the array of possible causes that induce the peculiar state of the lover that inspires poets. The poet who contemplates his character and the reader who deciphers the symptom with him are the ashamed physicians of Shriharsha's verse:

> Speaking of shame, the expert physicians
> who are treating him, shy as he is, for his high fever
> have nothing whatever to say
> about the etiology of his condition.
> Embarrassment apparently
> is contagious. (3.111)

It is, of course, a fool's game, because, like the goose, everyone knows that love is the root of his symptoms and that none of them are really threatening the lover's life. This feigned confusion keeps creation alive in a perpetual search for the true cause of a pair of lovers' odd behaviors:

> Allow me to restate this problem:
> 1) He's studying that painting of you
> 2) Unblinking
> 3) With deep attention and affection.
> 4) There are tears in his eyes.

5) Those tears are mine, says the eye. That's what happens
if you don't blink.
6) No way, says love. They're all mine.
7) This dispute remains
unsolved. (3.104)

Ativirarama Pandyan's
Tamil *Life of Naidatha*

TRANSLATOR'S NOTE AND TEXT

Ativirarama Pandyan, king in the far southern city of Tenkasi in the second half of the sixteenth century, gives his own version of the same passage from Shriharsha translated in the previous chapter but in a Tamil style rich and complex enough to rival its Sanskrit model. His *Life of Naidatha* is the key work in the Tenkasi Renaissance, arguably the first fully modern moment in Tamil literature. Together, both Ativirarama and his brother Varatungarama produced a library of masterpieces in Tamil, and their court was crowded with other gifted and innovative poets. In their works, we can observe experiments with highly individualistic and personal sensibilities, a radically ironic tone vis-à-vis the older tradition, a new empirical interest in the natural world, and a hypertrophied imaginative aesthetics.

ATIVIRARAMA PANDYAN'S *LIFE OF NAIDATHA* (4.107–23)

> "Whatever is inside will always rise up
> to the face. To read the signs
> and state these matters in words is a great
> talent: that's what messengers are for!
> No one *knows* with the clarity
> that is yours. So save me, sweet goose
> of fine feathers, before I wither away.
> Go now, and fast." (4.107)

> She spoke openly, her voice enough
> to make the cuckoo ashamed, and sweeter
> by far than ambrosia or liquid sugarcane
> or the honey in a flowering branch.

The goose saw into her heart and
was glad. He looked at her, drinking her in
with his eyes, as he spoke these measured words. (4.108)

"Ah, you whose full breasts are budding
with the pale signs of yearning and luminous
as cinnabar, though they've brought your tiny waist
to the breaking point, all that you've said is utterly
true. I don't think there's any need to broker
a meeting of the minds. Both Nala and you are ill
at heart with love. It's all the work of Desire,
who is also spreading the word. (4.109)

When that king of all the worlds asked us
which woman is the loveliest in this world
bounded by the ocean and in the Nether World
and the world of the gods, we of course said
it was you. You found your way
into his heart by following the arrow
the Love God fired. Lady with eyes
like the innocent doe: have you forgotten?
Or are you merely pretending
not to know? (4.110)

He, the warrior king, wants to paint
your portrait. He's collected many
precious stones and polished them
for this collage, each for one
of your perfect features.[1] But it's not
so easy. He grumbles: 'This damned canvas
is not wide enough to paint her breasts,' or
'The tip of my paintbrush is nowhere near
fine enough to paint her waist.'
He's frustrated: deep psychic
despair. All he can do is stare,
unblinking, yearning. (4.111)

This is what he says—the king whose honed spear
cut his enemies to pieces and spread a feast
for kites, hawks, and whole flocks of crows—'*You*
are the breath of my life, and *you* are the only remedy
for the sickness of desire that has possessed me
with all the suffering that entails.' He thinks
this thought in misery, with joy in his heart. (4.112)

This is that same person who is Death
to his enemies, his toenails polished to a glossy gleam
by the crowns of alien kings, and who is so dense
with beauty as he rides his huge elephant to victory
that men can't bear it and wish *they* were women.
Now he's a shadow of himself, and all five
of his senses hunger for nothing
but you. (4.113)

Listen to me, woman whose is hair is so dark
it makes the rain cloud look pale, woman
of dancing earrings: It's hard to say whether
he's been reduced to this state by the frontal attack
of the Love God with his five arrows dark with wasps,
honey-bees, and black beetles, or whether the white rays
pouring from the moon have undone him—since every time
he sees them, his body is further overwhelmed. (4.114)

The Love God keeps shooting long arrows of flowers
from his sugarcane bow at this king. That's one thing.
But beyond that, Desire has also apparently stolen his
good character. It's reached the point where if he had
to do something really wicked in order to lie on your breasts,
he'd do it without thinking. Whatever deep wisdom he once had
is gone. He's so unhinged by love that he would feel no shame
at becoming your abject slave. (4.115)

He stares at your beautiful body, starkly visible
in his mind. He's losing his grip, his very bones
melting down. He throws himself
at your young breasts. Then he decides
you must be angry and, as if trying to appease you,
laughs out loud. But when he sees you fading away
into empty space, he rushes after you like a lunatic,
awareness shattered, splintered, lost. (4.116)

He's the wild elephant of Nishadha who's crossed over a vast ocean
of enemy kings with spears reeking of rotting flesh. No one
could stop him. Now he's drowning in the waves of the river named
'Far From You,' with no place to stand. God help us!
He's passing out. Lady with the bow-shaped brow:
it's up to you now. Don't let him sink
to the final stage. (4.117)

Kings who fought him now sleep in the courtyard of his palace,
using their palms as pillows. We know he's a lion

among men when it comes to war. But look what's happened
to his mind, look at the state he's in. That's why he sent me
as his messenger to *you*, lady with breasts high
as the mountain slopes. But don't worry. It's all over.
You've won this destiny by whatever you did,
both of you, in some former life. (4.118)

Murugan's spear, the infant moon that three-eyed Shiva
wears on his head, the serpent that Vishnu, husband of Shri,
has taken for his bed—all these you have stolen
and made them over as your eyes, your bright forehead,
and your wide loins. Is it, then, any wonder that you
also robbed Nala, that lord of elephants in heat,
of his heart? (4.119)

'Golden girl, you who are the immortal sweetness
of speech, voluptuous goddess of the lotus:
how could I imagine sketching subtle sandal-paste designs
anywhere but on your luscious breasts, so heavy
that your waist, sleek as a streak of lightning,
has been worn away and may well snap?'
That's what your king said to me
in a garden buzzing with bees, so that I could
tell you. (4.120)

It will be my task to shake my wings
after my dip in the Ganges of the Sky, to sprinkle you
with a cooling drizzle and in this way to undo
your inevitable exhaustion after making love
in every possible passionate position.
That time is near, very near. (4.121)

I'd better go now, woman whose long black eyes
are deadlier by far than any lethal spear or fine-honed sword,
deadlier than Death himself or the fatal poison
that arose from the sea. While I'm rapidly
wending my way to the king, you mustn't worry.
I promise you he'll soon be riding his regal chariot
straight to your chambers, and he'll be here
before you know it, aflame with hunger
 for your dazzling breasts. (4.122)

So I'll be off, with your permission, to Nishadha, where conches,
heavy with child, drift through the channels in the fields
and give birth to pearls on the golden
inner ring of the lotus, and then white herons

perch over them, certain that these
are their eggs." Thus spoke the all-too-innocent
goose, and Damayanti of the long eyes
sharp as swords gently stroked its wings and,
courteous though eager with desire,
said, "Go." (4.123)

HEARING AND MADNESS: READING ATIVIRARAMA PANDYAN'S *LIFE OF NAIDATHA*

N. Govindarajan (Near Reader)

Ativirarama's *Life of Naidatha* is not just another version of the story of Nala and Damayanti. It is a Tamil version of Shriharsha's Sanskrit *Life of Naishadha*, but this Tamil poem does not follow the chapter divisions of its Sanskrit model. This is to good effect, and Ativirarama's version seems more logical and coherent than Shriharsha's. Indeed, the telling is straightforward and simple. It begins with a description of Nala's country and city, followed by an account of the two lovers' romance, how they overcame all obstacles to marry each other, and their subsequent happy marriage.

The passage translated here is from the fourth chapter of *Life of Naidatha*. This chapter narrates the errands of a goose as a go-between for Nala and Damayanti, including various dialogues between the three characters. The first is between Nala and the goose. Ativirarama breaks this dialogue into small units: Nala's meeting with the goose; the goose's portrayal of the matchless beauty of Damayanti to Nala; Nala's request that it act as his go-between; and the goose's departure on its mission. In this first dialogue, the main narrator is the goose, and Nala is a passive listener throughout. The second dialogue is a long exchange between the goose and Damayanti. After hearing about the beauty of Nala, Damayanti decides to marry him and asks the goose to convey her love to him. But the goose, before flying off, tells her that Nala is already in love with her and actually has been longing for her. Our selection consists of seventeen verses from this second dialogue in which the goose does most of the talking.

Hearing. When does love begin? The first treatise on Tamil grammar and poetics, the *Tolkāppiyam*, composed during the early centuries of the Common Era, suggests that love starts in the eyes, when the eyes of the hero and the eyes of the heroine meet, and especially once they can see the acceptance of love in each other's eyes. It is the eyes that initiate love, and it is the eyes that also acknowledge it. The *Tolkāppiyam* portrays this process as a subtle dialogical act, although no words are actually uttered. Sight is a soundless condition for and an expression of passion, so much so that another classical Tamil text, the *Tirukkuṟaḷ*, says that when two pairs of eyes meet and accept each other, words are useless.

In *Life of Naidatha*, love begins in a different way. It starts with words, the words of a goose. The goose promises to Nala that he'll paint his great beauty in the middle of her mind. The goose also describes Damayanti to him so effectively that Nala can see her completely with his mind's eye. Nala then says, in a passage that is not translated in this chapter:

> Many have spoken of her white smile, her mouth
> red as coral, her overpowering
> beauty, but your words have almost placed her
> before my very eyes. Seeing through
> the mind of a true friend is really
> seeing. Eyes that barely see
> what's right in front of them,
> especially something very fine,
> are only there to touch up
> the seer's face.[2]

This image of Damayanti in Nala's mind comes not from seeing but from hearing. Nala sees Damayanti right in front of him as he hears the goose speak. Apt words and astute ears become key in this context. A visual image is drawn inside Nala's mind by the goose's words. Hearing enables and then enhances what the mind's eye sees. This seems to be a deliberate break from earlier Tamil poetic models, one that may be influenced by Tamil Tantric culture.

In Tamil Tantric culture, sound has many important potentials and consequences. This is because the Goddess resides in sound, and in high-level Tantric practice, she inhabits sound to the point of indistinguishability: the Goddess *is* sound. The tenth-century *Tirumantiram*, the seminal text of the Hindu Tantric tradition, proclaims that the Goddess is *ōmkāri*, the "Om" sound; she is also *hrīmkāri*, the "Hrīm" sound. Repetition and rearrangement of particular sounds will reveal this hidden presence of the goddess. But how to repeat and rearrange these sounds is known only to a few. Only a competent guru will know this secret-coded grammar of language. Such a guru can transmit the properly arranged sounds directly into the ears of others, and their own minds will then visualize the image of the Goddess.

Ativirarama seems to assume such Tantric ideas and practices in his work. As we see in the verse just quoted, the goose speaks about Damayanti to Nala and vice versa. Nala has heard of her earlier. Many have spoken of her "white smile." They have spoken about her overpowering beauty. But only the words of the goose can make her appear before his mind's eye. In other words, the goose acts like a Tantric guru in this passage. Just as a skillful guru perceives the world better than others, carefully selects what is best for his students in that context, and also knows how to impart that to his students, so does the goose. Nala, in turn, acts like a Tantric practitioner who can see the Goddess thanks to his guru's accurate instructions. As Shulman has said elsewhere, "A very ancient South Indian notion of the pragmatics of poetic speech has merged with the Tantric practice of phonic magic."[3]

In the selection that opens this chapter, Nala tries to impart substance to his initial mental image of Damayanti by painting her portrait. Additionally, he collects many precious stones—one for each of her perfect features—and polishes them to use as ornaments for the painting. In the end his efforts to paint Damayanti fail:

> "The tip of my paintbrush is nowhere near
> fine enough to paint her waist."
> He's frustrated: deep psychic
> despair. All he can do is stare,
> unblinking, yearning. (4.111)

Here Ativirarama goes beyond anything in Tamil Tantric culture. In Tantric practice, once the image is evoked in the mind, it becomes stable and lives forever inside. Nala's mental image of Damayanti is unstable, and there is a constant rush of images in his mental "inscape," even as some fade away into empty space:

> He stares at your beautiful body, starkly visible
> in his mind. He's losing his grip, his very bones
> melting down. He throws himself
> at your young breasts. Then he decides
> you must be angry and, as if trying to appease you,
> laughs out loud. But when he sees you fading away
> into empty space, he rushes after you like a lunatic,
> awareness shattered, splintered, lost. (4.116)

For Ativirarama, the Tantric version of the metaphysical stance of nonduality or unity with the divine consort is set aside by a constant and conscious notion of split, or duality. Nala is "drowning in the waves of the river named / 'Far From You'" (4.117), and the goose urges Damayanti to save him.

Madness.   E. Valentine Daniel has said that in the Tamil worldview, "knowledge about the other, or object knowledge, is but an extension of self-knowledge." Self-knowledge attempts to know the other by establishing a relationship of sameness. In other words, it tries to know the self by seeing itself in the other. "At the point at which object knowledge is completely incorporated or engulfed in this manner," adds Daniel, "not only is there no longer object knowledge, but there is also no longer a self which is defined against object knowledge. What remains is pure knowledge."[4] But what happens when self-knowledge, rather than making a relationship with the other, comes about through distinguishing the self from the other? Is a relationship with the other still possible? And what happens when self-knowledge tries to fit the other, conceived in this manner, into its own phenomenal world? It is here that *Life of Naidatha* moves into the complicated Tamil world of knowing and its aftermath.

In both processes, according to *Life of Naidatha*, the ill-conceived other makes bare the rigidity of the projecting self and disequilibrates the resulting relationship between the self and its world. Nala's self-knowledge has conceived Damayanti, and "Damayanti found her way into his heart" (4.110). She is the breath of his life (4.112). Now she is in Nala's world. It is the world of valor, firmness, blood, flesh, victory, and so on. He is the king of all the worlds (4.110), "the king whose honed spear / cut his enemies into pieces and spread a feast / for kites, hawks, and whole flocks of crows" (4.112). He is "Death / to his enemies, his toenails polished to a glossy gleam / by the crowns of alien kings" (4.113). Likewise, "he's the wild elephant of Nishadha who's crossed over a vast ocean / of enemy kings with spears reeking of rotting flesh" (4.117), and "he's a lion / among men when it comes to war" (4.118). But Damayanti slowly deprives him of all such embodiments, even though she is also the only cure to his disease:

> "*You*
> are the breath of my life, and *you* are the only remedy
> for the sickness of desire that has possessed me
> with all the suffering that entails." He thinks
> this thought in misery, with joy in his heart. (4.112)

Nala's good character is stolen, and "Whatever deep wisdom he once had / is gone" (4.115). His kingliness is gone, and he has become an "abject slave" to Damayanti (4.115). He is no more a king, he is not even "Nala" anymore. Everything about him has been destroyed by her. "He's losing his grip, his very bones / melting down" (4.116). He is like a "lunatic, / awareness shattered, splintered, lost" (4.116). "He's passing out" (4.117). "He's frustrated: deep psychic despair" (4.111).

Certainly madness has overtaken him. But why? In Tamil culture, any woman who has come of age is thought to be filled with sacred power, *aṇanku*.[5] This sacred power is an invisible and ever-potent force. It resides inside women and is always at work in them. "Aṇanku is the power of fertility inherent in woman and it represents a value more significant to her affines, primarily to the men-folk, than to herself."[6] In the Tamil notion of femininity, *aṇanku* is sacred yet dangerous. Ativirarama makes a secret alliance with the ancient tradition of *aṇanku*. Damayanti or perhaps her very own "sacred power," the *aṇanku* in her, pervades the surrounding atmosphere. Damayanti's hair is so dark that it makes the rain cloud look pale (4.114), "her voice [is] enough / to make the cuckoo ashamed, and sweeter / by far than ambrosia or liquid sugarcane / or the honey in a flowering branch" (4.108). Usually a dark color symbolizes fertility in Indian culture. In Tamil love poetry, this color is inherent in the heroine. Damayanti's potency has taken possession of the whole cosmos and enslaved all of it as her own. She turns Nala's environment into an enemy, acting against him.

The goose wonders whether Nala's state of deprivation might have been caused by "the white rays / pouring out of the moon" (4.114). Ativirarama draws our attention to the insanity of Nala in a way that highlights Damayanti's power. Her *aṉaṅku* possesses Nala. "He throws himself / at your young breasts," the goose tells Damayanti (*aṉaṅku* is often said to reside in the breasts of a young girl; 4.116). Then, according to the goose, Nala decides "you must be angry and, as if trying to appease you, / laughs out loud" (4.116). In his madness Nala becomes a poet (4.120). He has not even a place to stand (4.117). Nala is dying, although his death is not physical, but rather the uprooting of his own being. At the same time, Damayanti's power over Nala is also benevolent and protective, and Nala knows this too (4.112).

The goose foresees a good future for Nala. In that future, Damayanti will unite with him. Her power will be pacified. On that very occasion, the goose will come again and, after dipping in the Ganges of the sky, it will shake its wings and sprinkle her with a cooling drizzle to alleviate her inevitable exhaustion (4.121). This sprinkling will, once again, rearrange their respective worlds, bringing them and their love into an equilibrium and allowing them to live peacefully and eternally.

Medicine for Poets.   When Ativirarama Pandyan, the author of *Life of Naidatha*, sent this poem to his elder brother's wife, a poetess in her own right, he probably expected her approval. Instead, she sent a sarcastic note saying that the poem was like a hunting dog that started running fast but then suddenly stopped, panting excessively and completely exhausted, without catching its quarry. This is usually taken as a note on the abrupt change of pace and style toward the end of the work, and the irregular, barking-like manner in which the later story of Nala and Damayanti (including their tragic separation and eventual reunion) is told. It may also be taken to signal a rift between an older poetic order, represented here by the family of the older brother, and new poetic ideals of the younger brother (the two, by the way, were also at war with one another). We do not know what the reaction of Ativirarama Pandyan was, but we do know that others saw in it far more than his sister-in-law did. In fact, his book has had a distinguished place in Tamil literary history since it first appeared, so much so that there is an old saying: *Naiṭatam pulavarkkōr auṭatam* (*Naidatha* is a medicine for poets). That is to say, *Life of Naidatha* cures whatever may afflict a poet, perhaps thanks to its combination of hearing, madness, and its promise of the goose's return, and with it, a pleasant shower from the heavenly Ganges. In this, the Tamil *Life of Naidatha* stands unique.

HOW WE READ

Sheldon Pollock (Far Reader)

> *All that glitters is gold*
> SMASH MOUTH

The question prior to "What is sensitive reading?"—the question the title of this book implies—is the one implicit in my own title. A silly one, many would say, since reading is something, like walking, that we do without much thought once we learn how. Do we ask ourselves what it means to read when we sit down with our coffee and the morning newspaper? Of course not, but we might well, because it is no straightforward matter.

By "reading" I don't mean what the dictionary tells us reading is: "mentally interpreting the characters or symbols" of which written matter is composed. I mean making sense of the text made up of those characters (I will be speaking here of a literary text, but my observations are meant to apply to all texts, religious, legal, historical). And sense-making becomes more complicated, becomes more of a problem requiring second-order reflection, the further in time and space the origins of the text are from the reader. A "classical" work of Indian literature—by which I mean any work composed prior to the coming of Western colonialism and the break in Indian literary culture that colonialism effected—is perhaps the limit case of this problem. Such a work poses questions of meaning at the extreme, and in fact one use of exposing ourselves to such literature is that the lessons learned in trying to make sense of it apply to any act of reading of any text any-where. As Heinrich Heine said of us Jews ("Jews are like everyone else, only more so"), classical Indian texts are like all others, only more so. The surfeit here is due to the fact that making sense of an Indian text requires the full range of meanings that "sense" can possess. Let me explain what I mean by this.

The morning paper comes, or appears to come, in a kind of pure presentness: it has no past (indeed, who wants yesterday's papers?). A literary work from, say, sixteenth-century south India, however, has a past; it has, in fact, what for analyti-cal reasons we can describe as two distinct pasts. One is the deep past of its moment of creation, where the text possessed various meanings for the original audience of the work. The text also has a shallower past, the three centuries following its pro-duction, where again it possessed a range of meanings for its readers. It also of course has a present, our own direct confrontation with the work here and now.

My basic argument is that none of these meanings, those of its origin or recep-tion or now, is a truer meaning—more closely corresponding with, or a better rep-resentation of, the essence of the text—than any other, for the simple reason that a text *has no essence*. The one true meaning of the text lies in none of those three readings, but rather in their sum total, in their full diversity itself. Particular read-ers—whether primary, traditional, or present-day—have by definition no access to that full diversity. Excavating that true meaning by assembling those readings is the work of the specialist in making sense of texts, namely, the philologist.

Accordingly, neither the "context-near" nor the "context-far" modes of reading, to adopt the idiom of the editors of this book, can ever stand independently for us philologists. We cannot read responsibly—that is, with the scholarly, even ethical, orientation of understanding not only that we impose our meaning on the world but that we must allow the world to impose its meaning on us, without which read-ing itself actually would become superfluous and hence meaningless—if we do not tack between them: between what a work meant in its historical moment and what it means to me here and now, with a third plane of meaning, that generated over the history of its reception, situated somewhere between "near" and "far." None of these meanings can simply be avoided. Presentist reading is not some optional practice; it is how we do, and must, first approach a text, which only subsequently we address more complexly. Contextualizing, or historicizing, reading, by contrast, is something we only learn to do, but once learned—and it is now universally learned—it cannot be unlearned. The meanings offered by a tradition are less often accessible to us unless we look closely. Few people, I suspect, bother any longer to read Shakespeare in the old Furness Variorum editions (which excerpts editor and commentator exegeses over several centuries), though Indianists always read, as people in India used to read, embedded in tradition. In any case, tradition has a way of seeping into our consciousness whether we know it or not; it helps constitute our prior hermeneutical situatedness, Gadamer's famous *Vorurteile*, or prejudgments (Shakespeare does not drop down right out of the sky to any contemporary reader, he comes trailing traditional clouds of glory). There is not only the potential for conflict among these meanings, but every likelihood of conflict. And that is so because of the inevitable cleavages in consciousness of readers as historical beings, and as a result the very different ways features of the text will address themselves to them.

For the philologist in me, then, my reading here and now—what I have taken to calling the presentist reading (a descriptor that of course applies to every earlier reading viewed in its historical moment)—can never stand alone as it is being asked to stand here. But, of course, it cannot stand together unless and until it has first tried to stand alone. For the exercise assigned to me here, however, I have to pretend to be far separated from the context of the selection: from its sixteenth-century social-political context (which I know something about); from its cotextual context (including the various Sanskrit originals with which the Tamil work is in conversation, and the vast body of Indic literary theory it is aware of, about which I also know something); from the textual context of the selection (like every other Indianist I know what finally happens in the Nala-Damayanti story—and I know it is a *poem* as defined by Indian tradition, and not a historical or religious or legal document). Here I am asked to consider the text completely denuded of all these contexts, as if I.A. Richard's were handing me the poem, or it came to me on the New York subway wall as part of the MTA's "Poetry in Motion" series, or better yet, as a reading assignment in a Great Books class I will pretend I am taking as a freshman in college. What meanings can the text have for this sort of me here and now?

The fact that has primacy for me in any *theoretical* analysis of reading, "sensitive" or otherwise, is that my presentist reading will have an irreducible and ineluctable dimension of my historically constituted subjectivity, and for that reason will only ever access one plane of the truth of the text. The *methodological* question, by contrast, is only a subsidiary fact, namely that all presentist readings, if necessarily partial and equally partial, are not all equal. Some methods unequivocally reveal or explain more of the text to our presentist eyes than others do. This is obvious in the case of lexical and grammatical methods, where knowing (that is, knowing how to figure out) what the words mean and how they best construe is unequivocally more illuminating of the text than not knowing at all. Less obvious but potentially equally illuminating are narratological, rhetorical, discourse-analytical, and other such methods that help us to look more deeply, to seek patterns, to discover and put pressure on tensions, to excavate more systematically the world that the text is conjuring, its vision of human being.

So then, with the proviso we acknowledge that while "sensitive" reading is a fine thing, it is a partial thing, we can happily inquire into what we come to understand about our selection when we ask about, say, its narrative organization, formal features, discursive tensions, and orientation toward the world.

Poetics and Patriarchy.   Like the other selections in this book, *Life of Naidatha* comes to me in a contemporary translation. But all translation is a form of reading (just as all reading is a form of translation)—an especially and visibly transformative form of reading. And as such it is subject to the many constraints I have already described. All the issues about subjectivity that I know I am facing when reading in general, and when reading this particular selection, had to have been faced by the translator. The text thus comes to me preread, prepresentist, so to speak; we are already—and as I claim, we are always-already—distant from the possibility of some single textual truth. (Some who argue "against world literature" tell me to learn Tamil; a noble sentiment, but remember that that only offers another plane of textual truth, and cannot bring us closer to The One Truth, because it does not exist.)

The selection is just that, a selection, and it is impossible to extrapolate, in some Auerbachian fashion, to the whole work (and beyond) since ex hypothesi I do not know the whole work. Is it possible that, as is the case in this selection, in the whole work too, and others of its genre, *nothing much actually happens?* Nothing at least on the surface. It is just a dialogue between a lovelorn girl and a talking bird (some theriomorphic concretization of the girl's hopes? some prefigurement even of her soul?), elaborating in multiple ways on her longing and her lover's. Just below that surface, however, a great deal indeed is taking place: the workings of overwhelming desire, assertions of political power, threats of dangerous transgressions, battles, violence, death. We seem to be in a world of poetry very different from what I am familiar with, where action occurs not so much in a narrative mode but in a figurative one: the story seems to be in the rhetoric, while rhetoric itself is part of the story. And what rhetoric!

The level of figuration here is overwhelming, comparable to nothing in literature known to me. I have seen Indian paintings in museums that seem jewel-encrusted, burnished with gold, resplendent with color, and which in that sense are very like the ornamentation of this selection. In fact, the text itself seems to call attention to this shared aesthetic, when the poet describes the "precious stones" polished for use in the portrait of the woman, which is itself a figure of the lover's quest for union. But figures of this sort are not part of my world—no more than the ornamentation on the seventeenth-century building where I once lived in Brussels could adorn my former Mies van der Rohe apartment in Chicago. It is their very density that prompts me to think about these figures and the kind of work they are doing.

For this poet, literature itself seems to be, in some very significant measure, precisely an exploration of the outer limits of language, here of describing otherwise indescribable objects or themes: the ineffable beauty of a woman, say, or the near-death experience of unfulfilled love. Matters such as these cannot be directly expressed but can only be captured in language that somehow bends reality to its purposes. Thus, the woman's voice or hair or eyes are not meaningfully described as "beautiful": no, her "voice [is] enough / to make the cuckoo ashamed"; her "hair is so dark / it makes the rain cloud look pale"; her "long black eyes / are deadlier by far than any lethal spear or fine-honed sword." Who piles up figure upon figure? (Well, maybe more than we take time to register—or took time to register before this selection forced us to; consider now the line "its fins like blades, its milky skin and wool-grey eyes," in a Dave Eggers novel.[7])

Things figurative can get very complicated very quickly: for example, the woman's eyes, forehead, and "wide loins" are actually things she has stolen from others—the spear of Murugan, the moon of Shiva, the serpent-bed of Vishnu (gods I guess, but I am ignorant)—so she's a clever and audacious and even impious thief, too, who can steal a man's heart. In general, however, these figures remind me of standard similes I already know. Yet the poet goes further in his figuration, seeking a way to capture a thing's ineffability not only by comparison but also by hyperbole. Vassals don't just bow down to a king; they polish his toenails with the gleam of their crowns; they find him so beautiful they wish they were women. The king himself is so lovesick that the rays of moon overwhelm him like the arrows of the god of love; his very bones melt. I feel certain there is far more going on in the figuration in this text (including the last verse, which is too allusive for me to understand), and I am led to wonder if they have ancient handbooks explaining how these complex figures work.

The hyperbole of figuration is complemented by what seems to be hyperbole of description. The king is not just in love: he is utterly overwhelmed by love. But here something curious begins to show itself, in that this extreme state is repeatedly expressed by the conjuncture of political violence and sexual desire. Juxtaposed to Nala's cutting "his enemies into pieces and spread[ing] a feast / for kites" is his declaration that his beloved is "the breath of my life." The man who is "Death to his enemies" is himself dying of love; he who has crossed "a vast ocean / of enemy kings with spears reeking of rotting flesh" is now drowning in longing for his beloved.

The hyperbole takes us into even stranger, darker areas, where we no longer feel certain that the poet is rhetorically exaggerating—where we are no longer sure this is still poetic play. How are we to take the following?

> . . . Desire has also apparently stolen his
> good character. It's reached the point where if he had
> to do something really wicked in order to lie on your breasts,
> he'd do it without thinking. (4.115)

The repeated references to violence, not just legitimate violence against enemies but what to my modern mind is criminal violence, when conjoined with references to desire produce an odd concatenation, one that asks us to pause and think. Of course, the god of love, in this old and far-off world as in my own, is himself an archer (he shoots arrows, five of them, "long arrows of flowers," at the king), and so violence and desire are linked in a primal figure. But is the poet here not pushing us, especially in this last verse, beyond this innocent mythological convention?

Since I am context-far, I know nothing about any aesthetic reflection in the tradition over tensions such as that between violence and love (is the copresence of such emotions common in this literature?). More broadly, I do not know whether King Nala is characteristically prone, or somehow driven, to reckless action; whether other kings in ancient Indian literature are shown to be tempted to evil by desire; or whether the poet—who was himself a king, according to the headnote—may be reflecting on the precarious balance between public justice and private fulfillment. All I do know is the text, and this suggests—however rhetorically meant the last verse may be, for remember that a "rhetorical question" provides an answer even while not expecting one—it was perfectly possible in this world to imagine, and to fear, the most dangerous kind of desire: one embodied in an authority that can simply *demand* fulfilment.

As unsettling as the intimation here of unconstrained power is the poet's reduction—as I see it, who know nothing about gender relations in ancient India—of the woman to her sheer physicality. Of course, modern English poets I am fond of have reflected analogously on the mystery of body and soul; "love comes in at the eye,"[8] we're told; "only God, my dear, / Could love you for yourself alone / And not your yellow hair."[9] Is it the same here? Nala has fallen in love with Damayanti only because of her physical beauty—he sought the woman who is "loveliest in this world," one whose "full breasts are budding" so much so as to bring her "tiny waist / to the breaking point" (more hyperbole for the ineffable). And it is that beauty that constitutes the sole focus, the core, of his fantasies and obsessions. The canvas of his painting is not wide enough to accommodate her breasts, his brush not fine enough to draw her waist. He stares in his fantasy at her beautiful body, throws himself at her young breasts, breasts "high as the mountain slopes," "luscious breasts, so heavy / that your waist, sleek as a streak of lightning, / has been worn away and may well snap." The king is "aflame with hunger" for nothing the woman possesses beyond her "dazzling breasts."

I know nothing about Indian moral thought and so the idea that physical perfection is a visible manifestation of moral perfection would not even rise to consciousness; neither would the idea, since I know nothing about Indian religions, that perhaps some perfect unity at the core of such a physical fixation could be thought to prepare the way for greater spiritual unity. A context-far reader like me will instead be inclined to see this as a sector of the long shadow of male power—here poeticized, normalized, and thereby endorsed—reducing woman to her body, a body the man can grab because he is a star; a shadow reaching back, from Yeats, and indeed, *from me*, here in the present, further and further into the past. The only difference between the text and me in this regard is that I can see and acknowledge that shadow—perhaps precisely, in part, thanks to such a distant text as this.

Practices of Reading and a Theory of Meaning.   In the persona of a general, context-far, nonphilological reader, I have tried to offer some sense of the narrative of this selection, its figuration, dualities, political ethics, and gender dynamics. Others will read differently, probably deeper, probably better. But their senses, any more than mine, are unlikely to be borne out by the interpretations found in the deeper past. This is so because "sensitive reading" is no single thing throughout history; it discovers no truth that transcends time and necessity. The sensitive readers of old India, the *sahṛdayas*, never read the way I have been reading here; they never attended, or described, or *saw* the way I have done. Like other early readers (Romans such as Servius, say) they tended not to read works as wholes, for example, instead concentrating their exegetical energies on the single verse. And the sensitivity of *sahṛdayas* themselves was by no means self-same through time: later readers found meanings that were never shared by earlier ones, like the fifteenth-century *Ramayana* allegorists, whose readings would have seemed outlandish to fifth-century readers.

While it may seem self-serving to say so, then, the methodological question, whether my "sensitive" reading is sensitive enough, is not for me the important one to ask (it isn't even coherent given that "enough" is incoherent). Method is a second-order question. The primary one turns on the *theory* of meaning and what, therefore, according to the theoretical viewpoint I set out earlier—the scholarly, or better, philological, viewpoint—we are to do with that reading.

It is not the task of philology, or of my philology, to test my presentist understanding of the text against its meanings in the original context and its meanings over the centuries of its reception. Its task rather is to conjoin that understanding with those others. It strikes me as illogical to say that a subjective sense of a text, which (as philosophical hermeneutics has powerfully argued) is ineluctable, can be *wrong*. By all means let's agree with Auerbach that from his historicist

perspective it will be "unhistorical and dilettantish." But it remains the consciousness summoned forth in me—and in every presentist reader, which means *all*
readers everywhere, a present consciousness is summoned forth—by actual features of the text. Yet at the same time, however, that sense, however necessary a
condition of understanding it is revealed to be, cannot be a sufficient one.

That is the real *Ansatzpunkt* of criticism, to use Auerbach's term, where we
grasp that such sufficiency can be achieved not by methodological refinements—
close reading or distant, surface reading or symptomatic, formalist or discourse-
critical, all of them useful, and better or worse depending on the purposes we
want them to serve and the skill with which we execute them—but only by the
expansive transhistorical synthesis performed by philological scholarship. You
cannot become Auerbach unless you first become yourself. And even Auerbach
was not the Auerbach you think, given his consistent failure even to acknowledge his ever-present presentist self and so to exorcise the ghost of metaphysics—
the reader's own historicity—that haunts historicism. While scholars are readers,
readers *qua* readers are not scholars. They only make their present (or historicist, or traditionalist) sense. Scholars by contrast acknowledge, with the humility
that comes from philological understanding, the actual, astonishing, plenitude of
senses. They know, or should know (though how rarely they actually acknowledge
it) that they will never discover the one true meaning of a text, that they will never
finally crack the code, because *there is no such meaning, there is no such code*. There
is only the panoply of meanings the text has evoked in readers over time. Truth lies
in none of them individually, not even in their triangulation toward some single
consensual meaning. It lies in the very assemblage of all of them, which the philologist holds—entirely possible if difficult though it is to hold—in a kind of non-
evaluative equipoise.

My meaning, like every other, is conditioned by my consciousness as a being
in history and is a consequence of the fact that that consciousness, my world, will
often be radically different from worlds gone by. Learning those older meanings,
by reading texts like the *Life of Naidatha*, helps me to understand just how different other ways of literary being—other forms of consciousness, other worlds, in
short, other ways of being human—have been in the past, and thereby to grasp
how I have become who I am.

Malamangala Kavi's Malayalam
Naishadha in Our Language

TRANSLATOR'S NOTE AND TEXT

Malamangala Kavi, writing in Malayalam (in the so-called Rubies and Coral style, mixing Sanskrit and Malayalam) in the sixteenth or early seventeenth century, shows us a slightly earlier moment in Nala's passionate imagination of Damayanti in his *Naishadha in Our Language*. These two people have fallen in love with one another by hearsay; it will take some time (and the help of the talking goose) before they actually meet. Nonetheless, one could argue, as Malamangala Kavi seems to, that their mutual imaginings provide them with their most fulfilling moments. This poet belongs to the creative period in which the self-awareness of Malayalam as a distinct and autonomous literary language was crystalizing.

MALAMANGALA KAVI'S *NAISHADHA IN OUR LANGUAGE* (1.22–23, 29–31, 33, 35, 37, 39–40)

> [Nala and Damayanti can't sleep:]
>
> First they drew from the depths of their hearts
> the person newly loved, and very beautiful.
> Then they placed him or her before them
> with the help of their imaginations, doing away
> with all other thoughts. Thus they happily fulfilled
> their desires, obsessively practiced and repeated,
> as little by little they submerged themselves
> in an ocean of joy. (1.22)
>
> The goddess Sleep came to them over and over,
> but each time she thought to herself,
> "I'm not about to create an obstacle

to the intense joy they're feeling
by making love in their imagination"—
so each time she went away,
as a tactful friend should. (1.23)

[Nala, lovesick, tries to divert himself in his garden:]

Puffs of wind were scooping up and scattering
dust of pollen, more and more,
blowing them here and there,
but what was amazing was the way
they lit the fire of love
in his heart
like the dry sap of the *payin* tree
that bursts into flame when you blow on it. (1.29)

In that garden, the generals of Desire—
the cuckoos and others—taking note of Nala's
long-standing, bitter enmity with their master
and imagining, in their minds, that this was the last
chance Desire could defeat him, issued a clarion call
to a final, fateful battle. (1.30)

They poured out sweet sounds
to the utmost limit of what a person
can hear, as if twisting red-hot rods
heated in rage by Love
in his two ears. (1.31)

Rows of trees were awash in torrents
of fresh honey, far sweeter than fresh milk
and heavy with the thrill of passion,
like a cloudburst aimed at killing
all on earth who were in love. (1.33)

Inside himself, he couldn't bear it—this awkward
and violent state. The fire of desire hit
the summit and kept on getting worse.
"It was a big mistake to come here," he thought.
"What misery." Everything his heart had once desired
now made him turn away. It was all because of that
princess who had robbed him of his heart. (1.35)

"Love's fire flares higher, generating ash
and more ash, rising up to the heights.

By comparison, dying would be easy.
Isn't there someone, anyone, some good soul
who now, or later, would touch my chest
and utter the great mantra that is Damayanti's
name, saying it slowly and sweetly
so that love wouldn't hurt so much?" (1.37)

"My dear delicate gust of wind: I hope you're well.
As for me, it's time to die. But I still have one wish
that I can't help but tell you. Go at once
to the city called Kundinapura. Come to rest
in Damayanti's sweet hair. There's a feast
waiting for you there. Enjoy it, and come back soon." (1.39)

"It's stupid that I should be talking to this
disembodied being, the wind. There's nobody
listening to my sad story. No one but me
and the wind outside. I've heard that when
the power of desire reaches down into
the depths of the mind, lovers
speak their delusion." (1.40)

I TALK TO THE WIND: MALAMANGALA KAVI'S NAISHADHA IN OUR LANGUAGE

Sivan Goren-Arzony (Near Reader)

What does it take to fall in love? And how much input is needed for love to develop into one of those scorching, all-consuming fires? Nala and Damayanti's love story, first told in the *Mahabharata* epic and then retold time and again in a variety of genres and languages in South Asia, depicts one such burning love initiated only by words. But to say "only" might be misleading in this case. For speech in South Asia's many literary cultures is a uniquely powerful entity, even a divinity. It is capable not only of making two people who have never met fall desperately in love, but also of conveying their story in such a compelling and powerful way that listeners and readers experience a singular sense of happiness, even if, like us, they are removed from it by hundreds of years.

The verses David Shulman selected and translated from Malamangala Kavi's *Naishadha in Our Language* share this power. They were written around the late sixteenth century in the region of Kerala, located on the western tip of the Indian peninsula. Like much of Kerala's medieval poetry, *Naishadha in Our Language* was composed in the Rubies and Coral style (Maṇipravāḷam), a blend of Sanskrit and Kerala's local language (which later came to be known by the name Malayalam). As the name suggests, the decision to narrate the Nala and Damayanti story in a local idiom was self-conscious: a bold response to one of the most beautiful and complex poems ever to be written in Sanskrit, Shriharsha's twelfth-century *Life of Naishadha*.

What was Malamangala Kavi's motivation for this composition? Was he trying to simplify Shriharsha's formidable text and present it to an audience less versed in Sanskrit? This was probably not the case since to read the *Naishadha in Our Language*, or, for that matter, any work in this unique linguistic concoction, requires the command of both Sanskrit and Kerala's local language. Rather, I believe, it was his faith in this idiom, both its rubies and its coral, that prompted him to convey an old story in new and appealing ways.

The Nala and Damayanti story is extremely popular in South Asia, and thus it is common knowledge that this couple fell in love by merely hearing of one another. But how could this happen? Malamangala Kavi turns our attention to the couple's inner world and allows us to see that it was in their imaginations that this took place. There, a meticulous process of visualization unfolds: first, each seizes the newly loved person from the bottom of their hearts; then each places the other in front of them, shaking off all other thoughts; finally, they make love so intensely that even Sleep lets them be. In other words, dreaming makes way for daydreaming and external reality makes way for an inner life that becomes the couple's central mode of being. The contrast between imagination and sleep, two mental states that are commonly bound together and that are both different from our "normal" daily perception, is more than just a literary turn. Malamangala Kavi's words are like a lamp thrust into a dark room, to adapt Dandin's famous analogy for language, and they allow us to see for ourselves what is really happening inside Nala and Damayanti's minds.

The next verses describe an almost fatal mistake on the part of Nala. As a reader of Sanskrit poetry (which, as we see next, he most certainly was), Nala should have known that for a lovesick man, the garden is a dangerous place full of unbearable sensual pain. This is a common motif in the extremely prolific South Asian genre of "messenger poetry." In messenger poems, lovers who are separated by life's harsh circumstances send messages to their faraway beloveds, often using odd go-betweens such as a cloud, the breeze, a bee, or some bird or another. In this sense, the Nala and Damayanti story with its episode of sending a goose as an envoy is already linked to the genre of messenger poems. In the literary messages sent to their lovers, generations of forlorn characters have portrayed pleasant and passion-inducing elements such as the cry of the cuckoo, cool moonbeams in the middle of the night, and the mild, fragrant southern wind as dangerously unbearable in their current situation. Malamangala Kavi animates these elements as "the generals of Desire," who are unwilling to let their lord's bitter enemy, now that he has finally set foot in their territory, escape with his life. The nature of this bitter enmity, explains the commentator, lies in the fact that Nala is so beautiful that he outshines Desire, the god of Love, known for his beauty. He is, in fact, "the agitator of the world's agitator (Love) before our very eyes."[1] Love surely seems agitated to act, then, and so are his "generals."

The four verses starting with 1.31 (not all are translated here) depict attacks on four of Nala's senses: hearing (31), sight (32), taste (33), and smell (34). All four verses end the same way with similes that exemplify Nala's dire state: just as "twisting red-hot rods," just as "a cloudburst aimed at killing," and so on. Taken together, the four verses are a cohesive unit that consists of a direct unfolding assault on Nala's senses.

Moreover, and this is something that cannot be gotten from any translation, there is a clear divide between the two verses describing Nala and Damayanti's lack of sleep (1.22–23), and the four depicting the attack on Nala's senses (1.31–34). In terms of lexicon and morphology, the former pair is entirely in Sanskrit, while the latter set of four is almost entirely in Malayalam, the language of Kerala, with only an occasional touch of Sanskrit. So even in the Rubies and Coral combination, there are variations: sometimes we find more rubies, other times more coral.

But let me return to the passage at hand. Verse 1.35 opens a new section in the narrative (something also signaled, in the original, by a change in meter). The campaign of Love's generals has turned out well, and Nala is on the brink of defeat. Now we hear his own words as he realizes that his short stroll in the garden has turned into a disaster for him. A common South Asian literary template describes love in separation as a gradual process of an intensification of one's mental and physical pain that culminates in death. Nala is fully aware of this and gives voice to this process as he himself experiences it. In verse 1.37, for instance, this intensification is expressed by a verbal chain that abounds with repetitions: Love's fire "flares higher, generating ash / and more ash, rising up to the heights."

In his anguish, Nala desperately looks for some relief. At this very moment, the poem turns, once again, into messenger mode: Nala talks to a "delicate gust of wind" and asks it to travel to Damayanti's town Kundina, enjoy a "feast" in her hair, and return scented. Will this fragrant wind, once back from Damayanti's hair, be a life-saving remedy for Nala? Or perhaps this is merely another death wish, also to be executed by Love's generals? As is common in messenger poetry, we never get that far. The sender asks the courier to carry the message, but whether it is delivered or not is typically left for the readers' imagination.

Indeed, Nala immediately reflects on his act of talking to the wind, "this disembodied being," and comes to see it as strange because there is no one actually "listening to my sad story." Yet here Nala reveals himself not only the hero of a messenger poem, but also a reader of such poetry. He thus finds comfort in a paraphrase from one of the most famous verses in all of Sanskrit poetry, the fifth verse of Kalidasa's prototypical messenger poem, the *Cloud Messenger* (Meghadūta). "I've heard," Nala remembers, "that when the power of desire reaches down into /

the depths of the mind, lovers / speak their delusion" (1.40). In fact, the original highlights the fact that this is something that happens to all those who are in love (*akhila-kāminām*). This comforting thought, which comes straight from a meta-poetic reflection in Kalidasa's poem, encourages Nala to continue his seemingly irrational behavior. In the very next verse (which is not part of the selection), he asks a mango tree to bid farewell to its own lover in the form of a creeper, and then rush to Damayanti to tell her all about his (Nala's) misery.

Kalidasa's words, then, frame Nala's understanding of his own feelings. We could even say that Malamangala Kavi portrays a hero who is to some extent aware of himself as a literary character, much as Cervantes did with Don Quixote. More depth is added by the temporal looping taking place here: Nala, a character from the ancient epic, the *Mahabharata*, understands his actions through a verse from Kalidasa, a fifth-century poet and playwright who is situated far in the future from the epic's perspective. Such playful intertextual moments also reveal the intimacy that the language of Rubies and Coral shares with Sanskrit poetry. The whole system of texts has been submerged in it through allusions and quotations for the purpose of creating a literature that is nonetheless entirely new.

In early works in Rubies and Coral, one can sense an anxiety to keep Sanskrit in check; this is most clearly expressed in *The Mark of Lady Grace* (Līlātilakam; fourteenth century?), the pioneering manifesto of this new form of literature. In Malamangala Kavi's poem, however, this anxiety is no longer present. Here, Sanskrit and Kerala's language are playfully bound together, syntactically, thematically, and temporally, to create a poem in which the linguistic borders become obscure and irrelevant.

In the very final verse quoted here, Nala is aware that there is no one to hear his "sad story." This is not only the regret of a lover who has no one to turn to (one goose, a delicate wind, and a certain mango tree notwithstanding), but perhaps also that of a poet, wishing that his beautiful verse be heard outside of himself. David Shulman's short selection enables readers who don't read Sanskrit, Malayalam, or their unique combination in Rubies and Coral to imagine just how powerful this poetry can be. Shulman has always been a "delicate gust of wind," ready to pay attention, listen, and spread the beauty of the words he has heard.

IN THE GARDEN OF LOVE: AN ESSAY ON *NAISHADHA IN OUR LANGUAGE*

Meir Shahar (Far Reader)

Many years ago I had the privilege of being David Shulman's student. As a Hebrew University undergraduate, I took several of his introductory classes to Sanskrit language and literature. The attraction of the Indian creative imagination notwithstanding, my academic career carried me elsewhere. I chose to specialize in Chinese literature, and it is the latter that offers me clues for understanding a Malayalam poem. In the brief essay that follows, I compare the *Naishadha in Our Language* to one of the greatest works of Chinese romantic literature, *The Peony Pavilion*. The Malayalam poet Malamangala Kavi and his Chinese counterpart Tang Xianzu are equally concerned with the role of mental construction in the experience of love, and their respective protagonists languish from desire to creatures of their own imaginings. Another theme that unites the two works is the centrality of the blossoming garden as the setting and metaphor for love.

Composed at approximately the same period as *Naishadha in Our Language, The Peony Pavilion* (Mudan ting) is considered among the greatest works of Chinese romantic literature. It is a play—or more accurately an opera—whose verses were intended for singing and reading alike. Contemporaneous with Malamangala Kavi, its author Tang Xianzu (1550–1616) designed it as an exploration of the power of love. Like Malamangala Kavi's Nala, Tang's heroine Du Liniang is brought by love sickness to the brink of death. Unlike Nala, she actually perishes from unfulfilled desire, only to be brought back to life by the force of reciprocal love. Having descended to the netherworld, she is summoned back to the world of the living by the tender supplications of her beloved. In Tang's masterpiece, love is not only as strong as death; it is stronger.

In the *Naishadha in Our Language* and *The Peony Pavilion* alike, the battle of love is fought in a blooming garden. The Indian and the Chinese Cupids accomplish their mission by leading their amorous prey to flourishing groves where the radiance of blossoming flowers and the music of warbling birds engender desire. The Indian god of love, Kamadeva, pierces his victims' hearts with flowery arrows shot from a bow made of sugarcane with a string fashioned of honeybees. He lies in wait for his innocent prey amidst flowering trees that intoxicate. He attacks them with legions of singing birds that beguile the senses:

> They poured out sweet sounds
> to the utmost limit of what a person
> can hear, as if twisting red-hot rods
> heated in rage by Love
> in his two ears. (1.31)

Like his Indian counterpart, the Chinese Eros sows the seeds of love in a budding grove. In *The Peony Pavilion* he is identified as a Flower Spirit, who lures his hunt in the season of their bloom. The spring is the time of love, the very word being synonymous in Chinese with desire: "Spring feeling" (*chunqing*) is love, and "spring intention" (*chunyi*) is desire. When the meadows are filled with colorful blossoms, and the bees and butterflies chase each other in erotic pirouettes, the Flower Spirit stabs his victims with the agony of unrequited love. The beauty of the season brings no joy to the tormented lovers. On the contrary, it serves to intensify the pain of unbearable desire, as if nature is intent on simultaneously titillating and mocking its helpless prey. Here is how Flower Spirit describes his mission as he appears on the stage of *The Peony Pavilion*:

> [I am the] Commissioner of the Flowers' Blooming,
> come with new [Spring] season
> from Heaven of Blossom Guard
> to fulfill springtime's labors.
> Drenched in red petal rain
> the beholder, heart-sore,
> anchors his yearnings
> amid the clouds of blossom.[2]

No wonder that the garden excursion brings no relief to Nala and Du Liniang. The blooming park that was thought to assuage the pangs of desire turns out to intensify them. The blossoming flowers and chirping birds do not slake the thirst that they themselves arouse. The riotous colors of spring contrast with the lover's drab loneliness. "It was a big mistake to come here . . . what misery," laments Nala. "Bright the morn, lovely the scene, listless and lost the heart" concurs his Chinese counterpart. "Ah Heaven," she cries, "I begin to realize how disturbing the spring's splendor can truly be. They were all telling the truth, those poems and ballads I read that spoke of girls of ancient times 'in springtime moved to passion, in autumn to regret.'"[3] The cravings wrought by the beauty of the flourishing garden are insatiable. Nature engenders desire, even as it is indifferent to the torments of those inflicted by it.

In the Chinese case, the anguish of the spring scene is twofold. Even as she is tormented by spring fever, Du Liniang laments the season's decay. The cravings wrought by the beauty of the flourishing park are inseparable from the pain of its imminent demise. Reading herself into the flowers, Du Liniang mourns their future withering at the very moment of their bloom. In the prime of her youth, the heroine laments her future fading. The tradition of mourning for fallen blossoms runs through Chinese literature. The greatest Chinese novel has its heroine bury them lest they be trodden upon by unfeeling feet. In Cao Xueqin's *Dream of the Red Chamber* (Honglou meng; ca. 1760), Daiyu goes rake in hand into the blooming garden to collect the fallen petals. She accompanies her lyrical task by a poem on her own sad fate:

> The blossoms fade and falling fill the air,
> Of fragrance and bright hues bereft and bare.
> Floss drifts and flutters round the Maiden's bower,
> Or softly strikes against her curtained door.
>
> The Maid, grieved by these signs of spring's decease,
> Seeking some means her sorrow to express,

Had rake in hand into the garden gone,
Before the fallen flowers are trampled on.

. . . .

Can I, that these flowers' obsequies attend,
Divine how soon or late *my* life will end?
Let others laugh flower-burial to see:
Another year who will be burying me?

As petals drop and spring begins to fail,
The bloom of youth, too, sickens and turns pale.
One day, when spring has gone and youth had fled,
The maiden and the flowers will both be dead.[4]

The resonance of the *Naishadha in Our Language* and *The Peony Pavilion* extends from the imagery of the garden to the centrality of mental construction in the experience of love. Nala and Du Liniang both fall in love long before they ever meet the objects of their desire. In this respect, the Malayalam and the Chinese poets similarly explore the origins of love in the depths of one's self. Malamangala Kavi and Tang Xianzu shy not from emphasizing that their protagonists are enamored of the creatures of their own imagination. Nala is brought to the brink of death by love sickness to a woman he never met face to face, and Du Liniang perishes from unrequited cravings for a man that appeared in her dreams alone. That they are figments of the imagination does not diminish the pain of longing for them. Psychologically, the imagined beloved is as real as the flesh and blood one. It might even be argued—to quote the title of one of David Shulman's books—that he or she is *More than Real*.[5]

In the verse, the word *imagination* reveals that the object of love is not a flesh and blood person but a mental construction. Malamangala Kavi tells us that Nala and Damayanti "drew from the depths of their hearts / the person newly loved . . . Then they placed him or her before them / with the help of their imaginations" (1.22). The Malayalam poet goes on to describe the pleasures of fanciful lovemaking, as delicious as—if not more so—than the meeting of carnal bodies. Sleep refrains from intervening with the lovers' chimeric encounters lest he disrupts "the intense joy they're feeling / by making love in their imagination" (1.23).

In the Chinese play, the idiom of "dream" (*meng*) is used to convey the agency of the self in the creation of the beloved. Tang Xianzu has his heroine fall in love with a man (Liu Mengmei) who is revealed to her in her dreams. Du Liniang perishes out of lovesickness for a person whom she never meets in real life. And yet the dream comes true: the creature of the imagination turns out to be a real person. Miraculously, the object of Du Liniang's reveries simultaneously envisages her. Liu Mengmei dreams of Du Liniang, just as she dreams of him. Arriving at her former residence and discovering the self-portrait she left behind, he is convinced of the veracity underlying his fantasy. He resolves to call upon the goddess of his dreams and the two engage in imaginary lovemaking, "a mating of shadows, consummation within the mind."[6] Their mutual devotion is such that it moves the judges of the netherworld to pity. Du Liniang is brought back to life and the meeting of shadows turns into the lovemaking of real persons.

Tang Xianzu's preface to his masterpiece reveals his primary concern with the role of mental constructions in the experience of love. The opening words of *The Peony Pavilion* challenge the distinction between dream and reality in the realm of emotions:

> Among all the amorous young women of this world, is there anyone comparable to Du Liniang? Having dreamed of her beloved, she fell ill. Her illness grew severe, so much so that she drew her self-portrait and died. She was dead for three years. Then, from the depths of the netherworld she sought the object of her dreams, coming back to life. A person such as Du Liniang might truly be said to have experienced genuine love. The origins of love are unknown. Having appeared, it deepens. Love might lead a person to his death, and it might bring a dead person back to life. If the living are not driven by it to death, and the dead are not brought by it back to life, it is not utmost love. And why should not the love in a dream be real? Aren't there many people in the world who are moved by dreams?
>
> . . . .
>
> Alas! The affairs of the human world surpass human comprehension. Since we are not geniuses, we employ logical principals (*li*) as our yardstick for everything. By logical principals, Du Liniang's story is unreal. However, by the standards of love it might be real. Who knows?[7]

I have relied upon the example of *The Peony Pavilion* to highlight two aspects that—as a far-removed reader—struck me in Malamangala Kavi's *Naishadha in Our Language*: the imagery of the garden and the significance of the imagination in conjuring the beloved's image. It might be fitting to conclude my brief comments with an allusion to another poetic tradition in which David Shulman is versed. Writing some two thousand years before Malamangala Kavi and Tang Xianzu, the Hebrew author of the Song of Songs (also known as the Song of Solomon) was, like them, obsessed with the crushing power of love: "Love is as strong as death; jealousy is cruel as the grave," he observes. The biblical verse and the Malayalam poem similarly draw upon the metaphor of fire to render the vehemence of consuming desire: "Mara's fire flares higher, generating ash / and more ash, rising up to the heights. / By comparison, dying would be easy," laments Nala (1.37). "The flashes of love are flashes of fire, a most vehement flame. Many waters cannot quench love, neither can floods drown it," concurs the ancient Hebrew poet.[8]

In the Song of Songs—as in *Naishadha in Our Language* and *The Peony Pavilion*—the blooming garden is the site of the erotic encounter. But it is more than that. The tempting grove functions not only as the physical location of the lover's tryst, but also as a metaphor for their very bodies. She is his private garden, and he is her secluded grove. He eats her luscious fruits, and she slakes her thirst in his embrace. He sings:

> I come to my garden, my sister, my bride,
> I gather my myrrh with my spice,
> I eat my honeydew with my honey,
> I drink my wine with my milk.

And she responds:

> As an apple tree among the trees of the wood,
> so is my beloved among young men.
> With great delight I sat in his shadow
> and his fruit was sweet to my taste.

What Does It Mean to Be "Modern" in Telugu?

EDITORS' NOTE

THE PLEASURES OF READING SOUTH ASIAN LITERATURE in translation are not to be found only in texts from a distant past. In this unit, the reader will find translations from works that are firmly rooted in South Asia's modernity, all from a single language: Telugu. Telugu speakers make up one of the world's largest linguistic communities today. There are about 100 million Telugu speakers, the bulk of whom live in the southern Indian states of Telangana and Seemandhra (parts of what was once the state of Andhra Pradesh) and many of them in the various diasporas. Telugu has a rich and longstanding literary tradition, with its own illustrious version of the Nala story and numerous classics, including *Vasu's Life*, a portion of which is translated in unit 4. Yet it also has its own vibrant modernity that is open to literary inspiration and models from elsewhere, as is evident in Abburi Chayadevi's short story "Touch," or Ismail's blank-verse poem "Rembrandt," and also in the first selection, *The Story of the Four Dervishes*, although it is a modern anonymous retelling of a Persian and Urdu premodern tale in the tradition of *Arabian Nights*. Modernity, it could be argued, is defined by its complex relation to the past and to forms of art from other cultures and regions. Rabindranath Tagore once said, while visiting Bali in the 1920s, "I see India everywhere, but I don't recognize it." Among the pleasures of reading these selections together is their own interplay of similar perceptions and nonrecognitions. In short, they and the responses to them together take up David Shulman's own question: "What does it mean to be 'modern' in Telugu?"

4

"Khwaja the Dog-Worshiper" from *The Story of the Four Dervishes*

TRANSLATOR'S NOTE AND TEXT

The story of Khwaja the Dog-Worshiper is a much-condensed Telugu retelling of the extremely popular stories of the four dervishes, best known from the elegant Urdu version by Mir Amman (early nineteenth century, based on earlier Persian versions). The four dervishes are picaresque travelers who undergo many unnerving, nearly fatal adventures, much in the style of *Arabian Nights*. Like the latter, the stories of these dervishes were widely diffused in all the South Asian languages. The Islamic frame shares the geography of the medieval Islamic cosmopolis, but in the section translated here we find recognizable south Indian landscapes and cityscapes.

"KHWAJA THE DOG-WORSHIPER" (61–72)

[A young and beautiful woman, daughter of a vizier wrongly imprisoned by the king of Turkey, sets out, disguised as a man, in search of a merchant from Nishapur, in northeast Iran, whose dog has twelve rubies sewn into his collar. If she can produce this man within a year, her father the vizier will not be executed. She goes to Nishapur, where she indeed finds the merchant and his dog, who is treated with utmost devotion, kept on a golden leash, resting on a velvet pillow, and whose collar is studded with twelve rubies. Near the dog, two unkempt men are imprisoned in cages; they eat the dog's leftovers. She manages to bring the merchant, known as Khwaja the Dog-Worshiper, together with the two caged men, back to Istanbul, where the king of Turkey summons him and commands him to tell his story. Khwaja the Dog-Worshiper begins by describing how his two elder brothers kept trying to kill him. After one such assault, which nearly succeeded in slaying both him and his dog . . .]

"Near where we, my dog and I, were lying wounded, there was a large city ruled by a Hindu raja. He had a daughter. She used to go into the wilderness to hunt with her father's permission. She happened to come toward the place where I was lying

67

two days after the attack. Her companions, riding near her, reported that they had seen me, groaning with pain, and my dog, too, lying on their path. She came and saw me and, overcome with compassion, had me carried to a nearby garden; she summoned the royal physician and promised to pay him generously if he could bring me back to life. He was truly a great doctor. For four days he had me bathed in a healing solution, and during those four days there was no limit to the care the princess lavished on me.

"Then one evening, while I was busy with my prayers, she came, looked at me, and asked, 'What is it that you do?' I told her the whole story. 'And what is your religion?' she asked. I told her everything. She secretly adopted Islam. She said to me: 'My parents are thinking of marrying me to an unworthy man. But my heart is fixed on you. So please take me away from this place to your own country, without anyone knowing.' I immediately accepted this command along with the bundle of jewels that came with it. I rented a room in the Turks' inn that existed in that town. Many merchants who came on business from Rum were staying there.

"A month passed. All of them wanted to go back to their country, so they summoned a boat and, since they were all very fond of me, they were glad to take me on board and even gave me a small cabin of my own. On the appointed night, in the second watch, I sent word to the princess, and she came, carrying a chest full of jewels and ornaments. With her, and together with the merchants, I went on board the ship. By dawn we had already sailed some distance when there was a sudden volley of cannon fire. The captain let down the anchor and raised a white flag in order to save the ship.

"All the merchants were terrified. They locked the slave girls they had brought with them in big chests—and I, too, locked the princess in her chest. Meanwhile, the captain of the port arrived in a small boat and boarded our ship. Our captain said to him: 'You can search our ship as much as you like.' When the captain of the port couldn't find even a single girl, he turned to a rather innocent merchant and pressed him to tell him the truth—which, indeed, he did, secret and all. At once he examined all the chests on the boat and took all the girls he found back to shore. By dawn the next day, he sent all the girls back to the boat—all, that is, except my princess.

"I tried my best to figure out what had happened. The merchants said to me, 'There's no point in thinking further; your slave girl is in the hands of the port commander. We'll take up a subscription and raise the money you paid for her.' They did their best to comfort me, but I couldn't go along with their idea. I said: 'I'm not traveling anywhere on this boat.' I disembarked, and my dog came with me.

"For a whole month I searched through the town but couldn't find the princess. Finally, I came to the conclusion that she must, indeed, be in the house of the captain of the port; there was no other possibility. Dressed as a woman, I managed to get into his house and, after searching through it, I saw my beloved. She was praying to God to save her from her misery. When she saw me, she quickly finished her prayers and rushed to embrace me. 'I never thought I'd see you again in this lifetime,' she said. 'My father, not knowing what has happened to me, has announced that I am ill; in a few days, he will announce that I have died. The port captain is pestering me to give myself to him. Seeing that I'm unwilling to do so, he is so far still patiently trying to possess me, somehow or other, without showing anger; he knows I'll kill myself if he tries to force me. There is only one way to get me out of here. Listen. There's a temple in this town, with a big image of the god. A Brahmin woman, two hundred years old, is in charge of it. Not even my father can disobey her command. Anyone in this town who becomes bankrupt goes to that temple; before going inside, he removes his shoes; then he sits there, covering himself with a blanket. Pilgrims who come there to see the god throw money, clothes, and other items at him, as they see fit. After three days that Brahmin lady comes there, blesses him, gives him the whole pile of money, and gives him leave to go. You, too, must go there and do as I have described. But when she gives you leave to go, stay, bow to her, and say, *The port captain has kidnapped my wife. I beg you to see that he is punished and that my wife is returned to me.*'

"I followed her instructions. The Brahmin lady turned to the young boys who were standing beside her and ordered them to take me to the king, to tell the whole story, and to demand justice. At once they took me to the king. When the king saw them, he cleaned their feet with pure cloth and seated them on his throne. After hearing the whole story, he said, 'I'll have the port captain brought here and investigate the matter.' When I heard this, I was terrified that the secret of the princess would come out. The Brahmin boys, seeing from my face how scared I was, angrily rebuked him: 'You're going to summon the port captain instead of following our mother's order?' The king trembled with fear. 'Punish the port captain as you wish,' he said to his soldiers, ordering them to follow the Brahmin lady's command.

"The Brahmin lady sent five hundred soldiers of the king with me with orders to execute the port captain and make over all his properties to me. They killed him with a single stroke of the sword and gave me his office and his wealth. After that I was reunited with my beloved. At her advice I rewarded all the soldiers and the clerks in the port, and from then on took over the authority of ruling, to the delight of all the citizens.

"The Brahmin lady in the temple and the king received many gifts from me. Those who worked for me, and indeed all people, were always treated with respect. Once a month I would go to the royal court and to the temple to show my respects. I married the princess. I had no further worries or doubts; all was joyful. My wife and I prayed to the Lord to let this state of happy satisfaction continue.

"Thus two years passed. One day a caravan arrived from the land of Zerbad. After finishing their business, their sardar brought me many curious gifts from all kinds of lands and invited me to a meal on the following day. I came to the feast; after dining, we were chatting when two men clothed in rags came in carrying trunks. Studying their faces, I realized that they were my brothers. The next day I summoned them, gave them good suits of clothing, and treated them with affection. But this time, too, they sought to kill me. They came one night at midnight, entered my bedroom, and tried to slay me. This dog of mine, who was lying near the bed, started barking and fell upon them. My servants rushed in and tied them up. The dharma texts tell us that one can forgive once or twice, but after that the evildoer must be punished. So I had to punish them; a single blow would teach them nothing. Dogs are infinitely more trustworthy than human beings. This dog saved me many times, and I take very good care of him. Such is my story. If your highness punishes me or protects me, it's all the same to me." The Khwaja now fell silent.

The king of Turkey, having listened intently to story, said, "Your brothers' wickedness is evident. They deserve whatever punishment you gave them. I pardon you. But this dog of yours has twelve rubies on its collar. How is that?" The Khwaja began to tell the story.

"One day, while I was serving as the port captain, as I was sitting at ease on a high balcony overlooking all directions, two people emerged from the wilderness. They were moving with great difficulty. At once I sent my servant lad to fetch them. One was a woman, the other a man. The woman was carrying a bundle in her hands, and the man was carrying two bundles and a child. When they reached my house, I sent the woman to my wife. I asked the man: 'Where are you from? How is it you've been struggling like this in the wilderness?' His appearance was utterly strange. The clothes he was wearing were hard as leather, and his hair, fingernails, mustache, and beard had grown very long. He was as thin as a thorn.

"He replied, 'My mother and father died while I was a child. My relatives made off with the house and the doorway as well. Driven from my home, I went through many hardships. And though I survived, I was once imprisoned in a tomb.' I asked him to tell the whole story in detail, and he began: 'My country is Azerbaijan. My father used to go often to the Hindu land and to China on business. When I was ten years old, he took me with him on a journey to India. Though my mother, aunts, and others tried hard to dissuade him from taking me, he wouldn't listen to them. *I'm getting old*, he said, *and my son has to be trained in business. If I don't teach him, later no one else will instruct him in the secrets of commerce.*

"'So off we went to Hindustan, where we sold all our merchandise and purchased some other goods. From there we went to Zerbad. There, too, we made a large profit and then set our course, by boat, for home. For a month the voyage went well. We never even used the word *hard*. Then, all of a sudden, a huge storm arose and dashed the boat against a mountain. The boat was shattered and everyone perished. Our money, too, was lost to the sea. My father went to heaven. I alone survived. A plank came my way and, clinging to it, I was carried by the waves for two days until, in the end, I reached a shore.

"'Looking around, I saw a field with some people in it that was not too far away. I went there as quickly as I could and saw that they were black and naked. They asked me something, but I couldn't make out their language. They were eating parched horse gram, and they gave some to me, too. When I had appeased my hunger to some extent, I took some of the horse gram in a bundle and went off along a road they showed me. A fort appeared—though no one seemed to be in it. I went on until I came to a hill, its earth black as collyrium. Beyond it I saw a city surrounded by a wall with many gates, though only one gate was open. A big man was sitting there on a chair; he beckoned to me to come near. Judging by his clothes, he seemed to be a European. He commanded me to sit down on a chair and gave me bread, meat, and wine. No sooner had I eaten and drunk than I fell sound asleep.

"'It was evening when I opened my eyes. After he had once again fed me well, he asked to hear my story, and I told it all. He showed me a place where I could sleep.

When I woke at dawn, he again brought me food and asked me to bring him a spade and a wicker sieve. I thought to myself that he was feeding me so lavishly in order to prepare me for some hard labor. At once I brought the tools to him.

"'*With these implements,* he said, *go to that hill and dig a hole a yard deep. Pass whatever you dig up through the sieve. Whatever is left over put in this bag and bring it to me.* I did as he ordered. What came to light were jewels without price. I put them in the bag and brought them to him. He said, *Take all of these and leave this place. It's not good for you to be here.* But—I didn't feel like going away without seeing what was in the city, and I told him so. He said, *Like me, you are from Persia. That's why I felt compassion for you and tried to save you from death. It's impossible to know what will happen to you in the future. I have helped you as much as I could. I'm giving you a ring. In the bazaar you will find a big man who looks just like me, but with a long white beard. He'll be sitting in front of a shop. Show him this ring—he is my elder brother. Do exactly what he tells you to. My jurisdiction ends here, but he has authority over the city. Your luck will be as it has to be.*

"'I took the ring and entered the city. Men and women mixed freely together there. There were women's shops in the midst of men's shops and men's in the midst of women's. Without any embarrassment, men and women bought whatever they needed wherever they went. I watched, fascinated, for some time and then proceeded farther until I saw the man with a beard and gave him the ring. He was very angry: *Even if my younger brother is an idiot, have you no intelligence? Why have you come to this wicked city?* I told him my whole story. He took me to his home and there, in a private room, he said: *You have walked yourself into a burial ground. The king of this town and all its inhabitants have very odd ways. The king takes every foreigner who happens by to the temple. The image in the temple announces the caste, the religion, and the name of every foreigner. The king commands the guest to prostrate himself before the image. If he refuses, they cut off his arms and legs and drown him in the river. So worship that image without protest. If you do so and then ask even that the king give you his daughter in marriage, he will. The big men in this town, and the king and the vizier, all have great respect for me. All of them go twice a week to the temple to worship the god. Tomorrow is the day they go there.* He then fed me again, and I spent the night in his house.

"'At dawn the next day he set out with me for the temple. By the time we got there, the king, his viziers, and the *umarā* nobles were already sitting there along with their servants. Young men and women, far more beautiful than *gandharvas*, those heavenly musicians, and the women of heaven, were also there. All of them, the king included, had removed their head coverings and were squatting on their knees. My host took me closer and said, *Do exactly what I do.* First he kissed the king's feet and then held the vizier's hand. The king looked at him and asked, *What's going on?* My host replied: *This man is a relative of mine, from a very distant land. He came here wanting to kiss the king's feet and wanting to marry the vizier's daughter.* The king was overjoyed. *As soon as he embraces our religion,* he said, *there will be no obstacle to fulfilling his wish.* No sooner had he said this than the elders of their religion initiated me into the faith, dressed me like a bridegroom, and married me to the vizier's daughter, who was more beautiful than any star.

"'I prostrated at the feet of the image. The god himself then spoke: *You have joined our faith. Thus you are very much in luck. You have our fullest blessings.* Hearing this, everyone honored me. The following day I got to see the king, who bestowed fine clothes on me and ordered me to attend his durbar every day.

"'After a few days, the king would no longer convene his advisors unless I, too, was there. Two years passed. I can't describe in words the splendor that was mine. I was, in fact, a king—only I. Meanwhile, my wife became pregnant. In the ninth month she gave birth to a stillborn boy and then died herself. When the midwives came to give me this news, I was overwhelmed by grief; I went to my wife's side and sat there, weeping.

"'Hearing my crying, women came from nearby; each one slapped me on the forehead and stood there, crying. After a while the man who had got me married came and said, *Why are you crying, you fool?* I replied, *Have you no heart? My wife, half of my body, is gone, and you ask me why I weep?* He laughed and said, *There's no point in your crying for someone else. If you want to, it might be a good idea for you to weep for yourself.* Some young boys came and carried me off to the temple. The king was there together with people from all thirty-six castes. Everyone took whatever he wanted from the property of my wife, leaving its cost in front of the god. With that sum, they purchased jewels and put them in a box. In a second box they placed bread, halwa, meat, bottles of liquor, and fruit. Afterward they put my wife's body in yet another box and set off in procession.

"'The boys then brought a camel and, at the raja's command, first put the box of food on its back and then made me mount the camel; they handed me the box of jewels, and off we went, with Brahmins singing bhajans and blowing conches along the way. Afterward, many of them shouted to me: *śubhamu, Good Luck!* After a while I arrived at the first gate together with the bhajan singers. The man who had given me his ring was sitting there. When he saw me, he said, *You unlucky man, if you had listened to me, this disaster would never have happened. You are the cause of your own death.* I was so confused that I gave him no answer.

"'All of them turned back, except for one Brahmin who led me into the fort and, with the help of the man who had given me the ring, took me and the box off the camel and said, *Man is born on one day and dies on one day. This is natural. Your wife and your son have been brought here before you. This box that came with you has food for forty days. You can survive by eating it. If our god has mercy, you may live.* Then he left.

"'I saw the bodies of my wife and child, and I grieved for them. Many others had been brought there and perished before me: there were countless boxes of jewels like the one they gave to me. Tortured by heat and cold, I broke open the box and ate the bread that was in it. But what about water? I looked here and there and saw a small trickle flowing from a rock. I drank that water.

"'After some days, the food was finished. I cried, *God—what am I to do?* Again, that same Brahmin appeared, bringing an old man and a box full of food; he left them there and departed. When things go wrong, is there any creature more cruel than man? I split open the old man's skull with a single blow; then I survived by eating the food they had brought with him. I ended up killing five or six who were brought there like him and eating their food.

"'Then one day that Brahmin brought a drum-shaped box and left it there. Inside was a girl more beautiful than the dancing girls of heaven. I at once took her provisions, but I couldn't bring myself to eat them without giving her some. After five or six days, we became fond of one another. A few days later I married her with God as our witness. We lived for a long time by killing everyone who was brought there and taking their food. She became pregnant and gave birth to a boy. I took him—the child born in that burial ground—in my arms. My wife explained to me that in that town they brought to this fort any woman whose husband had died and any man whose wife had died.

"'When our son was three years old, I said to my wife, *Is there no way we can get out of here?* She replied, *Except for God's grace, there is no way out.* That very night God appeared to me in my dream and said, *There's the water drain, isn't there?* I got up at once and told my wife. She was overjoyed. The next day both of us prayed to God and, using the metal spikes and nails from all the old chests, we managed to widen the drain. It took a full year for me to enlarge the drain to the point where a human being could pass through it. My wife and I took a selection of the precious stones that were in those boxes and, with our son, slithered out through that drain. We've been wandering in the wilderness ever since, hoping to catch sight of some person who would lift us out of this ocean of misery. The woman you sent to your wife's quarters is my wife. That's our story.'

"I felt sorry for him. I cared for him and his wife in my own home. Not only that, I made him my main assistant. My wife, the princess, gave birth to many children, none of whom survived; one boy lived to the age of five. My wife died out of longing for him. I could no longer bear to stay in that place, so I handed over command of the port to my assistant, took leave of the king, and returned home to my own country. As a sign of gratitude, my assistant gave me these twelve rubies. I had them tied into the collar of my dog, as a sign of *my* gratitude. Those who know nothing of my story say I'm a dog-worshiper. For that same reason I pay double taxes to the Padshah of Iran.'"

[Needless to say, the vizier's life is saved and he is freed from prison, while Khwaja the Dog-Worshiper is raised to high office in Istanbul.]

HOW NOT TO SEE A DOG-WORSHIPER

Jamal A. Jones (Near Reader)

Effectively buried alive in a fortress-tomb, the titular Khwaja's future assistant despairs. Who wouldn't? He has found himself in this pitiable position after suffering many trials and the deaths of many loved ones. Freshly locked away with too little food, he observes the remains of those who'd perished before him, along with "countless boxes" of worthless jewels that each had been given.

These "countless boxes of jewels" emerge as a particularly haunting image of loss, despair, and futility. In reading "Khwaja the Dog-Worshiper" we are not in such dire straits. But we may find the selection curious, the significance of its intertwined stories obscure. How then might we make our way through its narratives of misfortune, cruelty, and compassion?

The assistant, for his part, cruelly kills to survive until he is visited by God in a dream and presented with an exit route: a drain pipe which he digs into an escape using the nails and spikes that held together the mocking treasure chests. He—along with a new family—is able to emerge from the tomb, bringing along jewels that may now have value in their new life. Here, I hope, are a few implements for digging our way through the story, to extract some jewels into new life.

Countless Boxes.   Cages, caskets, and coffers: these and other boxes are littered throughout the present selection. Some hold treacherous kin. Some hold precious loves. Some hold priceless jewels rendered worthless. The prevalence of such containers is particularly appropriate in this story. As our translator tells us, the tale is an inset, encased by the larger tale of the King Azad Bakht and that of his vizier's daughter out questing incognito. Not merely a piece contained, the story is itself inlaid with interlocking tales of estrangement and exploration, of cruelty and compassion. We have the main story of the Khwaja and his dog-aided survival; this story is in turn inset with the harrowing tale of the man who would be his assistant and successor. So the story both presents us with significant boxes of *stuff* at key junctures and comprises interconnected boxes of story that are mostly unlocked in the course of the tale.

Such use of frame stories—also called narrative emboxment—is common the world over: one story contains another, which contains another in a process that can be repeated indefinitely. This narrative device is characteristic of South Asian narrative traditions. But beyond noting the family resemblance, we should also see what emboxment can do.

As instruments of both concealment and revelation, the boxes of narrative and the literal boxes contained therein drive the tale's unfolding. In this regard emboxment serves an explanatory function. Each frame or box is built from questions and provocations: Who would dare worship a dog? Who are the two men the Khwaja keeps in cages, and why does he keep them there? How does a man buried alive escape his tomb? Each narrative section springs open to answer the question or defuse the provocation. The second half of "Khwaja" offers the clearest example. Having been told why the Khwaja keeps two men caged like animals, the king of Turkey remains curious about how and why a dog should wear priceless jewels. In reply the Khwaja doesn't actually tell his own story. Instead, he speaks of how his assistant and successor told him a story of travel, shipwreck, and survival. This story is precipitated when the Khwaja himself encounters a puzzle: a man, woman, and child emerging from the wilderness, much worse for the wear. He asks the question and the man opens up.

Faced with a text that answers a question with a question and substitutes one story for another, we might profitably read the Khwaja's tale as a shell game: the boxes never quite reveal what we're led to expect, and sometimes they come up empty. For instance, the tale itself promises a dog-worshiper but fails to deliver.

The Khwaja's epithet proves to be a misnomer. Instead of meeting some kind of apostate, we quite circuitously come to know his more devout character. Or, in the selection's first half, note the movements and machinations of the Khwaja's beloved princess. She is quite literally emboxed in her treasure chest, then seemingly kidnapped and trapped, but ultimately stands as the engineer of her own and the Khwaja's rescue. There's an elemental pleasure in tracking the movement of people and their powers in the surprise of revelation.

But this shell game and its work of revelation are only possible because each box—each of the stories—resembles the others. Recognizing this fixes our eye on emboxment's flipside: repetition. The great scholar and poet A. K. Ramanujan deemed repetition essential to Indian epic traditions specifically, and his central point bears repeating here. Repetition, he teaches us, is not just a characteristic of such stories but their driving device: it constitutes the structure, allowing the narrative to grow and even go forward.[1] The "Khwaja" story is no different. Our translator and the Khwaja himself allude to the key repetitions in his personal tale—that is, his brothers' trying to kill him time and time again. But the repetitions more powerfully cut across the nested narratives. The repetitive structure, however, shouldn't be mistaken for the simplistic replication of identical units. Instead, we should observe the ways that repetition entails variation and intricately elaborates the story's central themes and figures.

What Is It That You Do?   Moving toward the particular, what are the subjects of these repetitions and variations? And what does the elaboration offer? In the broadest terms, the tale primarily recounts movements toward and away from misfortune, and the way that these movements are modulated by cruelty and compassion. But this broad concern is refracted through the figure of the foreigner—the Persian trader, represented by the Khwaja and his assistant—abroad in the Hindu land.

To speak of Persian Muslims in the Hindu land is schematic, no doubt. Yet we are reminded at every turn that the central characters are foreigners, and that their lives are marked by insecurity. For one, both the Khwaja and his assistant are driven to misfortune (at least in part) by shipwreck. Travel abroad is thus immediately shown to be dangerous. The assistant's story takes the dangers to the particularly harsh extremes already summarized. At the same time, the Persian transplants are always longing for their homeland or, at least, never feel quite at home in the Hindu land. We see this as the Khwaja attempts to elope back to his home country with his newly converted beloved. His desire turns out to be common enough that he is able to secure passage on a ship chartered by a party of traders who are homesick much like himself. The assistant's story reveals the commonality of the plight, too. Much of the compassion he receives comes from other Persians who recognize another in need.

All the same, the tale is ambivalent on this point. The Khwaja's situation underscores the fact that danger may just as well appear at home, with one's kin. By the same token, compassion can come from total strangers. We see this quite clearly as the Hindu princess rescues the Khwaja and when the assistant is saved from hunger by the people of the parched gram.

Generally speaking, the world of the tale would be constituted by both "Hindu" and "Muslim" cultural practices. As the narration of the Khwaja's tale demonstrates, this does not mean that individuals fail to distinguish between Hindu or Muslim practices or affiliations. Such labels plainly mark characters throughout the story. But we would do well to see that the story reveals a world more ambivalent and complex in these relations.

Religious differences do appear starkly at times, with the foreigners' identities marked most prominently by their Islamic character. The most intense moment is the assistant's public debut in the strange Hindu city. Here, his foreignness—precisely defined by his religious affiliation—is proclaimed and interrogated by the local god. This later scene has a gentler parallel, wherein we see the princess observe the Khwaja at prayer during his recovery. Apparently unacquainted with Islam, she plainly asks, "What is it that you do?" Their highly elliptical conversation ends in her conversion. The assistant, too, becomes an agent of conversion, bringing his second wife to Islam while they were entombed. On this account, they are not only marked as Muslim but are arguably (and sometimes quite literally) exemplary in their practice.

Still, the characters' religious commitments are complex. Their decisions to marry locals notwithstanding, the two men settle into their south Indian worlds, even if they do not undergo comparable conversions. First, the Khwaja, in service of the plan to extricate the princess from the corrupt port captain's control, integrates himself into the local temple culture and assumes the role of a pauper to gain an audience before the old Brahmin woman. He gains her favor and, as a result, the force of her one hundred henchmen-sons, and, through them, the king himself. The assistant's story repeats this process of entanglement. Following the Persian bazaar master who grudgingly helps him navigate the strange city, the assistant submits to the local deity and religion that seem to stand as the nexus of local affairs. While an exaggerated depiction, no doubt, these incidents do speak to the political importance of the south Indian temple and its administrators.

Such events might appear to be superficial or cynical since neither man seems to have truly relinquished his commitment to Islam. We can note that the Khwaja and the assistant both enter the temple because doing so is expedient; indeed, in the assistant's case, it is the only way to avoid certain death. All the same, I would suggest that these decisions and events are quite consequential to their stories—so much so that superficiality or insincerity cannot do justice to what we find here. Their participation in the local world runs deep. Further, once the king installs the Khwaja as the new port captain, he repays this favor regularly with gifts and respect to the court, the temple, and those who serve him at the port authority. The assistant, for his part, offers an even more extraordinary example. We have already noted the revelation of his foreign identity in the temple scene. But it is worth emphasizing that there is a proper epiphany here: the city's god is fully present in the assistant's audience. Thus, we find both the Khwaja and his assistant as full members of the religious economies of the kingdoms.

Both men also deploy basic idioms of the local religious order. The assistant frequently figures beauty in the image of *gandharvas* and the like, the beings who populate heavens and who are expert in all manner of pleasurable activities. The Khwaja, to take a more integral example, frames his unusual treatment of his brothers in terms of dharma, a concept that is difficult to translate with a single term, but which picks up notions of morality, law, and more fundamental cosmic orders.

In these, even as the narrative has an Islamic core, the narrative and its figures are thoroughly embedded in locales that have their own concrete legitimacy and veracity. In this, the narrative moves away from either/or and instead favors both/and.

Those Who Know Nothing of My Story.   Though the assistant's story often dramatizes the story's themes in more extraordinary terms, the dog-worshiping Khwaja remains the central image of the story's complex representation of narrative and identity. In this, he does not just represent the characters' simultaneous foreignness and intimate connection to the worlds they find themselves living in. His story and the others it contains model a kind of idiosyncrasy and interiority that is otherwise difficult to comprehend.

In suggesting that a dog-worshiper exists, the narrative presents a problem. What would it actually mean to worship a dog? The denomination is more or less absurd. It is so unimaginable as to be ridiculous and defamatory. Thus the Khwaja has achieved a portion of infamy for his aberrant behavior. But, as I mentioned earlier, we do not in the end take away a portrait of a true dog-worshiper. Yes, he honors the dog extraordinarily but he is, we know, quite devout, even a champion of Islam. What's more, the tale actually undermines this title explicitly in the end, with our narrator offering a defensive summation: he obliquely asserts that he is not a dog-worshiper by noting that only "those who do not know his story" defame him so.

Yet few know the character of his belief. We can safely assume that this is by the Khwaja's own design, that the act of narration presented in the tale is rare if not completely unprecedented. He has let this misinformation—or really slander—survive unchallenged. But, when he is otherwise utterly transparent with his dog-and-man exhibit, why does the Khwaja effectively conceal his truth? The problem is not raised repeatedly or very explicitly, but still it stands. Not only does he preserve his own infamy by failing to share his story, but he is also materially punished for the behavior in having to pay double taxes to the Padshah for his apparent heterodoxy. Why, then, has he not tried to clear his name? Why has he not narrated himself before?

One answer could be that, despite his more orthodox devotion, he recognizes the complexity of his behavior and experience, and therefore wishes to acknowledge some kind of deviancy. Still another and more fundamental one may be that he places some value on secrecy or privacy. The situation implied by this final summation—a man living in intentional infamy—highlights how the story's narrative strategies offer a sense of interiority and depth of character. The Khwaja lives as a kind of open secret—his actions apparent but their true significance concealed. He thus represents a tense relationship between concealment and truth in the story. (On this we might also recall the assistant's story: it is only when he is trapped in the desert tomb that he can both recognize his own inherent cruelty and move along some arc of compassion.) Given such open secrets, we can't easily answer the question presented by his character, but we might just barely grasp it by the opening out of his story.

A HISTORIAN READS A FABLE

Muzaffar Alam (Far Reader)

The Story of the Four Dervishes is originally a storybook (*qissa*) in Persian, rendered into Urdu by Mir Amman Dehlavi as *Bāgh-o-Bahār* in the early nineteenth century.[2] It is comprised of tales told by four dervishes about their wanderings and the experiences they encounter in spaces which the author portrays as actual parts of the world of Islam. Interestingly, the story "Khwaja the Dog-Worshiper" is a subplot that does not figure in any of these dervishes' narratives and is narrated by a fifth character, as will be explained. In fact, I and perhaps many other readers and scholars generally skip this subplot while reading this storybook. I originally read it in my school days as it represents the first standard work of Urdu prose. I read it a second time as a historian of Mughal India, and then, too, my attention was drawn only to the main plot of the four dervishes and the world of Islam in which their stories were set. I thought, obviously wrongly, that the *qissa* of the *Four Dervishes* moves only within the Islamic lands. It is only now after I read this English translation of the Telugu version of the Urdu rendering of this Persian subplot that I realized how the story of Khwaja the Dog-Worshiper is key to the larger structure of the *Four Dervishes*, which indeed moves well beyond Islamic geographies.

The translation alerted me to the fact that in the *Four Dervishes*, we also have significant depiction of southern India and its neighboring regions where a part of Khwaja the Dog-Worshiper's story is set. I then read for a third time Amman's Urdu version, and was delighted to virtually discover the Hindu and Buddhist spaces therein, although I was also appalled, as a historian, to note the many inaccuracies. In addition, I felt the need to revisit some commentaries on the *qissa*, in particular on the portions dealing with this subplot.

The Frame Narrative of the Qissa.   The story of Khwaja the Dog-Worshiper (part of which also relates the experience of a young man of Azerbaijan) is narrated to the dervishes by a fifth character in the book, Azad Bakht, the king of Rum ("Rome," whose reference is actually Istanbul in present-day Turkey). The story takes place mainly in pagan countries, imaginative realms that seem to tally with Sri Lanka (Sarandeep) and a country on its borders, south India, where Brahmins hold high position.

Azad Bakht, the king of Rum who narrates the Dog-Worshiper's tale, was an ideal ruler, "as just as Noushervan and as benevolent as Hatim. . . . Everyone was happy under his rule. . . . Every day was festive and every night full of joy. . . . He had all the pleasures . . . but no son and this worried him constantly," until he reached his fortieth year and decided to retreat from his duties.[3] However, his chief counselor persuaded him not to do so. He remained watchful of the affairs of the kingdom but constantly longed for an heir. He would also often visit graveyards at night to pray and remember that all that is in this world would ultimately perish. One night, despite the strong winds, he noticed a flame burning in the distance. As he went closer, he saw four dervishes wearing shrouds and sitting with their heads held between their knees. The king hid and eavesdropped while they shared their tales with each other. Each dervish told a tale of the calamities that had befallen him and how he was driven to the point of suicide, only to be prevented by a masked man who instructed him to go to Rum where he would find the local king and his troubles would thereby come to an end.

By the time the second dervish finished his tale, it was already dawn. Not wanting to be noticed, the king returned to his palace and then summoned the dervishes to his court. Recollecting what the veiled rider had promised them, the dervishes realized that the time had come when their troubles would end. They reached the court, where the king first related his own story to them, that of Khwaja the Dog-Worshiper. Thereafter, he requested the third and fourth dervishes to narrate their own tales, which he was eager to hear.

Just as the fourth dervish finished his tale, news arrived from the palace that the queen had given birth to a son. The king was delighted, but the newborn prince came with a story of his own. Whenever the child was brought to the king, he mysteriously disappeared only to miraculously reappear. This worried the king to no end. It was discovered then that the prince was taken to the land of Shahbal, king of the jinns. The king of Rum decided to meet King Shahbal along with the four dervishes. With Shahbal's help, their wishes, too, were fulfilled, which is the happy ending of the story and the solution sought by all five narrators.

The modular nature of the story, divided into five different parts, all disconnected from each other, implies that we have five heroes instead of one. There is no presence of a typical quest motif; rather, the king accidentally chances upon the four dervishes. All the four stories by the four dervishes center on love (*'ishq*), but there is no place for love in the life of the king. The stories of all the principal characters get integrated at the time of the birth of the prince, which symbolizes the fulfillment of their individual quests and wishes. This happens with the intervention of a supernatural element, the king of the jinns, which reminds us that the *qissa* is still narrated in *dāstān* (fable, romance) form. The accounts of the supernatural world, however, are not beyond human grasp.

Versions of the Story. It is difficult to identify the exact period when this story was first composed. Mir Amman Dehlavi says that it was first narrated by the noted Persian poet and prose writer, Amir Khusrau (1253–1325), to entertain his Sufi preceptor Shaikh Nizam al-Din Auliya while the latter was sick. Amman also mentions that upon hearing this story, the Shaikh made a speedy recovery, and then blessed the story and announced that whoever hears it would live in good health. "Since then," adds Amman, "the story became current in Persian."[4] It is Amman's version in his *Bāgh-o-Bahār*, however, that spread this story far and wide in the Indian subcontinent and beyond. Nearly all the translations that exist in other vernaculars draw on Amman's version, although there are many unmistakable variations between them. This is especially the case in the story of Khwaja the Dog-Worshiper, in which different versions situate parts of the story in very different places: on the frontiers of *Firang* land; Zerbad land (Southeast Asia); and a south Indian city. From comparing these variations, we can conclude that the story, before it was written down, circulated far and wide for quite some time in various oral forms. There also seem to be some large variations between the Telegu version, from which comes our translation, and the Urdu one. I compare and contrast the two in the following sections.

Glimpses of Mughal Delhi in Amman's Urdu Version. I remember reading Mir Amman's *Bāgh-o-Bahār* the second time when I was already a historian of eighteenth-century north India. I found in it a virtual *muraqqa'* or album of Mughal India. It contains glimpses of Mughal Delhi culture—the culture that emerged in India following the convergence of the different traits of global Islamic culture with indigenous traditions—marked by pomp, opulence, and also a decadence that carries forebodings about the dire future of the Mughal order. After all, Mir Amman grew up in eighteenth-century Delhi and had seen the last days of Mughal glory. Until his death he identified himself as a Delhiwala (Delhi man), which explains why we find reflections of the city throughout the story. The images of Delhi dance in front of our eyes: its nobles, its crowds, and its fairs; its promenades and spectacles; its delicacies and festivals; its customs and traditions, rites and rituals. In sum, there is everything in here that was or could have been in Delhi of those days.

Whether the incidents take place in Iran, Turkey, or Basra, they actually reflect the life of the Mughal capital. There is no difference between Delhi and Basra in Mir Amman, for instance, when he describes a wine and drink party (*mahfil*), or any other ritual and social practice. As we see in the context of the first dervish's story, the merchant's son is hesitant to stay in his married sister's house, which is actually a taboo in Indian culture. And while describing musical parties, Amman makes the Dervish, who is from Yemen, somehow namedrop two legendary singers from Mughal India: "So delightful and absorbing were their songs that even Tansen would have forgotten his strains, and like Baiju Bawara, he had been driven to distraction on hearing them."[5] Or consider the decor of the party: "Rich carpets were spread in all the apartments; and there were big cushions, betel and scent boxes."[6] The details of many varieties of food, fruits, sweetmeats, and confectionary provide a distinct taste of the Mughal Delhi palate. We also see a glimpse of customs like washing hands after eating *pān-gilaurī* wrapped in a sheath of gold and silver foil. The women who guard the princess's mansion are mentioned as bejeweled Qalmaqinis, Turkanis, Habshinis, Uzbeknis, Kashmirnis—reminders of the varieties of female guards of the Mughal harem.

Khwaja the Dog-Worshiper's Story.   We also have hints in Mir Amman's version of the story of controversies within the palace and the negative features of court life. For instance, at the beginning of the story of Khwaja the Dog-Worshiper, when king Azad Bakht gets angry at the claims of the vizier and gives orders for his execution, the *firangī* ambassador is depicted as the only wise advisor who preaches caution. Perhaps this detail reflects Amman's own experience in early nineteenth-century Calcutta and is a reference to the British sense of social justice. I combed through the translation of the Telugu for such details and couldn't have enough of them.

But being the historian that I am, I discovered plenty of inaccuracies in Mir Amman's account of south Indian Hindu ritual and culture, which form a major part of the story of Khwaja the Dog-Worshiper. David Shulman writes in his brief note that the Telugu version shows "recognizable south Indian landscapes and cityscapes." But Mir Amman displays no accurate or scientific knowledge of the geography, culture, and religion of the places mentioned in this section of the story. The people and practices of Zerbad and, more astonishingly, of the city on the borders of Sarandeep (Jaffna and the eastern parts of Sri Lanka), read like they are set in some wonderland (*'ajāyeb*). For example, Mir Amman refers to idol houses, but, strangely enough, these seem to have no connection with actual Buddhist or Hindu temples, even though mention of Brahmins is made. Instead, Mir Amman hints that the people of the land worship Lat and Manat, deities worshiped in Mecca before the coming of Islam.[7] Likewise, consider the tale of the young Azerbaijani who is supported and patronized by the Khwaja. He is dressed as a European but he clearly is a Persian Muslim, and it is he who guards the magical city of the idol worshipers. If the Khwaja's appointment by a Hindu raja as the port captain echoes Mughal political culture, Mir Amman's portrayal of him as a Muslim missionary who married a Hindu woman only after her conversion does not tally with the Mughal culture that Mir Amman knew well.

The Telugu version mentions only the part of the story that takes place in the neighborhood of Sarandeep, "a large city ruled by a Hindu raja." In the Urdu version, in contrast, the Khwaja encounters trouble twice, once in Zerbad (somewhere in Southeast Asia?) and a second time, in a country near Sarandeep. It seems that the details of Zerbad may not have been included in the Telugu version. Why? I am curious about the portrayal of this particular story and its setting in the Telugu version. Does the Telugu telling accurately depict particular locations in south India, where Telugu is actually spoken? Also, the Telugu version refers to the princess's conversion very briefly as "she secretly adopted Islam," with none of the details available in Urdu.

Since the Telugu version does not mention particular locations and the two women whom the Khwaja marries, the reader does not get an opportunity to evaluate the characters involved. In the Urdu version, since these details are available, we can comment on the Khwaja's character and on the roles of these women as well. Initially, the Urdu Khwaja appears to be the embodiment of virtue. He suffers twice at the hands of his wicked brothers, and twice he is rescued by initially hostile infidel women who eventually fall in love with him. He also impresses upon them the benefits of embracing Islam after extended conversations on religious truth. But the readers can see that his religiosity is aimed at these women only for the purpose of enticing them and making them elope with him. We then know that there is a different Khwaja under the veneer of this religiosity, whom we can find in his cruel behavior toward his brothers. The women's characters in the Urdu version, too, deserve special attention. They grow as characters through their transformative encounter with the Khwaja and emerge as strong individuals.

There is an ulterior motive, then, behind the Khwaja's seeming piety. He also performs non-Islamic rituals, which further shows that he is interested only in his own expediency. He ends up a true dog-worshiper, not merely in name. Notice Azad Bakht's expression of shock when he hears that the Khwaja was feeding his brothers with the dog's leftovers. He says, "You are a devil in the garb of a man! What is this devilish net you have cast! You have dug an infernal pit for yourself! What is your religion and what rite is this? Which prophet do you follow? Even if you are an infidel, what is the idea behind all this?"[8] In response to the king's anger, he relates the whole story and focuses the narrative on his religiosity in an attempt to divert attention from his heinous crime. Further, Mir Amman shows the shallowness of his character and the superfluity of his religiosity when he promptly agrees to marry the Vizier's daughter, a teenager whom he had earlier imagined to be a boy and intended to adopt as his son.[9] He shows no qualms breaking the sacred bond of a father with his child. He only follows the letter of the law and has no regard for its true meaning. He does not represent the Islam that Mir Amman projects more generally in his story.

The qissa of Four Dervishes as told by Mir Amman, even if it reads like a fable (dāstān), is different from other such traditional tales, like the Dāstān of Amir

Hamza, for instance, where supernatural elements are integral to the storybook (*qissa*), and where proselytization and conversion is celebrated and projected as an achievement of the hero. Together with some elements of a traditional *dāstān*, we have some glimpses of innovation and change in Mir Amman. It combines historicism and temporality with idealism and ethicality.

There are some important details showing ethical and social life in the Urdu version not found in our translation, possibly because they may not have been available in the Telugu version. Still, reading the Urdu version and its Telugu translation side by side, I was able to get a comparative understanding of the two versions of this story both as a reader of literature and as a historian. Others may also read the various versions of it to relish the literary flavor and also draw historical insight. It is interesting to note that the part of the tale that appealed to the Telugu audience was the part that was set in a cultural context very similar to their own. Just like Mir Amman's version provided its readers with a glimpse into the social and cultural setting of Mughal Delhi. Similarly, David Shulman's translation of the Telugu gives a taste of the local flavor of southern India that is absent in the Urdu. Having read his translation, I now feel an urge to read the entire Telegu *Story of the Four Dervishes*. The historian is always thirsty for more local context and flavor.

"Touch" by Abburi Chayadevi

TRANSLATOR'S NOTE AND TEXT

This short story in precise and elegant Telugu prose comes from the contemporary writer Abburi Chayadevi's outstanding collection *Her Own Way* (Tana mārgam). A highly individual voice in modern Telugu, Chayadevi writes with restraint about the nuances of feeling and awareness in modern, mostly middle-class Telugu families. Born in the Godavari delta in 1933, she created a niche for herself as a feminist writer at a time when feminist sensibilities were only beginning to take shape in Telugu. She published several collections of powerful short stories, a novella, and a set of children's stories. She died in 2019.

"TOUCH" BY ABBURI CHAYADEVI

When I went in, Father was lying on a cotton mattress, facing the wall. Since I left my sandals at the door, I made no sound of any kind. I approached the cot and said, "Sleeping?"

"Who's that?" He turned toward me.

"It's me."

"Come sit here," he said, still lying flat. I started to drag a steel chair to that side, and he heard the noise and said, "Why so far away? Come, my dear, sit close to me." He raised himself to a sitting position and, tapping the cot with his hand, pointed to a place near him.

I sat down on the cot's wooden frame.

Groping with his hands, Father touched my back. He patted the cot and said, "Sit up."

I shifted slightly away from him, finding my place.

He was feeling around with his hands; he found my hand and held it between his. "I've been expecting you every day. Are you all right?"

"Um," I said, softly.

He said nothing more. He went on caressing my hand in silence.

Once, a while back, that is, when I was already old enough to get married, he and I were going somewhere together in a rickshaw. Although there was plenty of room, I sat there, shrinking well away to one side.

"Sit up straight," Father said, "you could fall out."

With some hesitation, I moved an inch closer to him.

When I was learning to read, he would usually speak to me from a certain distance as he drilled me in the letters, or out of concern for ritual purity, signaling to me with his eyes. I didn't dare come too close to him, to assume too great a familiarity. Whenever I saw him, I felt like I should take a bath and put on freshly washed clothes; I would fold myself into myself, and this became a habit. So how could I sit close enough to touch him in that rickshaw?

When we kids would come home from school, he would bring us close and question us about this and that, and the kids would tell him the news, like parrots. Not only that, he would be standing there on the threshold, glowering at us, scowling, asking: "What marks did you get in arithmetic? Did you bring me the mark sheet?" All of us were terrified of him. I lived with that terror to the age of twenty. Even now, fear hasn't left me.

Father is now past eighty. Too old to have an operation to restore his sight. Though in other areas his health is good, the loss of his sight has rendered him helpless. For the last two years he's been in bed.

When we heard that my mother-in-law was not well, we took leave and came to spend a few days with her. Whenever I'm in town, somehow or other I make time to see Mother and Father. I sit and talk with him for half an hour and leave.

I still have a childhood memory of sitting close to Father, of being close. Now, when he took my hand in his and touched me lovingly, I remembered how, ever since my childhood, in my innermost heart I'd ached for his touch. I could see it all clearly before my eyes, and tears welled up. When I tried to speak, I choked. Would he ever know how much I once yearned for his loving touch?

Was it because of his distant dignity and his fierce glances that the flood of love flowing between us in our letters evaporated when we met? Ever since I was a child, I couldn't cope with his eyes, which burned like the rays of the sun. Since I couldn't bear them, I avoided them. This, too, became a habit. Why can't I come close to him now, though I know that his eyes are like burnt-out lamps?

The first time I came from my town and sat down on the edge of his cot, I noticed bugs were crawling on it. I caught one or two and silently threw them under my feet and crushed them.

After that, whenever a bug would turn up in our house, on the bed, my husband would get upset. I'd say that maybe it got there because it somehow got into my clothes when I was sitting on Father's cot. So whenever I was about to set out to visit Father, my husband would caution me not to sit on the cot but to stay on a chair at some distance from him as we talked.

But if I moved my chair away and was about to sit down, Father would say: "Come sit closer." How could I refuse? He would not be satisfied until I was leaning against him, with my hand in his.

All his life my father yearned to have sons, but in the end only we girls remained. In the final stage of his life, there was one son who was like a strong tree holding up the whole family; he died. If you say the word "fate," I guess that's what it means. After my brother's death, I hesitated even to go see Father—as if some notion that I'd made a mistake was pulling me back. I wanted to hold him tight and say, "Don't cry, I'm here for you." But I was afraid to touch him. That was how he'd brought me up.

After we'd been sitting and chatting for a little while, he asked me to trim his fingernails and toenails. There was no point in even mentioning such things to Mother; she had her hands full. It would be like the mortar, struck by one hand, complaining to the drum that was pounded by two hands on either side. I couldn't ask my brother; he's no more. His kids lived somewhere else. No way to ask my sister-in-law. Maybe he'd asked me because he ached to have me perform some such service. It was a gift. I trimmed his nails carefully, with great joy.

I think Father's mind was not at peace. Caressing my hand, he said, "It would be good if you were to move to this town, I would come stay with you." I looked at him helplessly. He couldn't see my eyes. My words brought him no comfort.

Father asked nothing more. Silently, he went on caressing my hand as he sat on the bed. At that moment, all my studies, my job, everything—all seemed to me like mere window dressing. I sat there a little while more, then I stood up and said goodbye.

Father's soft touch seemed to follow me as I was going home in the rickshaw. My eyes filled. The road ahead turned dark.

HOW TO TOUCH "TOUCH"

Gautham Reddy (Near Reader)

As a story, "Touch" is rather uneventful, describing little more than a half-hour visit. A daughter takes a seat near her father, exchanges a few pleasantries, clips his fingernails, and takes her leave. The setting features little more than an old wooden cot, a steel folding chair, and a few pesky bugs. These events are narrated in a colloquial style that is marked by a conspicuous minimalism. Yet within this austere frame, Abburi Chayadevi weaves together a series of highly evocative memories and reflections that illuminate the tremendous feelings of loss and helplessness that result from a daughter's confrontation with her father's vulnerability and mortality. In this regard, the simple everyday language of the story poignantly reveals the protagonist's struggle to express the great depth of her emotion, grief, and sense of connection with her father.

The story opens with the daughter announcing, "It's me," as she takes a seat next to her blind father's cot. Her father questions the distance she has set between them and insists that she join him on his cot. Taking her hand in his, father and daughter sit together in silence. The daughter's mind wanders to memories of her father and the distance that has always existed between them. This distance, a mark of respect as much as a habit of fear, structured her interactions with her father from her earliest years. As the daughter's recollections suggest, this was a distance that permeated all aspects of their relationship but was articulated primarily through physical touch. There are two ways readers can make sense of the "distance" between father and daughter. The first, a direct and more existential reading, offers itself through the first-person perspective of the daughter as she narrates her experience of distance through memory and personal reflection. The second, an indirect and more sociological reading, emerges through the ways distance has been formally encoded into the father-daughter relation through Telugu social norms and cultural expectations.

Let us begin with the first existential reading. The daughter recalls that, during her younger years, the mere sound of her father's voice or the sight of his piercing gaze was enough to make her instinctively shrink. A stern disciplinarian, the presence of her father inspired a "terror" that she would live with until she was twenty years old. Even as an adult, when practical circumstances such as sharing a seat in a rickshaw demanded proximity, the daughter found herself retreating to the seat's edge, risking falling out of the vehicle rather than infringing upon her father's presence. The daughter's terror, we gradually understand, was not born of an apprehension of danger or violence, but rooted in a desire to honor a person she understood as occupying a role of great dignity and prestige in the home. It was a fear that acknowledged the reality of a parental role considered sacrosanct, born of a deep respect coinciding with love and admiration. The daughter remembers how she ached for her father's touch as a child—for a gentle pat on the back, a stroke of her hair, to fold her hand in his—but that his formidable presence precluded any of these familiar gestures as everyday forms of affection. In later years, when she was older and had left her childhood home, she forged a closer more familiar connection with her father through an exchange of letters. Yet this disembodied flow of intimacy "evaporated" whenever she returned to visit him in person. Even now, though he was past eighty, blind, and bedridden, she found herself still hesitating to approach him. When her father asks her why she hasn't visited more frequently, she becomes tongue-tied, unable to mumble little more than a helpless "um."

Touch is a proxy for all the forms of distance that have grown between daughter and father, for the way they hold her hostage and prevent her from knowing or reciprocating the love she seeks. Her father, his piercing gaze eviscerated with age, now looks for his daughter's touch and freely offers his—we see him affectionately clasping her hand, requesting her to sit near him, and asking her to perform the highly intimate act of cutting his nails. Yet as the distance between them has diminished over the years, so too has the cherished hallowed image of her father as a powerful and capable authority, the very image that necessitated and maintained the distance between them. The father's open approach to his daughter, a sign of his growing vulnerability, disrupts the daughter's knowing of her father. She suddenly finds herself at a loss to understand her inability to draw closer to her father.

Though flooded with feelings of love and concern for him, she chafes against the great barrier of history, unable to offer him the warmth or connection he desires and needs. Burdened by a feeling of estrangement, the daughter's memories and reflections on the nature of this distance are thickened by a painful sense of help-lessness and despair. She sees that her father now needs her, that he aches for her touch as she once ached for his. And yet, although the vulnerability of her father has opened up a possibility for a new type of intimacy, the daughter does not feel she can engage with him in the way they both long for. She was "afraid" to touch him; as she explains, "That was how he'd brought me up." And as she admits this, a feeling of inevitability emerges, a resignation that this distance has not only been unassailable but unavoidable.

Now let us turn to the second, sociological reading. Even as the daughter draws us into a web of private memory and reflection, we are also exposed to some of the greater social and cultural realities that structure her world of feeling. Through casual references and subtle details, a dark portrait emerges of the powerful ways the conventions of caste and patriarchy have determined the possibilities of inti-macy between daughter and father.

As in many upper-caste Hindu homes of the mid-twentieth century, con-cerns around ritual purity determined the degree of familiarity that was accept-able among members of the daughter's family. One of the reasons her father maintained a physical distance from her was to avoid "pollution." The daughter acknowledges that she was instilled with an anxiety around ritual purity from a young age, aware that her mere touch could jeopardize her father's piety. While young children were not in and of themselves considered "polluting," their inabil-ity to recognize sources of pollution meant that they were often at risk of con-tracting and then spreading impurity. The daughter remembers how her father would fastidiously preserve his distance from her potentially polluting touch as he taught her the alphabet, speaking cautiously from afar and signaling with his eyes. As a result of such constant vigilance, a stiff sense of formality and a preoc-cupation with cleanliness were instilled in the daughter as forms of deference and respect. Ever alert to caste considerations of ritual purity, she notes that as a child, "Whenever I saw him, I felt like I should take a bath and put on freshly washed clothes." As the daughter grew older, taboos and cultural associations of unclean-liness around menstruation would have intervened and increased the distance between father and daughter. In the ritual universe of Brahminical life, a woman's touch was believed to be intrinsically impure during menstruation. As such, it was customary in upper-caste households to sequester women on their period from participating in cooking, domestic chores, and family life for several days as a means of quarantining the menstrual dangers of ritual pollution from "clean" members of the household.

While there is only one direct reference to caste and the considerations of ritual purity in the daughter's narrative, there are several references to the patriarchal limits of Telugu society that conditioned the daughter's sense of self and her relationship to the men in her life. Once daughters married out of their childhood homes, they were deemed strangers to their parents and male siblings in many social respects. Until relatively recently, Telugu families were organized along the joint family system that followed the male line. This meant that while sons were expected to stay at home and provide for the welfare of the family and its elders, daughters were expected to marry outside the family and integrate into their husband's households. In this regard, the distance between father and daughter was structured by the social protocols that dictated the relationship of daughters to their natal home. After their marriage, daughters were expected to disidentify and distance themselves from their childhood home and family. We see this informing the way the daughter imagines her visits to her father after her own marriage. She frames such visits as originating in "my town," by which we are to understand the town she lives in with her husband. This suggests that she now entirely identifies her home, town of origin, and family with her husband. Consequently, the daughter does not conceive of her visit to her father as coming home or a return to her *ur* (native place), as a son who has left his childhood home might, but as a polite social engagement carried out in a less familiar place.

Throughout the daughter's narrative, we see that she was expected to orient her primary social obligations and affections first and foremost to her husband and his extended family network. In fact, even the purpose of her present visit was in relation to her husband's family. She mentions that she had actually arrived to the town of her childhood in order to accompany her husband on a visit to his sick mother and not, as it initially seemed, to pay her respects to her father. In the daughter's social world, visits to her own parents and hometown were not a priority. It was a conventional idea that women who visited their natal homes too often were considered to be negligent in their duties as a wife, daughter-in-law, and mother. As the daughter herself remarks, "Whenever I'm in town, somehow or other I make time to see Mother and Father." It is with great effort that the daughter is able to excuse herself, "somehow or other," during such visits to her husband's family in order to attend to her own sick father. We may infer that her husband did not accompany her on such excursions and that the daughter's time away from her husband's family on trips "home" was perceived as something of a personal indulgence not only by the husband's family but also by the daughter herself. In consequence, the daughter's visits to her father were infrequent and limited to little more than "half an hour."

As in most Telugu families, the daughter recalls that her father "yearned to have sons." A son would have provided her father with a sense of security and been responsible for his care during his old age. The daughter remembers her brother, the family's sole son, as a proud man "who was like a strong tree holding up the whole family." Her brother's untimely death during the prime of his life not only wreaked the devastating loss of a child for her father, but the loss of the family's security and sense of future. With no other sons, the daughter's father and mother were left to fend for themselves in a highly vulnerable financial and social position. During rare visits to her parents, the daughter is pained to discover insects crawling over her father's bed, shocking signs of the negligence and decrepitude that had entered into a home once marked by its concern for purity and hygiene. The daughter's own commitments to her husband and his family meant that she was unable to take an active role as caretaker or provider in her father's life. The daughter's visit concludes with a simple appeal from her father, "It would be good if you were to move to this town, I would come stay with you." In a social context where daughters could not freely spend more than a half hour with their parents, the father's impossible request is emotionally stirring. His words highlight the daughter's inability and unwillingness to transgress her social and personal obligations to her husband's family. In this regard, the distance between father and daughter has become permanent and insurmountable.

In a field of literature historically dominated by men, Abburi Chayadevi invites us into the interior realms of Telugu women. Set within the confines of an upper-caste and middle-class Telugu home, "Touch" is a powerful short story that highlights the range of anxieties and emotions that accompany a married woman's visit to her elderly father. It contains unmistakably autobiographical elements and reflects Chayadevi's own strained relationship with her father. Born in family of orthodox Brahmins in Coastal Andhra, she spent most of her professional life away from her father working as a librarian based in New Delhi. As a child, Chayadevi recalls that she was discouraged from writing by her father and chafed under his strict authoritarian personality. Father-daughter relations are a reoccurring theme in Chayadevi's work and she later published a short novel entitled *Mrityunjaya* (1993) based on letters exchanged with her father.

Chayadevi achieved renown as a short-story writer during the mid-twentieth century, a period when women were first beginning to emerge as a powerful new voice in Telugu literary life. She published short stories and poetry in popular periodicals, served as an editor of a women's monthly, and compiled several collections of contemporary poetry. Today, Chayadevi is considered a forerunner of feminist writing that challenged upper-caste gender norms and her work was included in the landmark anthology of Telugu feminist poetry, *Nili Meghalu* (1993).

Here, however, Abburi Chayadevi's "Touch" stands on its own, providing a powerful glimpse into the nature of many father-daughter relationships in contemporary India. Chayadevi artfully explores existential aspects of universal human themes relating to childhood, aging, and mortality through the sentiments of a child who is confronted by the vulnerabilities of her aging father. At the same time, her universalist meditation is situated within the particularities of gender and caste and foregrounds the patriarchal values that constrain the affective horizons of modern Telugu women. Saturated by a sense of deep despair, "Touch" leaves the reader haunted and unsettled by a sense of things that could have been but never will be.

"DON'T STAND SO CLOSE TO ME!": REMARKS ON CHAYADEVI'S "TOUCH"

Sanjay Subrahmanyam (Far Reader)

Touching and distance are a part of everyday preoccupations for many Indians, especially those who belong to the upper castes. This can seem a paradox. If you have ever stood in a line to buy a train ticket, or taken public transportation in India, you will know that people press on you constantly, eating away at any notion of a comfortable distance, even when it is extremely hot and humid. For a woman, this can turn into a not very subtle form of harassment. If you push away, or express your discomfort, you risk being taken for a snob or a disagreeable person. Analysts of crowd behavior have even suggested that this too-close proximity may in part be responsible for the stampedes and deaths that happen periodically in contemporary India in the great fairs, festivals, and such, from the Kumbh Mela to the Mahamakam festival in Kumbakonam. But when one turns away from these public spaces to the interior of the household, things can change rapidly. Again, matters are far from simple. Space in many households is desperately limited, and so too is any notion of separation or privacy. Many married Indian couples must find intimacy in the most difficult and surreptitious of circumstances then, with siblings, in-laws, and others constantly breathing down their necks. This of course generates a certain quantity of bawdy humor on the one hand, but also results in deep tensions that few are willing to talk about, let alone properly analyze or dissect.

Abburi Chayadevi's short story addresses this question of touching and distance at a more metaphorical level, from the point of view of a young or middle-aged woman who is visiting her elderly and ailing father. Past eighty, the once formidable father has lost his sight and is confined to a small and somewhat dirty room, lying on a wooden bed crawling with bugs. She, like the other characters, is given no name; everyone is referred to simply in terms of their familial relationships: "father," "mother," "brother," "husband." The woman, who is well-educated and has a job, has moved to another town with her husband, and so she sees her father infrequently now. After she enters the room, the father insists that she come closer, and holds and caresses her hand. This leads to her remembering many other moments in her upbringing, when such closeness and intimacy would have been wholly inconceivable. In earlier years, before his illness, the father had insistently kept his distance, ostensibly because of concerns with ritual purity. With his "fierce glances," he instilled a sense of shame in his daughters, to the point that they almost felt dirty in his presence, as if they "should take a bath and put on freshly washed clothes." It is implied however, that earlier still, perhaps when they were infants, they did once enjoy a greater physical closeness, if only for a short while.

The whole relationship between father and daughter is characterized by an oppressive tension. The father would have preferred sons rather than daughters, but has had to make do with what he had. The one son he had counted on died early, and the son's family is now indifferent to the old man. There is a sense that finally, in holding and caressing the daughter's hand, and insisting that he would gladly move in with her and her husband if he could, the father is clutching at straws. The gestures are at last there, rather too little too late, for a deeper and more real affection seems absent. The daughter tries to console herself in small tasks such as trimming the father's nails, but it seems that she too is just seeking some meager consolation for missed past opportunities rather than living in the moment.

The tension between father and daughter is, as noted in the contribution by Gautham Reddy, a theme that has been visited earlier in Chayadevi's writings. The father who withholds his affection is of course a classic modern figure, of which the most striking instance may be Hermann Kafka, who apparently ensured (in Saul Friedländer's words) that his son Franz "felt humiliated and shamed" by him.[1] But unlike in Kafka's *The Metamorphosis*, here it is the father rather than the child who has been transformed, not by becoming a bug but by being surrounded by bugs. In his lectures on Kafka, Vladimir Nabokov tried to bring the skills and cold gaze of an amateur entomologist to render the transformation anodyne, but the truth is that the reader is meant to feel both sympathy and revulsion for Gregor Samsa.[2]

Underlying all this is a deeper problem with touch, distance, and cleanliness. One is given to understand by Chayadevi that these preoccupations look different to men and women, with the former being far more conservative in the face of the challenges of modernity and its threat to bridge distances that had previously been unbridgeable. For, now that the father is ailing, it is the daughter's husband who has taken over his role as the guardian and guarantor of distance and cleanliness. From a safe distance, he advises his wife not to sit too close to her father when she visits, out of fear that she be contaminated by him and the bugs on his cot. Ironically, blindness has made the old man indifferent to the obsessions that characterized his attitudes before; but these have simply been passed on as obsessions to someone else—another man, of course.

The short story has no clear spatial location, and could also be taking place at any time over the last half-century, with only a few direct markers such as the young woman's education and job, and the presence of a steel chair, suggesting that this is probably in a small town in post-Independence India. But it is certainly a time when the old ways regarding touch, distance, and purity were gradually being questioned. As a child in a Tamil Brahmin family, growing up in the 1960s, I can recall the complications that these old ways posed to us. (It may be noted that Chayadevi comes from a Brahmin background in coastal Andhra.) Our parents considered themselves "modern," and had stepped away from many of the older ideas. We directly sipped water, juice, and tea from cups and glasses, rather than pouring them into our mouths from a safe distance above. We had become just a little bit careless about using our left hands at the table. Ideas of *eccil*, or pollution through saliva, were still familiar to us, but meant much less than they used to. And so on. But whenever we left Delhi to visit our extended family in South India, or spent time with the older generation, our behavior would become the subject of reproach. We did not easily understand, for example, why at certain moments people observed *madi*, a form of ritual purity which meant that you could not touch them, say between the time they had their bath and finished their rituals and prayers in the morning. For an extended time, an old widowed aunt— a former child widow with a shaven head, who wrapped herself in a single piece of white cloth—lived with us and observed an even more complicated set of such rules. With her and others of her ilk, there were lots of other prohibitions and regulations regarding food, leftovers, and so on. Indeed, food was nothing short of a mania in this world; one talked endlessly about it, spent inordinate amounts of time preparing it, and it became an area where for women like this widowed aunt, sensuality (largely blocked from other obvious spheres) effectively came to be sublimated. To be sure, infants were largely exempted from the rules and proscriptions that applied to others. But as one grew up, things became far more convoluted, especially for women. Again, in some of the distant parts of the family, people still observed older rules concerning the segregation of women during menstruation, or at least their exclusion from the kitchen. Some of my female cousins, who came from "modern" families, were deeply shocked by radical versions of this when they married into traditional families in Thanjavur or Tiruchi even within the same Brahmin subcaste.

I do not see in Chayadevi's story a simple tension between a more traditional father and a more modern daughter, although I suppose that reading is certainly permissible. In a variety of ways, often having to do with the movement of people, modern India does cast a shadow on this kind of parent-child relationship. But for me, the story is largely about fathers who prefer sons to daughters and starve their female children of affection, in a way that certainly had a different meaning in the second half of the twentieth century than it might have had a century earlier. At the same time, it seems to me (both from personal experience and from observation) that some habits regarding distance persist even across the so-called modern-traditional divide. Despite his assertive modernity in some matters, my own father maintained a marked physical aloofness with his children once they had left infancy. However, unlike Chayadevi's female protagonist, none of his children (whether female or male) necessarily felt a great sense of deprivation at this, perhaps because we came to internalize such attitudes, and perhaps because we also realized that this did not have to do with a lack of affection. Unlike our European friends, many Indians of my social background and generation do not (and did not) find it distressing if couples do not make ostentatious gestures of affection in public, or if family members do not embrace when they meet or say goodbye. Old habits die hard, and this is especially so when the habits are deeply inscribed in the body. The touch and its deeper significance remain mysterious, yet full of meaning.

6

"A Street Pump
in Anantapuram" and Five Other
Poems by Mohammad Ismail

TRANSLATOR'S NOTE AND TEXT

These short Telugu poems have the pointed meditative quality typical of this
maverick Muslim poet from the Godavari delta—a modernist, profoundly familiar with the modernist canon of the West, but with a sensibility informed by a
Godavari-style nature-pantheism.[1]

The latter can be described as an idiosyncratic strand of nondualism informed
by the yogic and tantric teachings of Telugu- and Urdu-speaking mystics of the
last three hundred years. Ismail's ancestors came to Andhra—specifically, to
Konasima—from Iran; they were learned Shi'a Muslims of wide-ranging taste
(his grandfather, Shah Wazir al-Din, was a well-known Sanskrit scholar). Ismail
(1928–2003) was educated in Madras and Kakinada, and for much of his life taught
philosophy, from Plato to Shankara, at P.R. College, Kakinada, one of the primary
intellectual sites in the Andhra world throughout the twentieth century.

REMBRANDT

> On the cheeks, on the arms,
> on the jewels on the neck,
> on the finely woven hems—
>
> how to capture on canvas
> that shimmering
> gold sheen?
>
> First, summon the darkness.
> Very thick darkness.
> With a knife, cut into its skin

without mercy.
From those wounds
golden blood gushes

under the cheeks, under the arms,
under the jewels on the neck,
under the finely woven hems
and turns solid.

A STREET PUMP IN ANANTAPURAM

At sunset
you can hear women coming
carrying heavy pots
full of darkness.

When they go,
after emptying out the darkness,
they take back
pots full of water and,
floating on top,
droplets of evening.

DHANIYALA TIPPA

A white sheet of paper.

At its edge
a horizontal line
a vertical line—
a boat and its high sail.

River, below.
Sky, above.
Maybe.

LEFT BANK, PARIS

A man
sits on the bank of the Seine,
casting a rod.
Swimming in the depths of his eyes:
the hope to catch an amazing fish.

On the opposite bank
Notre Dame hopes to catch something
in the depths of the sky,
casting its high steeple.

On this bank,
a street artist
casts his brush
into the depths of his paper
and lies in wait.
Hoping to catch
some strange species?

LACE

When I was little
and my mother was weaving lace
I used to stare in wonder.

With needle and thread
she created shapes in the air.

As if she were weaving my eyes
into the lace.

Wherever I looked, beautiful shapes
were floating before my eyes.

As if she had woven into the threads of lace
all living beings.

I think that's when I learned
how to write poems.

TWO DONKEYS IN ANANTAPURAM

A pair of donkeys
standing for hours in meditation.
They never ever
face each other.
One looks one way,
the other, the other way.
"You look eastward.
I'll face west.
Who can say from what direction
wisdom will dawn?"

Suddenly
one donkey brays,
runs around himself
once or twice
and comes back to his place.

The second donkey never moves.
Never asks what happened.
He knows that wisdom dawns only
in the east.

SPEAKING OF LANDSCAPES, REVOLUTIONARIES, AND DONKEYS: ISMAIL'S WORDS AND IMAGES

Afsar Mohammad (Near Reader)

This selection of Ismail's poems begins with a tribute to the seventeenth-century Dutch artist Rembrandt, famous for his distinctive palette of colors along with many experiments in portraits and landscapes. In this poem, Ismail focuses on a painting that fits well in life and reflects his worldview. What the Dutch artist did with paint, Ismail does with words: depicting nature and people in particular local spaces. When we pause as we read this poem, however, we come to see that Ismail's poetry is not only about local spaces. It is also about other life-worlds that coexist with these spaces and the conversation between the local and the global that takes place in our everyday experiences.

Ismail has published extensively in Telugu, and these six poems are representative of the range and depth of the central themes in his corpus. Ismail wrote during times of radical political movements and social activism between 1968 and 2003, and his is a voice that affirms individual freedom and subjectivity. Against the backdrop of most modern Telugu poetry that tended to demand political and social change, Ismail successfully created a space for private voices and interior perceptions. He thus heralded the coming of an era of poetry of personal experience, or *anubhavika kavitam*, to use his own Telugu term. Ismail was one of the few poets in Telugu who assertively defended his poetic vision in critical essays (sometimes taking part in extensive debates about it), and these essays provided a counternarrative to the political writings of the times.

It is fitting that this selection of Ismail's poems begins with one about a painting of Rembrandt. Ismail often reflects on Imagist poets and Impressionist painters in his essays and poetry. He wrote numerous prefaces to collections by other poets from his generation, and most of these include stories about poets and painters. Ismail specifically celebrates the centrality of images in his poetry, and like Imagist poetry in Europe and North America, his preference is for sharp and clear language. When reading his poems—beginning with the earliest collections such as *The Tree of Death* and *Tree My Ideal* and going all the way up to the final ones such as *The Mysterious Rain of the Last Night*—we are drawn in again and again by his simple language and accessible metaphors. He steers away from the elaborate poetic tropes and complex styles of his contemporaries and chooses what he calls a "clean language."

Two poems in the selection here are about a key moment in creativity—the first is about Rembrandt; the other "Left Bank, Paris." Both poems are about a similar mood in front of a painting. In the first, Ismail explores the moment of origin in the imagination, the moment when Rembrandt struggled to paint the "shimmering gold sheen" of twilight. Those acquainted with the paintings of Rembrandt will recall noticing this gold sheen when viewing his works. Rembrandt's use of color— the gold, the yellow, the black, and the different shades of gray—may capture the viewer's immediate attention, but it is the gold sheen that holds it. Delving deeper into his own imagination, Ismail brings that visual experience of being held by the colors into his poem, painting with words, as it were, both the artist's and the viewer's state of mind:

> how to capture on canvas
> that shimmering
> gold sheen?

For Rembrandt and Ismail, it's a single aesthetic moment. Nevertheless, they both embark on separate journeys and arrive at different emotional destinations. Ismail as a poet is creating his own idiom that is capable of articulating the colorfulness and liveliness—the gold sheen—of ordinary life in south India as his home. Before setting out on his inner journey, Ismail begins a simultaneous conversation with both Rembrandt and the viewer. Then, Ismail imagines Rembrandt speaking to himself as well as to us: "First, summon the darkness. / Very thick darkness. / With a knife, cut into its skin / without mercy. / From those wounds / golden blood gushes . . . "

Ismail turns our attention to the identity of two key aspects of this painting: the moment of its creative inspiration and the moment of its reception. In effect, this strategy invites the reader to open her mind for a fresh encounter with the artwork. In his literary life, Ismail tries to follow a similar mode of connecting the same two moments, and he encourages his readers to come with him in his journey inward. For Ismail, a literary text is more like an image, and the term he uses for such writings is "open poems."[2] To draw us in, he uses a stylistic strategy that requires his readers to enter into a poem with a mind open to what is to come. Most of his poems begin with a precise description of an object or a specific scene that a reader can visualize in her mind.

This is also true of "Left Bank, Paris," another poem in which similar dynamics of words and images are in play. Some might ask why a Telugu poet from south India seems fascinated by Paris, but Ismail's concerns are elsewhere. The poem opens with a simple image:

> A man
> sits on the bank of the Seine,
> casting a rod.

Both the Seine and the Left Bank represent key sites in our sense of Paris. As an imagined place, Paris represents bohemian possibility, promising happiness and fulfillment to artists and intellectuals. It's sometimes said that "Paris learned to think" on the Left Bank.[3] During my conversations with Ismail, he mentioned this place as "a symbol of freedom and [the] intense individuality of an artist." Reading this poem brings to mind Ismail's own place in the Telugu literary landscape as well. Like the artists and intellectuals who gathered on the Left Bank, Ismail too represented the possibility of alternatives in the Telugu literary sphere with his emphasis on freedom and the diversity of life.

The first two stanzas ("A man / sits on the bank . . . " and "On the opposite bank . . . ") are more indicative of the Telugu literary sphere in the late twentieth century than anything in the French capital. The third verse builds on this with an image of a street artist, although we now know that what he is writing about is the poet and his poem.

> On this bank,
> a street artist
> casts his brush
> into the depths of his paper
> and lies in wait.
> Hoping to catch
> some strange species?

What "strange species" could he catch? And is the street artist doing something different from the fisherman ("casting a rod") in the first stanza and Notre Dame ("casting its high steeple") in the second? Ismail's poems often convey the down-to-earth beauty of nature and everyday life. Rather than looking for extraordinariness, Ismail unveils an ordinariness that most poets and artists do not try to capture, and if they do try, they often fail. When Ismail looks at even the most ordinary aspects of everyday life, they seem to turn for him into something "strange." As a poet and person, Ismail brings his experience of strangeness back to his readers and tries to enable them to relive those moments in addition to similar moments of their own. Whereas these global images shimmer with their own local color, Ismail's poetry also explores another major aspect—he celebrates the concreteness, the lived reality, of local places filled with ordinary people, animals, and birds. In the process, he pokes fun at intellectuals who often drift off, away from the ordinariness of life.

From the Seine to the Godavari: The Everyday Cultures of Ordinary Life. David Shulman, in his introductory note to the translated poems, observes that Ismail's poems are "planted deeply in the Godavari landscape." The great Godavari River is featured in many of Ismail's poems. Likewise, in conversations I had with him, Ismail always showed immense pride when speaking about the Godavari. Of course, there is a history to this. Many Telugu poets and writers who grew up on its banks never tired of sharing their varied memories of life there.

For Ismail, the Godavari River is akin to the Seine: it represents both classical and modern Andhra in the same way that the Seine stands for Paris. This is a region with a long history: it was home to the beginnings of written literary traditions in Telugu, as well as the early phases of modern social reform movements in Andhra. The entire riverbank is dotted with sites where classical, medieval, and modern legacies come to mind and intermingle. However, the journey that Ismail takes us on is different. Ignoring the great memory sites of saints, warriors, and poets, he instead focuses on tiny, overlooked places and the often-invisible details of everyday life. He takes us, his readers, to this other side of the Godavari.

Again, Ismail's perception of this world is close to the way a painter looks at a landscape—watching it with the eye before the brush touches the canvas. For instance, the poem "Dhaniyala Tippa":

A white sheet of paper.

At its edge
a horizontal line
a vertical line—
a boat and its high sail.

River, below.
Sky, above.
Maybe.

The poem is about a tiny island in the Godavari, but it is not only a description. Ismail borrows images from a painter's actions to picture this island, allowing us to imagine the entire landscape. Trying to see things just as they are is one of the most striking aesthetic features of Ismail's poetry. Ismail is a participant observer and is extremely reflective about what he is trying to see in the landscape and what he wants us to take from it. He makes sure that his presence does not disturb the essential serenity of the scene. Having found the quiet beauty of the landscape in his mind, Ismail now invites people to its interiorities with his words. As he does so, he introduces us to the beings living there: children, women, and much more.

In his poems that are set further away from the river banks, Ismail touches on another distinctive theme of his: the urban life that is causing rural life to vanish, the encounters between city and village, and their conflicts. He often turns to the places that lie in between village and urban space to reveal everyday beauty. In the poem "A Street Pump in Anantapuram," Ismail describes an evening scene when women come to fetch the water. Anantapuram is one of the towns where Ismail worked as a college lecturer. Here he draws a beautiful image from a scene of ordinary urban life.

At sunset
you can hear women coming
carrying heavy pots
full of darkness.

When they go,
after emptying out the darkness,
they take back
pots full of water and,
floating on top,
droplets of evening.

The poem does not seem to need much explanation or interpretation. Ismail uses the images to tell an entire story in a few words. The key lies in the way he imagines such an ordinary scene. This very concrete scene seems to manifest something more intangible and full of deeper meaning.

Donkeys in Search of Wisdom. The poem "Two Donkeys in Anantapuram" generated a heated debate. On the first reading, it may sound like a parable. Ismail uses a narrative mode in many of his poems, which gives some of them satirical undertones. Here, Ismail again utilizes a scene from ordinary life to make fun of the overly political tendencies of other Telugu writers. Ismail's poem is straightforward: there are two donkeys who face east and west, anticipating the revelation of wisdom. Both donkeys have different dynamics in their search; one is restless, the other relaxed and confident about the inevitable result.

Suddenly
one donkey brays,
runs around himself
once or twice
and comes back to his place.

The second donkey never moves.
never asks what happened.
He knows that wisdom dawns
in the east.

With this comic scene, Ismail shows that both donkeys ultimately fail in their quest for wisdom. In another satirical poem titled "The Song of a Woodpecker" (not in this selection), Ismail returns to this mode of parable and comic imagery. At the time Ismail was writing satirical poems of this sort, Marxist approaches to everyday life and politics were ubiquitous in Telugu public life and literature. As a critical thinker and innovative poet who believed in the idea of freedom and the autonomy of the literary domain, Ismail had little sympathy for the leftist literary movements that he believed were overly concerned with their political mission. Ismail never tired of critiquing these poets and writers, and he often condemned the "political poetry" they produced. According to him, political poetry is "inane and repetitious." Poems like "The Two Donkeys" and "The Song of the Woodpecker" were indeed satires chiding such literary propagandists and, more specifically, both probably were written to mock a particular conference that Marxist writers held in 1975, when Ismail lived in Anantapuram.

Appreciating Ismail's Poems.   For Ismail, a poem is a "crucible of emotion and intellect, striving to close the gap between words and experiences."[4] How does he find a way to close the gap between words and experiences? Although all poets write using words, images, and metaphors, each poet sees the beginning of a poem in her own way. The understanding of a poem's source—before the words are inscribed on paper, before the artist's brush touches the canvas—can reveal the poet's philosophy of life. The poems translated in this chapter provide insight into the sources of Ismail's poetry and throw light on what he tried to do with his words. More than once, Ismail celebrates the process of writing a poem within a poem. In such pieces, we get a good glimpse of his self-understanding.

In his poetry, Ismail aims to share some of the most personal kinds of experience, to give an authentic statement of what he sees and knows, what he suffers and loves, and the heightened moments of his life. He always begins, however, with an object or action of an everyday nature and uses it as the central image around which to organize his vision. This can be seen vividly in "Lace," the last poem I will be discussing. In this poem, Ismail talks about his mother and the way she used to make lace. Making lace is not uncommon, but Ismail's approach focuses our attention on the doubling movement of his mother's mind and his own: his mother creates beautiful shapes with needle and thread, and her movements become interwoven with Ismail's imagination in the form of another set of beautiful shapes and beings. Seeing in her movements something more than the making of lace, the poem tracks the poet's journey from object to imagination to words, all the while weaving together the various experiences of his mother, himself, and so much more. Two stanzas stand out:

> As if she were weaving my eyes
> into the lace.

And:

> As if she had woven into the threads of lace
> all living beings.

Ismail shows here how a poem is prompted by an everyday experience, only to go further. Every poem is a world that weaves together objects and impressions, images and perceptions, and ultimately "all living beings."

BETWEEN SKY AND ROAD: THE WANDERING
SCHOLAR, MODERNISM, AND THE POETRY OF ISMAIL

Gabriel Levin (Far Reader)

Barely a week into his sojourn in Rajahmundry, where he would reside for the next six months, David Shulman noted in his journal, "What does it mean to be 'modern' in Telugu?" This is a subject that continues to resurface in his *Spring, Heat, Rains: A South Indian Diary*, often in the context of its complement, tradition, which is treated throughout with a mixture of reverence and foreboding: "Must the past be slain," the entry continues, "to make way for the new?"[5] It is 2006, and Shulman has ostensibly arrived in Andhra Pradesh both to improve his spoken Telugu and to embark on a prolonged study of two classical texts, Peddana's sixteenth-century Telugu *Story of Manu* and Shriharsha's Sanskrit *Life of Naishadha*. But it is the diarist of the everyday minutiae of life that soon takes over: on the one hand, the sheer, physical intensity of the Godavari delta—its colors and odors, tastes and sounds—and on the other, the lively network of social relations, consisting in large part of writers, publishers, local historians, ethnographers, geographers, and Carnatic singers. In short, the *sanghalu*, or literary societies of Rajahmundry, Hyderabad, and beyond. It is the latter band—and in particular his enduring friendship with the great Telugu scholar, essayist, and literary maverick and gadfly Narayana Rao, as well as the new ties he will forge with such local writers as Patanjali Sastry and the poet Smile—that will keep alive the notion of the "modern" in Shulman's mind.

Literary translation exerted a major influence on the English and American High Modernists. One has to think only of Ezra Pound's translation of the Romance troubadour poets while tramping through Provence, and his reinvention of China in *Cathay*; T.S. Eliot's forays into Sanskrit in *The Waste Land*; William Carlos William's experiments from Spanish, French, Chinese, and the Greek of Theocritus; Marianne Moore's versions of La Fontaine; Basil Bunting's versions of Ferdowsi, Sa'di, and Hafez, completed while living in Persia; or, for that matter, Helen Waddell's translations of the medieval Latin lyrics of hard-bitten, wandering scholars. The early Modernist poets were less engaged with translation as a literary exercise; rather, they were seeking out cultural, temporal, and geographical diversity in both the West and, increasingly, Asia as they endeavored to rejuvenate and radically innovate the means of their own production: the perception of difference became above all, in the words of the great French explorer and confabulator of Asia, Victor Segalen, "a personal point of departure."[6]

Which brings us back to Rajahmundry, in the spring of 2006. *What does it mean to be "modern" in Telugu?* needs to be examined in the context of Shulman's own peregrinations, scholarship, and translations from Tamil and Telugu, for have not the distinguishing features of Modernism in the West—cultural diversity, polyglotism, and esotericism—been at the heart of Shulman's own understanding of the imaginative reaches of classical South Asian thought? And yet Shulman has been equally clear-eyed about the fact that the transmission of the vast, oral literary tradition of south India may be gradually eroding under the banner of nationalism and modernity, at least as understood in India.

This dialectic is played out in Shulman's diary in the running exchange—albeit imaginary, since one of its interlocutors isn't physically present—between Shulman and Narayana Rao. Early on in his stay in Andhra, traveling on the train, Shulman reads an acerbic broadside by Narayana Rao in the Telugu Weekly: "The notion that poets should produce something useful for society has, unfortunately, taken root. It is truly a misfortune if a poet has the delusion that his poetry is meant to change society. The business of a poet is to write poetry." Shulman reads on: "For a long time now, Telugu poetry has stopped being poetry. Telugu literature has departed from all the so-called literary societies, *sahitya sanghalu*; only the *sanghalu* are left behind." This brings Shulman to muse:

> Historically my role is to defend, to offer hope; each time I come back from Andhra, we argue over the current literary scene. I see promise, fragile seedlings of innovation, and I can wait; it can take a century or two for a great poet to germinate and ripen. The twentieth century produced two giants, Gurajada Appa Rao and Viswanatha Satyanarayana, and three or four near giants—is that not a respectable harvest, almost on a par with the golden ages of the past? Such thoughts fail to comfort him; he [Narayana Rao] sees mostly a scorched landscape, a withered discourse, benighted critics or pseudocritics, vast rhetorical effusions, anything but the real thing he knew so well as a young man in Eluru.[7]

To defend, to offer hope. The marked difference between the two friends and coeditors of more than one anthology of Telugu poetry in English may be one of temperament as much as it is of origins and perspective. Narayana Rao, the éminence grise of Telugu literary culture, and Shulman, the peripatetic Western scholar, translator, and ambassador-at-large, may in the end reflect two sides of the same coin: the insider combatant, with more than a few scores to settle, and the romantic outsider, at one remove from the fray. The pair may be at loggerheads on the state of the arts in south India, but they are in perfect agreement over at least one critical point: namely, that right up to modern times the poets of south India had worked out of and were steeped in a poetic tradition in which "the word of the *cāṭu* poet"—I quote from the jointly authored introduction to their anthology, *A Poem at the Right Moment*—"is never empty of effect; it changes, or indeed creates, a reality in conformity with the vision implicit in the poet's speech."[8]

This is an astonishing statement for a Western, secular reader to come up against, and is elaborated in Shulman's more recent study, *Tamil: A Biography*. "Poetry was now [speaking of the premodern period, ca. 1500–1800], if anything, even more effective in working on the world: the grammatical pragmatics of the post-Chola centuries were integrated into musical grammars of 'auralization' and shamanic magic aimed at generating divinity and concomitant forms of understanding in the listener's mind. Tamil itself, one powerful and prestigious medium for such effects alongside its sister languages, was now a full-fledged deity, sometimes capricious, situated in the core of the speaker's inner self."[9] For someone nourished on the Western canon, wherein the medium of poetry is perceived primarily as mimetic and expressive, and, at its most daring, visionary or oracular, the notion that poetry might not only reflect but *change* reality is as alluring as it is suspect.

The allure may have been what drew so many of the early Moderns in the West, in the wake of World War I, to what they homogenized as "Eastern thought," "African shamanism," and the general exploration of the unconscious through dreams and automatic writing as practiced by the French Surrealists. One had at one end of the spectrum the self-referential, ironic vision of Auden's "For poetry makes nothing happen; it survives in the valley of its making," and at the other, Rilke's call for transformation: "You must change your life."[10] Shulman, perfectly aware of the challenges posed in the West and the East by modernity—fragmentation, cultural relativism, destabilizing notions of the self and reality—lands squarely on the side of Rilke's call for the reintegration of the self in poetic speech, or as Narayana Rao and Shulman will have it, in the continued survival of "the metaphysics of language"; poetry may no longer have claims on changing outer reality but it can still effect *the core of the speaker's inner self*. Herein lies the juncture between the old and the new, tradition and innovation. *Spring, Heat, Rains* is above all a record of Shulman's own vagabonding endeavors to find in Telugu poetry and song, in its ancient temples, and in his own daily, chance encounters, the elusive, essential core, the vital perception of difference—to come back to Segalen—in which we recover some unacknowledged part of ourselves.

One such encounter will be with the poetry of Mohammad Ismail, a major poet of the Godavari delta, who died in 2003, not long before Shulman's sojourn in the region, and who was still very much in the hearts and minds of the company of poets and writers Shulman had befriended in and around Rajahmundry. One day in late June of that year, Smile, one of these writers, recited a poem by Ismail after Shulman returned his bicycle, which he had borrowed to ride around town. The ride down Nehru Road is in itself important in the context of the poem he is about to receive as a gift, for Shulman's own observations border on the epiphanic: "The colors have changed again: green and dark blue (clouds), dark-red waterlogged earth, soaked brown thatch, pastel facades, red rooster feathers, mud-black buffaloes, white afternoon sun—no more gold. Relief."[11] Shulman records a transliteration of the poem in his journal as well as his own English version:

Am I taking it
or is it taking me?

Don't know.
Like my poetry.

Between sky and road
wheels revolve.
Mostly in the sky.
Only a finger's breadth
touches the earth.
Like my poetry.

Kites soaked
in evening tones
float down to rest.
After we reach our nest,
a wheel on the ground,
another floating into dreams,
It sleeps.
Like my poetry.[12]

The poem is a typical Ismail specimen, as I would soon discover in reading the handful of Ismail poems translated in this chapter. Such poems are composed of short, clear, declarative sentences. They are deceptively simple in their presentation and crystalize around a central, resonating image: in our case a bicycle, whose wheel revolves between sky and earth, dreams and reality, which in turn is compared in the refrain to the act of writing poetry. The poem comes as a poignant tailpiece to Shulman's bike ride with its own luminous glimpses of the twists and turns ("Am I taking it / or is it taking me?") of his surroundings.

Ismail came into his own as a poet in the fifties and sixties, soon after the establishment of the Republic of India. These were heady times in Andhra Pradesh as the literary community sought to establish the parameters of its own national identity in relation to, and not infrequently at odds with, the old religious and cultural hierarchies. Neo-Marxist theories, Surrealist manifestoes, and progressive, antipundit tracts were the order of the day. Ismail, descending from a family of Sanskrit and Telugu scholars on his mother's side, while his paternal grandfather, whose ancestors came from Iran, was a scholar and poet of Arabic, Persian, and Urdu—the sort of polyglotism dear to Shulman's heart—generally shunned the more strident sort of politically engaged poetry coming out of Hyderabad and Chennai in the sixties and seventies, and developed in its stead, while lecturing on logic and philosophy in Kakinada, an inward-turning poetry soaked in the local colors and sensations of the Godavari delta.

A STREET PUMP IN ANANTAPURAM

At sunset
you can hear women coming

carrying heavy pots
full of darkness.

When they go,
after emptying out the darkness,
they take back
pots full of water and,
floating on top,
droplets of evening.

Note the immediate appeal to the sense of hearing, made more acute as evening
sets in and one's surroundings are drained of color and the world of solid boundaries becomes less distinct. So the "double agency" of inward and outward reality
is quietly instantiated at the very onset of the poem. I cannot speak of the original
in Telugu, sealed as it is within the felicities of its own aural world. But Shulman
himself writes in his diary of the Borgesian notion in which the original may be
considered "unfaithful to the translation."[13] Although the notion is fully explored
in Walter Benjamin's seminal essay "The Task of the Translator," the literatures
of south India, if I am not mistaken, are the very embodiment of such a notion.
Major Sanskrit epics, such as the *Ramayana*, rather than being frozen in time, are
transplanted over centuries as independent works of art in Telugu and Tamil, Kannada, and Malayalam. These are not translations but re-creations, or as Benjamin
would have it, afterlives.

Ismail, to return to "A Street Pump in Anantapuram," isn't content to simply
record the coming and going of the woman at dusk. His imagination seizes the
moment only as the darkness of the empty vessels, filled to the brim on the wom-
en's return journey, sparkles with "droplets of evening," an image that is attentive
to the surface effects of fading light on water even as it silently probes deeper and
evokes in the reader's mind the unspoken, ominous braiding of light and dark
forces, presence and absence. Surely Ismail is drawing on a common pool of
imagery, which extends to the Telugu *cāṭu* tradition and further back, partaking
of the Upanishad's ellipses, but his imagistic verse is indebted as well to Chinese
poetry and to Japanese haiku—the latter of which he translated into Telugu—and
to Western contemporaries writing in French, Spanish, and English. Of the last,
William Carlos Williams, whom Ismail translated into Telugu, comes to mind as
a comrade-in-arms in the modernistic battle to rejuvenate the act of perception,
addressing directly, plainly, the "thing itself" within the boundaries of a sharply
particularized reality, even as both are equally alert to the dark side of the mirror
reflecting that reality.

In a like manner, Shulman's taking to Ismail's poetry might be seen as another
instance of shared sensibilities. Answering Shulman's question—"What does it
mean to be 'modern' in Telugu?"—requires embracing the double vision of East
and West in a Telugu poet's verse and an American-Israeli wandering scholar's

quest. Not surprisingly, two poems Shulman renders into English were written by Ismail in—or inspired by—the West: "Left Bank, Paris," and "Rembrandt." The latter meditates, once again, on the dialectic between surface and depth in a painter whose portraits testify to the dawning of isolate consciousness ("The human was no longer self-evident," writes John Berger of Rembrandt, "it had to be found in the darkness").[14] Men and women, old and young, indigent and affluent, emerge from the penumbra to fix us with their gaze, a brume of light and dark strokes calling into question the very notion of the self-materialized on canvas:

> On the cheeks, on the arms
> on the jewels on the neck,
> on the finely woven hems—
>
> how to capture on canvas
> that shimmering
> gold sheen?
>
> First, summon the darkness.
> Very thick darkness.
> With a knife, cut into its skin
> without mercy.
> From those wounds
> gold blood gushes
>
> under the cheeks, under the arms,
> under the jewels on the neck,
> under the finely woven hems
> and turns solid.

But one cannot leave Ismail without returning to his own locality where a man "bestirs himself to become awake," as Williams would have it, in a poem that speaks once again of the origins of the creative act, and in its unitary vision draws on Nagarjuna's philosophy, a major influence on Ismail.[15] Shulman too is drawn to Nagarjuna's writing and devotes a long passage—only days before coming upon Ismail's poetry—to "the Advaitic temptation," though coming from the West, he cannot help resisting, even as he acknowledges it, the longing in everyone for a "singular, godly aliveness hidden within us."[16] For Ismail, however, such inner aliveness is the *rasa*, the liquid essence released in the perception of beauty:

LACE

> When I was little
> and my mother was weaving lace
> I used to stare in wonder.
>
> With needle and thread
> she created shapes in the air.
>
> As if she were weaving my eyes
> into the lace.

Wherever I looked, beautiful shapes
were floating before my eyes.

As if she had woven into the threads of lace
all living beings.

I think that's when I learned
how to write poems.

The Love of Music and the Music of Love

EDITORS' NOTE

POETRY AND SONG ARE CLOSE KIN in many parts of the world but in South Asia, literature is inseparable from music. Writers and musicians often move in the same social circles, exchange ideas, and, indeed, lend each other materials. Written literary works typically were, and often still are, performed orally in courts, salons, concert halls, and even on street corners, just like music, and the musicality of a text has always been deemed just as important as its contents (if not more). Music performance, for its part, often features in literary texts, and as we see in the first selection in this unit, frequently shapes key plot junctures. In the first selection of this unit, from a tenth-century Tamil poem called *Chivakan's Gem*, the ability to perform and enjoy music is the only way to reach another's heart. Love and joy also pervade the second set of selections, two musical pieces by the composer Muttuswami Dikshitar (1775–1835). And although the love and joy are felt by the devotee and meant for god Shiva, the latter is expected, just like human beings, to open His ears and heart to them. Robert Frost's saying (cited by Donald Davis in his reading of the musical pieces)—"The ear is the only true writer and the only true reader"—never rang righter.

The Music Contest from Tiruttakkatevar's Tamil *Chivakan's Gem*

TRANSLATOR'S NOTE AND TEXT

Tiruttakkatevar's tenth-century *Chivakan's Gem* is one of the great Tamil narrative poems. It's hero, Chivakan, known from classical Jain sources in Prakrit, slowly finds his way to liberation via a seemingly endless chain of love affairs. Indeed, this massive tenth-century work is known in Tamil as the "book of weddings," since it tells of the many relationships and marriages of its hero, Chivakan. The present passage describes the bridegroom's contest for the hand of the celestial singer Kantaruvatattai, whose father has sent her to a port city in order to find a husband: whoever succeeds in defeating her at music and song will marry her. Chivakan, a highly accomplished musician, surpasses her by singing a set of three verses in the persona of the beloved's girlfriend, in a somewhat modernized version of the old Sangam style of love poetry. In this older corpus, the companion of the heroine often speaks on her behalf to the distant hero and describes her friend's lonely plight. In this passage, the author of *Chivakan's Gem* follows this convention, but when the bride-to-be replies, she acknowledges her defeat by replying with three verses of her own, in which the beloved speaks in her own voice. These are poems of desperate longing that go beyond the classical template.

THE MUSICAL COMPETITION FROM *CHIVAKAN'S GEM* BY
TIRUTTAKKATEVAR (722–37)

> Famous for his perfection
> in making music, Chivakan lifted his veena
> with its freshly painted golden gourd, its elegant frets
> of coral, its ivory tuning pegs studded with diamonds,
> and flooded the sea-circled world with the tremulous sound

of its strings, fluid as the draught of immortal life,
sweet as fine honey. (722)

Sound fused into sound as he played, a garland
of flowers falling from his hair, his fingers coaxing out
the song. No one could say if he was singing
or plucking the strings. Gods and people of this world
fell unconscious, birds and animals became faint,
trees and stones turned to water, absorbed
in the opening phrases.[1] (723)

"Need I say
that when lightning roars in the rain,
a little snake shivers in fear?
Need I say
that she, breasts chafing
under strings of gold, is sick
with lightning and with rain? (724)

Need I say
that when rain pours from clouds
in the sky, a waterfall rumbles
on the hill?
Need I say
that when she, lovely as shadow,
sees the waterfall rumbling
on the hill, her heart
breaks apart? (725)

Need I say
that when it rains, jasmine blossoms
in the forest like stars in the sky?
Need I say
that she grieves, her hair flowing
with honey, when she sees the forest
in flower?" (726)

His fingers flew along the strings
with infinite precision as he sang,
holding fast to the rhythm, and hearing
this brilliant performance, the gods
cast away their veenas, the professional musicians
in heaven could think no more, and all who live
on earth were bewitched by wonder

that penetrated the hearts of even
hard-core Yogis. (727)

His veena was graced by a garland, a little rumpled
by black bees that haunted its flowers and by streaks
of ivory, and as the prince played its polished strings,
his fine-pitched voice became one with their resonant tones
to the astonishment and dismay of the Kinnara singers
in the skies. (728)

He sang. The very gods were dumbfounded.
Fierce Vidyadhara sorcerers could only praise him.
In our world, people were happy. Birds
forgot their bodies, forgot their own songs.
The God of Love was put to shame. All the kings
on earth, hearing the melody, stood still
as painted portraits. (729)

"Like a hawk and its shadow, the song
and the veena's notes have come together
as a rich feast in this Chivakan's playing."
So she thought, knowing she was
going to lose to him. Still, lovely
as a young peahen, her eyes sharp as spears
tapering like leaves at the tip, she took up
her veena and, taking her seat, began to play. (730)

She sang as she played, her long hair cascading
down her back, her earrings and gold palm-leaf jewels
flashing on her ears, her charming brow stained
with sweat, her neck turned slightly toward the left.
She was beautiful beyond compare, her song
plaintive and sweet. (731)

"Pallid with love are my breasts, covered with jewels
crafted like leaves, and my brow, a bent bow.
The waterfall on the hill gleams like a sword.
Tell me, my sweet-spoken friend: how can *he*
fail to see? (732)

Pallid with love are my forehead, brilliant
as the crescent moon, my eyes limned with mascara
that are always ready to do battle, and my all-too-heavy
breasts. On the high mountain
the waterfall that gleams like a sword

flashes like lightning. Tell me now,
my friend with eyes like spears smeared
with poison: how can *he* fail to see? (733)

Pallid and bright are my perfect breasts,
my delicate, dancing arms, my forehead
like the crescent moon. The waterfall
teeming with precious stones flashes
high on the mountain. Now tell me,
my friend, your words sweet
as sugarcane: how can *he*
fail to see?" (734)

But her voice quivered, and her gentle fingers
couldn't move up and down the smooth strings,
so the sung melody and the sounds of the veena
never became one. The song fell, far from heaven.
She couldn't think. She sat there,
defeated. (735)

She let the jeweled veena slip from her hands.
Wounded, trembling, and very embarrassed,
this wide-eyed queen among women slowly
and truly lifted up the nuptial garland of gold
as if straining to lift a mountain, to adorn the prince
standing before her, his anklets
engraved with flowers. (736)

Her anklets were ringing softly, and her belt
was shimmering like lightning as she walked,
just a little hesitant, but with a grace that would put
even a graceful goose to shame. Then
she tossed the garland on her lord as if to say
to all of us who live in this world that being selfless
is its own reward. (737)

LOVE IN DEFEAT

Talia Ariav (Near Reader)

The musical competition between Chivakan and the divine female musician Kantaruvatattai is above all a nontrivial contemplation on love.[2] Love, it seems, is at its most beautiful, and at its most intense, in its asymmetries and moments of loss. More specifically, Kantaruvatattai's defeat, evident to her even before she enters the competition, is a unique take on the Tamil tradition of *akam*. *Akam*, often translated as "love," is the theme and title of a major corpus in the canonical collection of classical Tamil poetry (Sangam). As such, *akam* stands for a highly codified poetical language of love in various modes and contexts, classified and debated in the authoritative Tamil grammar and its commentaries. As I demonstrate here, this excerpt from *Chivakan's Gem*, which postdates the classical Sangam corpus by several centuries at least, relies on the *akam* tradition and alters it from within.

One striking feature of the dissonant chord with which the excerpt ends is that it is achieved via the concrete possibility of harmony. Chivakan's performance, in which his song and veena are invisibly connected (like a hawk and its shadow, in the eyes of Kantaruvatattai), is a prelude to, and somehow essential to, her defeat, in which her song and the veena never become one. Chivakan's sound is fluid and sweet, as all beautiful or good things are expected to be in the Tamil world. Quite appropriately, it "flooded the sea-circled world" (722). The solid state of the world as we know it—and of south India in particular—is surrounded by seas, and it can potentially be flooded at any given moment with intense beauty or emotion. It is not by chance that the word for "world" in the Tamil is *akam*: the very word used more commonly for love or in-ness. Chivakan's sounds have the capacity to make the world, which is also the inner state of his listeners and/or of Kantaruvatattai, liquid. This choice of word also suggests that Chivakan's sound literally floods, with its own liquids, the classical world of the *akam* tradition. As we shall see, this is a rather apt description of what Chivakan is doing in his song.

Chivakan's Gem is an early and influential Tamil poetical work of vast dimensions, featuring lexical and syntactical experimentation in the novel *viruttam* prosodic pattern. However, the embedded sung stanzas within this excerpt, of three to four verses each, are markedly different in register, meter, and texture from their surroundings, as the translation distinctly shows. Even knowing little about the classical *akam* corpus and its grammar of love, it is possible to identify its intertextual echoes in these songs. First, the most expected figures of an *akam* poem—namely, a hero, a beloved heroine, and the heroine's girlfriend—are present. The commentators suggest that Chivakan assumes the friend's voice when he sings, and in Kantaruvatattai's song this triad is made explicit. Moreover, their songs use loaded vocabulary and imagery from the *akam* tradition, such as rain, hill, waterfall, and jasmine. Such elements, when used in an *akam* poem, correspond with the inner state of the heroine, as they evoke one or more of the five landscapes of love. When using such descriptors, which function as an economical yet richly suggestive mechanism, each classical *akam* poem enfolds a specific and condensed situation between lovers.

Returning to our text, the mention of rain and jasmine immediately place Chivakan's song in the *mullai* (jasmine) landscape of early and painful separation after marriage. This is hardly intuitive, as we are contextually at a moment of promise, occurring right before a wedding. The rain and the jasmine therefore strongly suggest to the informed audience that the moment of marriage already holds the seed of painful separation. Such a notion resonates well with the *akam* commentarial tradition, which acknowledges that love, at any of its stages, inherently entails a measure of loss or separation. The hill and waterfall, however, which link the songs of the two lovers, appropriately belong in the premarriage landscape of stolen love. Such a mixture of landscapes is not uncommon in the classical *akam* context. Here, however, it sets the stage for further creative use of the old *akam* "grammar of love."

To begin with, the manner in which these evocative nouns are repeated calls for attention. The rain, the waterfall, and the hill reappear in clear and intensifying patterns throughout these stanzas, so that a usually suggestive and economical evocation of landscape in the *akam* grammar is replaced with deliberate repetition. What is the work doing when Chivakan asks:

> Need I say
> that when lightning roars in the rain
> a little snake shivers in fear?
> Need I say
> that she, breasts chafing
> under strings of gold, is sick
> with lightning and with rain? (724)

Chivakan (or the poet Tiruttakkatevar) is quite literally asking if these *akam* clichés are worth repeating. His answer is a resounding yes, and he goes on to demonstrate the creative possibilities that such a strong poetic tradition opens for the poet. Tiruttakkatevar's repetitions do not cancel out the content of the condensed evocation, but rather add to it and dramatically alter its effect. The evocative rain of painful separation becomes, increasingly, an actual rain that thickens the pain in question and a recurring sound that makes us listen to the music accompanying the words.

This repetition also creates a governing sense of associative connections, which resist a closed set of metaphors. In the verse quoted here, it is suggested that the suffering heroine is the little shivering snake. However, the repetition of the rain and thunder disturb this suggestion, as her breasts, with their strings of gold, bring to mind clouds and thunder. The heroine is sick because of the lightning, but she is also somehow the lightning itself, perhaps implying that Chivakan, when he speaks in the voice of her friend, is also suffering like the little shivering snake. These semantic loopholes should not be overstated. Rather, the repetition creates the sense of constant movement between images. It poses a demand for constant reflection and revision, which contribute to an effect of subtle and dynamic emotions.

As Chivakan's song evolves, the structure of repetition marks a shift to Kantaruvatattai's point of view:

> Need I say
> that when rain pours from clouds

in the sky, a waterfall rumbles
on the hill?
Need I say
that when she, lovely as shadow,
sees the waterfall rumbling
on the hill, her heart
breaks apart? (725)

The waterfall on the hill is first a result of the rain, and then repeated as the object of Kantaruvatattai's perception, which in turn causes her heartbreak. This repetition, even more emphatic in the Tamil, weaves the traditionally minimalist and suggestive force of a waterfall, in terms of an *akam* vocabulary, into a different aesthetic that includes naturalistic causality and explicit psychological dimensions. It also poses an articulate question of perspective, as Kantaruvatattai simultaneously sees the waterfall, and is herself seen by Chivakan, to be "lovely as shadow" (725). The irony is hard to miss: Chivakan sings in the female friend's voice, asking himself to see what she (Kantaruvatattai) sees. Note, in this regard, that this is all framed as a stanza within the text, with an archaic flavor of the *akam* conventions. Structurally, the use of a marked register of *akam* within a work from the tenth century makes for very apt grounds (some may say, the sine qua non condition) for irony to take place. By saying very little, and in a subtly ironic tone, the poet is effectively asking the following nontrivial questions: Can a lover see his beloved? Does seeing the beloved amount to seeing the world through her eyes? And, can a (renewed) grammar of love enable him to see?

Interestingly, Chivakan wins the competition while these questions remain very much open. Winning, it seems, is not very conducive to an intimate knowledge of love. The conventions of the *akam* dialogue allow for these structural asymmetries, in which Chivakan playfully sings in the girlfriend's voice, while Kantaruvatattai answers very openly in her own voice. Kantaruvatattai sings again and again the very question that Chivakan left open: can he see? It could very well be her predetermined defeat that allows for her lucid description of his shortsighted glance. The artist's failure, rather than his or her success, conveys the most penetrating insight about love. Within this extract describing artists at their performance, this readily reads as a striking metapoetic statement.

Kantaruvatattai's song, even more intensely than Chivakan's, is governed by repetitions, such that the three verses are slight paraphrases of each other. One is tempted to read something of a repetition compulsion into her song, as her few looping sentences brilliantly communicate her pain. In any case, all three verses return to the waterfall on the hill. It is an *akam* footprint, as described earlier, and a strong statement of her condition in which the waterfall tortures her like a sword. It is also a reference to Chivakan's song, paraphrasing what he stated, in the voice of her friend, to be the content of her glance. Her song, then, affirms and elaborates on his observations, but also implies that his very song is a torturing sword to her. If we take the dialogical situation in these verses seriously, this is only reasonable. His song was quite clear about his inability to see her; her song mourns this fact, tries to make him see her with elaborate descriptions of her beauty, and explicitly asks over and over again if he really cannot see.

As Kantaruvatattai performs her preordained failure, she asks her reverberating question, which sums up the inherent separation involved in love. To put it plainly, even in the most intimate of situations, there is never a true unity of perspective, and misperceptions of one another are bound to happen. The description of her failure, in which the song and the veena never become one, quite literally corresponds to the content of her lament. Love, the passage suggests, is not about becoming one. Only her condition of loss reveals this inner truth, which, as we have seen, must first be staged in an idyllic language of perfect accord. This accord, however, is produced by a man who cannot see. Of the two, Kantaruvatattai is the true artist who fails and therefore sees.

By way of conclusion, I should briefly mention that Tiruttakkatevar, the author of this text, is a self-professed Jain monk. The framework of the entire *Chivakan's Gem*, which follows that of various Jain Prakrit sources, supports a Jain philosophy of life. Chivakan, the serial groom, eventually marries Mukti, or Freedom, and renounces the world and its bodily pleasures. One question, then, is how does the extensive presence of erotic love, which makes for most of this vast work, support its Jain conclusion. If one were to seek cohesion between the erotic content of the work and its strong "Jain" framework, it is perhaps the attentive reflection on modes and conditions of seeing and feeling in the world, not of indifference to it, that somehow prepare the ground for the radical conclusion of renunciation.

It might, however, be altogether wrong to read this work through the lens of its renunciatory conclusion. The author of *Chivakan's Gem* is clearly invested in the poetics and dynamics of erotic love, and his work is a massive poetic endeavor that includes different elements and tensions. The excerpt discussed shows that, among other things, the poet is purposefully reusing the authoritative and nonsectarian Tamil grammar of love. In doing so, he is broadening that grammar to include a series of meditations on the noncoincidental relationship of love and defeat, and on the role of defeat in both a lover's and an artist's ability to see.

SWEETNESS THAT MELTS THE HEART

Kesavan Veluthat (Far Reader)

Indian aesthetics, particularly in Sanskrit, has always considered love as the "king of sentiments." Anandavardhana, a ninth-century literary theorist writing in Sanskrit, has gone to the extent of saying that reading about love in literature can cause the utmost pleasure. For Anandavardhana, reading about love can also render a reader's heart tender. Commenting on Anandavardhana about a century later, Abhinavagupta, another prominent literary theorist, says that love "melts the heart of a reader in every way." What we have in the passages from *Chivakan's Gem* is exactly that—an occasion for love to melt a reader's heart. The whole work in general and these passages in particular carry us to an ethereal world where it is all sweetness and where we find our hearts melting.

Chivakan's Gem follows the adventures of a prince, Chivakan, who wants to avenge the murder of his father. In the course of his wanderings, Chivakan encounters and marries many beautiful women, so much so that the poem has been called "the book of marriages." The passages at hand are from the third canto and are about a music contest between the daughter of the king of celestial musicians (known as *Vidyādharas*), Kantaruvatattai, who vowed only to marry a man who could defeat her in a music contest.

The contest begins. Chivakan lifts his veena, its golden gourd painted freshly, its elegant frets of coral, its ivory tuning pegs studded with diamonds. Note carefully what happens. The tremulous sound of the strings floods the sea-circled world with music—a music that is pictured as "fluid as the draught of immortal life, / sweet like fine honey" (722). It is the string of the veena (the word for "string" in Tamil also means "vein" or "nerve") that the musician touches; the music it produces is meant to go straight to your heart. Without our knowing it, we are drawn into the audience, alerted to the need to expect something out of the ordinary, something between fine honey and the nectar of immortality.

The performance proceeds. Sound fuses into sound, a garland of flowers falls from the musician's hair, celestial and terrestrial beings fall unconscious, birds and animals faint, trees and stones melt, all are absorbed in these opening notes. We in the audience are included in this process of utmost absorption.

Then follow three verses in which Chivakan sings in the voice of the girlfriend, one of the typical personas of this poetry. Usually in poetry of this type, the girl-friend addresses the male protagonist, urging him to show pity on her friend, but in this case the protagonist may be Chivakan himself. Nothing is said explicitly; the friend couches what she wants to say somewhat elliptically, if not allegorically. She tells the hero "that she, breasts chafing / under strings of gold, that she is sick / with lightening and with rain," like a little maiden snake shivering in fear "when lightening roars in the rain" (724). It is only natural to expect snake-like quali-ties in the princess of the celestial musicians: haughty, fearsome, and probably also venomous. But it is rather sweetness, beauty, and sacredness (serpents are the objects of worship in South Asia) that make the little snake attractive. The princess is attractive for the same reasons: she is tender and sweet, and she is even worthy of worship. By invoking the image of a maiden snake, all possible qualities of the heroine are hinted at: she is no ordinary person, she inspires awe; but she is also tender and lovable.

Equally suggestive is when the girlfriend, still in Chivakan's song, tells the hero that her mistress's heart breaks apart when she looks at the waterfall rumbling on the hill, a waterfall that increases in size and intensity in the rains. The friend also tells him that her mistress, hair sweet as honey, grieves when she looks at jasmine blossoming in the forest during the rainy season, "like stars in the sky" (726). The message is as clear as the medium is beautiful. Perspicuity and sweetness come together and so do her condition of loneliness and the lushness of the monsoon. No wonder "her heart / breaks apart" (725).

The performance continues. The precision with which Chivakan sings, the dexterity with which his fingers move along the strings, and the impeccable rhythm in which he does it all are hard to miss. Veenas drop from the hands of the gods, the celestial musicians are at a loss, and those who inhabit our world are bewitched by wonder. The effect penetrates "the hearts of even / hard-core yogis" (727). The last part is significant: the yogis are said to be devoid of any emotion.

It goes on. Chivakan plays the polished strings of the veena, a veena graced by a bee-haunted garland and decorated with ivory, and his fine-pitched voice becomes one with its resonant tones. The celestial male singers in the sky are at once astonished and dismayed. The very gods are dumbfounded. "Fierce Vidyadhara sorcerers could only praise him." People on earth are happy. Birds forget their bodies, forget their own songs. "The God of Love [is] put to shame" (729). All the kings on earth, upon hearing the melody, stand still as if painted in portraits. The music of Chivakan freezes its audience, including us, the readers, into a picture-like stillness.

What follows in the next two verses, which actually constitute a single song, is what could be expected. Once the song and the veena's notes have come together as a rich feast in Chivakan's playing, Kantaruvatattai realizes that she is losing the contest. His song and the music are "like a hawk and its shadow" (730). The simile is interesting. On the face of it, it may seem that this is not the most appropriate of comparisons. But look at it more closely. A hawk sets its eyes intently on the ground, on what it aims at, as it soars higher and higher in the sky. As it closes in, its prey coming within its reach, the prey is covered by the hawk's shadow. The coming together of the hunter, his shadow, and the game indicates an imminent union. The notes on Chivakan's veena and the lyrics of his vocal performance are now so perfectly blended that he has almost had Kantaruvatattai. And she was becoming aware of it.

Here is a situation where the two contestants are nearly matched. It is an apparent paradox that the daughter of the king of celestial musicians has to lose the musical contest—in fact, wants to lose it—if she is to win the hero. At the same time, she is too proud to give in so easily. She does not want to be a walkover, as it were. She has no time to lose. "Lovely / as a young peahen, her eyes sharp as spears / tapering like leaves at the tip" (730), she takes her seat, veena in hands, and begins to play and sing. As she sings and plays, her long hair cascades down her back, her earrings and gold palm-leaf jewels flash on her ears, and "her delicious brow stained / with sweat" (731). Her neck bends slightly toward the left. She is beautiful beyond compare, her song plaintive and sweet. While his song and the notes on his veena are compared to a hawk and its shadow, she is like a peahen, her eyes sharp as spears and tapering like leaves at the tip. The chain of imagery is complete, and the poet gives indications as to where we are headed. She knows she is losing; but she succeeds in turning her loss into a gain.

Her song is contained in the next three verses. Here it is the heroine who does the talking, responding to her friend, with the hope that the hero will overhear the conversation. It may sound as if she cannot wait anymore. She is eager to lose, albeit after putting up a fight. She asks her friend:

> "Pallid with love are my breasts, covered with jewels
> crafted like leaves, and my brow, a bent bow.
> The waterfall on the hill gleams like a sword.
> Tell me, my sweet-spoken friend: how can *he*
> fail to see? (732)

> Pallid with love are my forehead, brilliant
> as the crescent moon, my eyes limned with mascara
> that are always ready to do battle, and my all-too-heavy
> breasts. On the high mountain
> the waterfall that gleams like a sword
> flashes like lightning. Tell me now,
> my friend with eyes like spears smeared
> with poison: how can *he* fail to see? (733)

> Pallid and bright are my perfect breasts,
> my delicate, dancing arms, my forehead
> like the crescent moon. The waterfall
> teeming with precious stones flashes
> high on the mountain. Now tell me,
> my friend, your words sweet
> as sugarcane: how can *he*
> fail to see?" (734)

The contest is over and Kantaruvatattai has both lost and won. Her voice quivers; her gentle fingers cannot move up and down the smooth strings anymore. The sung melody and the sounds of the veena do not resonate; they fail to become one. The song falls, but not from heaven. She is simply not able to think. She sits there, defeated. She has accepted her defeat, but she has done it triumphantly. She lets the jeweled veena slip from her hands. She is wounded. She is trembling, and embarrassed out of shyness. "This wide-eyed queen among women slowly / and truly lifts up the nuptial garland of gold / as if straining to lift a mountain" and adorns the prince standing before her, "his anklets / engraved with flowers" (736). We see the shyness of a bride who is marrying the person she wanted even at the cost of her own pride. The complex emotions are brought out very effectively by the choice of words here. Her anklets ring softly, "and her belt / was shimmering like lightning as she walked, / just a little hesitant, but with a grace that would put / even a graceful goose to shame" (737). Then she tosses the garland on her lord as if to tell the audience, those of us who have been drawn into them and all of us who live in this world, that being selfless is its own reward.

Two things stand out. First and foremost, there is the conflict of emotions. Born as a celestial princess, Kantaruvatattai is an accomplished musician in her own right. It is unthinkable for such a person to lose a musical contest, much less to an ordinary human. At the same time, she had fallen in love with this prince of the human world, who had put "the God of Love to shame." By losing the contest, she wins him. The feelings of being wounded, embarrassment, shyness, the trembling—all show this very effectively. In the case of the much-married Chivakan, this is only one of his many conquests. A perfectionist in the art of music, he wins a contest and a bride.

Let's not forget how the narrative unfolded. The perfect performance by Chivakan, the one that wins the praises of heaven and of the entire world, comes first. Kantaruvatattai's accomplished but imperfect recital comes second, so that the competition ends not with the exclamation mark of victory but with the more complex and ambivalent response of the loser. True, the loss is a triumph of sorts, but the narrative structure may also hint at the gender inequality built into it and at the cost with which Kantaruvatattai's "success" comes. And where are we in all of this: Do our hearts melt completely in the sweetness of the performances and the success in matchmaking? Are we happy for Chivakan? Or maybe we feel more for Kantaruvatattai than for the hero? Such questions lead to metapoetic lessons for us as readers of translation, if we take the passage allegorically: Chivakan's performance may stand for the text in its original language, but it is Kantaruvatattai that stands for the translation before us. The latter is imperfect, perhaps, like any translation, but it is imbued with added complexity and richness of emotion. It may be that it is in response to this richness that our hearts finally melt.

WHAT'S GAINED IN TRANSLATION

Sonam Kachru (Far Reader)

>]prosperous
>]to listen
>]
>
> SAPPHO, FRAGMENT 85A

No doubt, you've heard tell of what's lost in translation. But in the best of times, there is something gained as well. If, that is, the translator has listened. Really listened. And if the translator allows us to listen in.

I think that the poem in translation before us can be heard making the necessary cognitive room. I think that the poem can also help us feel how it is that listening can change us.

Some might say it's there in the opening. Chivakan, who you will recall was "famous for his perfection / in making music" (722), lifts up his veena, and

> Sound fused into sound as he played . . .
> . . . No one could say if he was singing
> or plucking the strings. Gods and people of this world
> fell unconscious, birds and animals became faint,
> trees and stones turned to water, absorbed
> in the opening phrases. (723)

What we're told is that sense and sound can fuse in a consuming, absorbing perfection. The effect is a translation of a kind, an "absorption" of one variety of thing into another. Music, here, one might say, is a figuration of the limits of language used poetically. It's as if music can change the fabric of the world, changing us with it.

More than human, these are intimations of a very different mode of being. Chivakan's song is said to be "fluid as the draught of immortal life" (722). What's intimated here is the stuff of immortality, or, perhaps more precisely, a state of being not bound up with the passage of time and the consciousness of differences as is our ordinary, linguistically inflected experience. It is made real for those in the poem in the experience of sounds: the world, for a while, and its inhabitants, lose their edges, and their place.

Allow me to pause here and take a step back from the poem. As I read this, I can't but be put in mind of the thought that the fusion of sound with sound is a more visceral and a more embodied vector for the kind of cognitive absorption some traditions of Indian asceticism have long valorized, and for which metaphors of dissolving, melting, and even fusing have sometimes been used. The absorbing perfection of music, however, does not come from insulating the inside *from* external influence. Like desire, this is a wonder that seems to get *into you*, working on you inside out, a wonder "that penetrate[s] the hearts of even / hard-core Yogis" (727).

The blurring of the boundaries between sense and sound at the level of the production of music is crucial to the absorbing effect: "No one could say if he was singing / or plucking the strings" (723). The veena, mind you, can be played so as to conjure up a human voice; and voice, in song, may be modulated to suggest our sonorous and not our speaking parts. Perhaps you will be reminded of folktales where instruments speak. If you are anything like me, you might recall lessons learnt as a child from instructors in music. "Do not forget," intones the voice in my memory, "that the texts say that the human body is itself an exemplary variety of instrument. Your body is a corporeal veena." And the discipline necessary to realize ourselves in art, some of us were told, even counts as a way to freedom.

Listening, too, can change you. Let's return to the poem before us. The metamorphosis here of a person into its reverberating if unconscious parts is not given to the singer alone to experience. It changes those who hear it. And such a meta-morphosis results in a kind of attention that is close to unconsciousness:

> He sang. The very gods were dumbfounded . . .
> Birds
> forgot their bodies, forgot their own songs.
> The God of Love was put to shame. All the kings
> on earth, hearing the melody, stood still
> as painted portraits. (729)

Such listening, a variety of connection deeper even than corporeal, animating desire, can make us altogether strange.

Strong stuff, admittedly. But I have in mind a different variety of change to recommend to you. The invocation of music as a figure for the limits of poetry is altogether too much of a perfection. It invokes, in fact, precisely the variety of intimate familiarity of sound and sense that is most likely to put you in mind of what is altogether lost in translation. Forget the music, if you can. Listen to the voices.

The invocation of consuming perfection in the poem is interlaced with a far more intimate drama, one that is better suited to being enacted and not only invoked in translation. To hear it, we must allow ourselves to listen in a particular way to two set-pieces, each involving a triangulation. In the first, the heroine's girlfriend speaks to the hero, the lover, about the heroine, the beloved (724–726); in the second, the heroine, or beloved, speaks to her girlfriend, an address that, in principle, is capable of being overheard by the hero or lover (732–734).

I recommend reading these verses as you would a script in a play, whether silently, or out loud. You might try modulating your own voice to capture the different personae, the changing addressees, and the presence of the silent "third" party in each set piece. Notice the way in which who falls silent, and who is in a position to overhear themselves talked about, changes. You might even assign the speaking and silent parts to *actual bodies in the room*, the better to feel the weight of the silent, overhearing witnesses, and the possibilities for dramatic shifts in meaning.

Let's begin with the idea of change. Try reading the following without letting the overpowering displays of poetic power crowd out the scale of human response and sympathetic connection:

> Need I say
> That when lightning roars in the rain,
> a little snake shivers in fear? (724)

To make room for a shiver, we will have to modulate ourselves, attuning our attention to different scales of concern. But go on,

> Need I say
> that she, breasts chafing

under strings of gold, is sick
with lightning and with rain? (724)

Did you hear it? There is a transition here, even stranger, I feel, than the blatant metamorphoses we have been given to hear in the figuration of music and its overpowering effect on us. But it is far subtler. If sick with the majesty of roaring lightning and rain you might not hear it. Where there was a little snake, and a barely perceptible shudder, now a very different body heaves, or writhes, or moves, under strings of (serpentine?) gold. The change is one effected in the degree to which imagination can direct our perceptual awareness, a change in the intensity and the scope of how we bring the world under a description.

Such a change seems to me to be different than any connection in transition elicited by the sound of roaring lightning and the shiver of the snake. That is a movement of correlation, lifted up from the prosaic by that marvelous adjective, "little." But what comes next is invention and not description. You could say that to move from the snake to the breast moving from out under the strings of gold is a trope, a swerve in speech and perception. You could say that this involves a change in consciousness. Call it what you will. If you haven't felt it now, you'll surely feel it when you go on to say,

Need I say
That when rain pours from clouds
in the sky, a waterfall rumbles
on the hill?
Need I say
that when she, lovely as a shadow,
sees the waterfall rumbling
on the hill, her heart
breaks apart? (725)

The girlfriend is teaching you, the reader, how to listen to voices in poetry. This looks like a sequence. But yet again correlation (the waterfall after the rain) gives way to something that does not quite follow in the same way that a waterfall does rain. The girlfriend has put the witness back into nature, a consciousness, precarious and lovely as a shadow, capable of being changed by what it sees: "her heart / breaks apart"; unlike the rocks on the hill down which the water rumbles?

Something happens as the water moves from the sky to the earth, down the rocks of the hill and then through the mind of a particular kind of person. *There*— that's the precarious stage, and that's the intimate change I would like for us to hear. Note again how this drama is played out against the backdrop of awesome sounds that threaten to crowd out your mind. The roaring and the rumbling, I ask you now, to consider echoes of the absorbing perfection of music. These I hear as competing figures for power. What you must listen for, instead, is the sometimes softly spoken drama, one where the fragility of meaning and acknowledgment is staged in overheard conversations.

Consider the triangle made by the speaker, the listener, and the alternatively present and absent addressee for whom what is said is really meant. Music is a perfection of consummation. The play of voice, and what is meant by what we say, is a felicity of being in-between. Are our words heard? Do our meanings reach their intended target?

And being conscious of this, saying what you want heard while seized by this tense inbetweenness, can change you. As it does the heroine, "whose song," after speech, "fell far from heaven. / She couldn't think" (735).

Did *we* fail to see it? Listen to the change that occurs between these lines

and my brow, a bent bow.	On the high mountain
The waterfall on the hill gleams like a sword.	the waterfall that gleams like a sword
Tell me, my sweet-spoken friend: how can *he*	flashes like lightning. Tell me now,
fail to see? (732)	my friend with eyes like spears
	smeared with poison: how can *he* fail
	to see? (733)

When I first read the heroine's words, all too quickly, I am ashamed to say that I did not catch the flash of change: not the lightning; not the poison; not the accelerating shift in tone and stance. Rereading, slowing down, it now feels to me as if a sword has been unsheathed, as if one has talked oneself into readiness for war ("with eyes like spears smeared with poison"). You will need to try enacting this in different ways, even try to modulate your breathing, and play with your sense of dramatic timing if you are to do justice to the accommodation the speaker appears to reach. Take a deep breath before continuing:

The waterfall
teeming with precious stones flashes
high on the mountain. Now tell me,
my friend, your words sweet
as sugarcane: how can *he*
fail to see? (734)

The *gleam* of the waterfall in verses 732 and 733 is a play of surfaces. The flashing light now comes from the interplay of surface and depths, from reflections of what we now see revealed under the surface. As we speak, listening to what we say, more of ourselves, or new possibilities that we might yet have be true of us, is available to be seen. Is "see" the right word here?

Consider again the two complementary refrains of the two set pieces: *Need I say?* (724–726). *How can* he *fail to see?* (732–734). What does poetry ever need to say? What does it ever bring into view that we might otherwise fail to acknowledge? This is a question facing all of us experiencing poems, and all of us experiencing poems in translation. "Seeing" is a figure of speech for the experience of the bone-deep alchemy initiated by poetry at its best, and the expectation of acknowledgment that moves so many of us, so often, to speak. We speak at times because we wish to be seen by another, even if so often all that happens is that we speak, and listening to ourselves, we change, so coming to see ourselves anew.

Translation, the untwinning of sound and sense in one language, and the search for a new familiarity, a new relationship of sound and sense, in another, is a variety of triangulation, a variety of being in between. It is no less a site of possible change, of new possibilities for voice and self-consciousness. Possibly, it is a variety of unconsummated love. To experience it, you have only to allow yourself to form part of this triangle, allowing yourself full consciousness of the fragility of the sense of these words, and all that goes into making a voice, as they make their way from one world to another. (I'll allow you, so to speak, to construct your own triangles, each with their own possible apexes, each potentially changing the way in which you experience reading the poem.)

You have to be willing to experiment: to try and realize these voices as potentially your own, with their meanings coming to inform your possible experiences. Again, the criteria for success here is not that of consummation. It shall perhaps never be as it is with a hawk and its shadow (730). These words, and their meanings, will, perhaps, never be entirely your own. And perhaps these voices will only ever remain parts that you might play. The mere possibility of changing by listening in is everything.

To be sure, realizing such possibilities involves of us a kind of renunciation. And that is, "as if to say / to all of us who live in this world that being selfless / is its own reward" (737). We read translations not to learn about another world. We read to see as much as we can of who we might be, could we but momentarily overlook who we are.

What has reading this translation with me allowed you momentarily to forget?

Perhaps you have even, however briefly, forgotten that there is an "original" for what you have read? Such forgetting, in small doses, can act as an antidote for the nostalgia that too often accompanies our reading of translations. All of us are at times too quick to become attached to our presumptive sense of our place in this world, and our feel for the too-settled place of everything else in it. We are too quick to feel for our attachments what some among us feel for their place of birth. What the translator, and the enjoyer of translations, must work from is a contrary conviction: what will set us free is the unsettling wisdom that we might none of us be at home. Not yet.

Two Songs by Muttuswami Dikshitar, Performed by T.M. Krishna and Eileen Shulman

TRANSLATOR'S NOTE, TEXTS, AND RECORDINGS

Muttuswami Dikshitar (1775–1835) is the most lyrical of the trinity of classical composers in the south Indian tradition of Carnatic music, which also includes his contemporaries Tyagaraja (1767–1847) and Shyama Shastri (1762–1827). All three, by the way, came from the same village of Tiruvarur. Two of his compositions are offered here, both of them in Sanskrit, like the bulk of his work. The first is part of a set of five *kirtanas*, or devotional songs, one for each of a set of five *lingams* of Shiva, associated respectively with the five elements of creation. Dikshitar loved composing sets of intricately intertextual *kirtanas*, each building upon themes hinted at in others of the same (or a parallel) series. In this case, the *kirtana* is directed at the invisible *lingam* of space in the temple of Chidambaram, where Lord Shiva performs his dance of joy; it is appropriately called "Luminous As Joy in His Dancing" (Ānanda-naṭana-prakāśam), after its first line. Those familiar with Carnatic music will recognize that it is in Kedaram raga, and that the performer is T.M. Krishna, arguably the finest of the male Carnatic virtuoso vocalists in our time. The second piece is a particularly haunting, melodic composition devoted to the goddess Kamakshi in Kanchipuram. It is entitled "Friend of the Goddesses of Life and Learning" (Śrīsarasvatī-hite), also after its first line. The raga is Māñji, and the performer is Eileen Shulman.

"LUMINOUS AS JOY IN HIS DANCING" BY MUTTUSWAMI DIKSHITAR

Sung to Shiva, the lord of Chidambaram, the *lingam* of empty space.
Raga: Kedaram
Beat: Miśrajāti ekatālam

Rendition by T.M. Krishna. Streaming link provided by Charsur Digital
    Workstation.
Audio: https://www.charsur.com/song/detail/5394/1

Refrain:
I go to him, luminous as joy
in his dancing, Lord of the Chamber
that is awareness, lord of the goddess
who is his passion.

Pallavi (refrain):
ānanda-naṭana-prakāśaṃ cit-sabheśam /
āśrayāmi śivakāmavallīśam

Second refrain:
Bright as ten million suns,
the infinite space in the heart
that gives both love and freedom,
who protects those who are in trouble,
who has shown his bent foot, soft as a lotus,
to the serpent Patanjali and the sage
with a tiger's foot,
        luminous as joy in his dancing . . .

Anupallavi (second refrain):
bhānu-koṭi-saṅkāśaṃ bhukti-mukti-prada-daharâkāśam /
dīna-jana-samrakṣaṇa-caṇaṃ divya-patañjali-vyāghrapāda-
darśita-kuñcitâbja-caraṇam

Verses (*caraṇams*):
Black Neck with the moon and the river
in his hair, who lives in Kedara and other temples
and in the ragas Shri and Kedaram,
god of ghouls, dressed in a tiger's skin,
dressed in the space of the mind,
the one sage who went missing
from the three thousand Brahmins,
god of everything, his heart
soft as butter, father of Guruguha, that is, of me
who sings this song,
the first of all, the one the Vedas know,

beyond passion, beyond even the raga,
who can be brought very close

if you know anything about oneness,
and who has many parts that take your breath away,
parts that emerge from the singing and the playing
and the happy game of the dance,
luminous as joy in his dancing . . .

Caraṇams:
śītâṃśu-gaṅgā-dharaṃ nīlakaṇṭha-dharaṃ śrī-kedārâdi- kṣetrâdhāraṃ
bhūteśaṃ śārdūla-carmâmbaram cid-ambaram
bhūsura-tri-sahasra-munīśvaraṃ viśveśvaraṃ
nava-nīta-hṛdayaṃ sadaya-guru-guha-tātam ādyaṃ veda-vedyam

vīta-rāgiṇam aprameyâdvaita-pratipādyam
saṅgīta-vādya-vinoda-tāṇḍava-jāta-bahutara-bheda-codyam.

FRIEND OF THE GODDESSES OF LIFE AND LEARNING BY MUTTUSWAMI DIKSHITAR

Sung to the goddess Kamakshi in Kanchipuram
Raga: Māñji
Beat: Ādi tālam (4 beat-lines)
Rendition by Eileen Shulman
Audio: https://doi.org/10.1525/luminos.114.2

Refrain:
Goddess, friend of the goddesses of life and learning,
you are the thrill of awareness, fused into Shiva,

Pallavi:
śrī-sarasvatī-hite śive cid-ānande śiva-sahite

Second refrain:
Praised by Indra, king of the gods, and all the others, too,
free from the dark fragrances of the past,

Anupallavi:
vāsavâdi-mahite vāsanâdi-rahite

Verses:
You who live in the shrine of a million desires, in Kanchi,
your wrists decked with jeweled bangles,
your heart softer than anything soft,
the one hope of Guruguha who is me,
who sing this song:

have mercy,
care for me.

Caraṇam:
-koṭi-nilaye kara-dhṛta-maṇi-valaye
komalatara-hṛdaye guruguhodaye mām ava sadaye

BEYOND PASSION, BEYOND EVEN THE RAGA

T.M. Krishna (Near Reader)

Every subsuming musical experience carries the sensitive listener, or *rasika*, beyond thresholds. Raga, pulse (*laya*), light, color, stories, history, religion, belief, and even identity become irrelevant. Much like tools, rules, and methods that provide access to learning, these paradigms are doors that grant us entry into life's inner sanctum. Once inside, the doors disappear. The sensitive audience includes everyone present, even the musician. The subsuming or drowning is collective yet intimate, together *in* solitude. Perceived dichotomies are left behind in a moment of wonderment. The musician is a mere catalyst, the song not his or hers.

In the first composition, "Luminous As Joy in His Dancing," Muttusvami Dikshitar speaks of Shiva in one compound word (*vīta-rāgiṇam*) that has two meanings: he is "beyond passions, beyond even the raga." The composer may be referring to his own passion for the lord, but he knows that the lord is not trapped within his passions, just as when he speaks of being beyond ragas he implies that the lord is formless. In fact, he may be imagining the slow expansion of every raga particle much like the constantly expanding universe. When the smallest atoms become explicitly clear, in that moment of revelation, every raga comes together in unison. It is a unison, however, devoid of nomenclatures, structures, rules, forms: sound and melody become interchangeable, memory disappears, and living within the sound wave becomes a reality. At that moment, the raga underlying the composition, Kedaram, contains every sonic possibility.

Composed by a musical genius, "Luminous As Joy in His Dancing" is the first among five compositions dedicated to one of a set of five images of Shiva, each of which is thought of as the embodiment of one of the five primordial elements: earth, water, fire, wind, and space. Each of these is associated with a particular temple on the sacred grid of the Tamil country. The "Luminous" is dedicated to the "Space Lingam," that is, the invisible embodiment of Shiva in Chidambaram.

Any act of creativity is mystical. Every time we dip into its splendor, we discover multitudes of inner meanings as light enters through unnoticed crevices. This keeps happening at every encounter with the composition. Did the *vāggeyakāra*, that is, a single person as lyricist, composer, and arranger, know all this from the first moment when he conceived this art object? Is all this already laid out for us to stumble upon? We may never know the answer to these questions. But there is one thing we can be sure of: only in great art do we find both ourselves and the work anew every time. Even the very same line of melody that I have rendered a million times yields an unknown shade, the tiniest glide, or a subtle change in intonation every time I sing it. In these conversations between the composition, the composer, and myself, music occurs "beyond passion, beyond even the raga."

The "Luminous" opens with a soft glide from the *niṣāda* (*Ni*) note in the lower register to the *pancama* (*Pa*) in the same register. It is the enunciated vowel *ā-* that holds this flow within, and by the time we reach the second part of the word, *-nanda*, on the middle register *ṣadja* (*Sa*), we are cajoled into *ānanda*, or "joy." Muttusvami Dikshitar has Shiva oscillating between the temporal and the celestial. Shiva is performing his celestial dance, and his partner, Shivakamavalli, who is in unison with him, is also his witness. In the inner sanctum of the Chidambaram temple, Shiva, King of Dance (*naṭarāja*), is in ecstasy, and as he dances with abandon life happens. Very close to him, in that very same chamber, he exists as space. That root, primary form, is waiting to erupt and explode into resplendence. As space, he is known for being the "secret of Chidambaram" hidden in plain sight. The dancing god is the resulting extravagance in a state of aesthetic madness, while the invisible god is made approachable by the golden *bilva* leaves that adorn the space around him.

Space is real and unreal; it binds the real and the unreal to ensure that life is ever existent but never complete. Space is not empty, it is filled even when motionless, odorless, and tasteless. It is everything between and within the elements. It is unseen and unheard. It is the movement in the static and the stillness in movement that connects all of creation. The English word "ether" sometimes used to translate *ākāśa* does not capture its significance. *Ākāśa* is not just the limitless sky but also limitless time, both joined together.

In the secondary refrain (*anupallavi*) of this composition, Muttusvami Dikshitar shifts the tempo (*laya*) between Shiva as an indescribable, radiant, all-pervading ethereal nothingness, and as a physical and emotional being. This change in *laya* seems to demarcate the inner from the outer. The first line of the secondary refrain is:

bhānu-koṭi-saṅkāśaṃ bhukti-mukti-prada-daharâkāśam

Immediately after this line, Muttusvami Dikshitar sketches for us a kind, caring, almost human Shiva, whose lotus-like bent foot is blessing "the serpent Patanjali and the sage / with a tiger's foot." This line is rendered in a faster tempo.

dīna-jana-samrakṣaṇa-caṇaṃ divya-patañjali-vyāghrapāda-darśita-kuñcitâbja-caraṇam

For some, this line can bring back memories of gazing through that little window provided for devotees at the Chidambaram temple. Peeping through those small openings we witness in awe the glittering golden *bilva* leaves hanging in the foreground against the backdrop of the dark rock face. *Ākāśa* envelops the whole space between the gold leaves and the black stones, even as *ākāśa* seems to move with the mild breeze that caresses the golden flowers when the temple priest moves the lamp to illuminate the space within. With the contrasting play of darkness and light, the stark and the ornamental come to life as the lamp moves. A few steps away the image of Shiva, King of Dance, is as physical as can be, poised on one foot with the other carefully angled in space, a statue in motion.

David Shulman and I engage with works of art from what could be seen as two opposite poles. Shulman extrapolates the spirit of life from every syllabic form, word, phrase, line, suggestion, and explanation. As Shulman sees with his mind's eye and hears with his mind's ear, meaning takes hold of his hand at the limits of logic and reason and leads him into unimaginable realms. In that space he finds new meanings and rare perspectives. I, in contrast, know that the spirit of life in music exists just in sound. That is, it exists in every sound, from the level of consonants, vowels, extensions, and aspirations, to the level of *laya, tāla, rāga,* and *svara.* As each folds into the other there is an explosive burst (*sphuṭa*) of identity-less vitality, an all-pervading understanding of life. At no point do I devalue the pronunciation of every element or the articulation of lyrics, but I treat every syllabic expression as the primordial sound (*nāda*), the sound that is the source of all sounds. I believe that the great composers, too, traveled the path of the semantic only to transcend into language's inborn domain—sound itself.

Still, it may be that we are not so different. One has only to read Shulman's translations or, for that matter, the writings of any great writer, to realize that semantic meaning is only a gateway, a point of entry. Once it is entered, meaning reveals its own being and allows an experience that is devoid of any selfish emotional benefit. In other words, meanings are abstracted from meaning itself, leading us to a state of dispassionate, intimate rapture. While I come to this state through sound, Shulman dives into it as a linguistic artist. I say artist because only an artist can free meaning from its prison.

When I decided to record the full set of Muttusvami Dikshitar's compositions dedicated to the five *lingams,* I first searched for older versions of "Luminous." These older versions raise seminal questions about oral and written traditions. Almost all of Carnatic music is learnt through oral/aural osmosis. Music books and notations can be aids in the process but rarely serve as learning resources in their own right. It is also very difficult to capture in written form the musical movements of ragas. That said, the practice of writing musical notation has been present in the India for over a millennium.

In recent Carnatic music history, Subbarama Dikshitar is probably the most important musician, musicologist, and scholar. In 1904 he published the *Sangīta-sampradāya-pradarśinī* (SSP), a treatise that captures in theoretical and notational form the history of Carnatic music for the last three centuries. In over a thousand pages, the SSP gives modern Carnatic music an aesthetic anchor. It is also the first attempt to transmit this musical heritage using a descriptive notation system. Using innovative symbols Subbarama Dikshitar captured every musical

-movement. It is from his book that I learned the "Luminous" and, in fact, all five compositions in this set.

Those who inherit oral traditions can feel an organic flow of thought that is intrinsically interpretive. This means that a composition never remains "as it actually is" in a positivist sense. Every master musician receives it only by adding curves, shifts, colors, and even melodic cadenzas. A composition is a living art object that never grows old. But the oral tradition is not perfect. Musicians are human beings and hence at times things are changed because the musician's own ego and the need for asserting his or her own identity overpowers musical appropriateness. And this may also lead to the loss of historical traces that are ingrained in the aesthetic architecture of the musical art object.

Subbarama Dikshitar's notations are based on the oral tradition he received. He put on paper what he heard and knew, and as a result the notations fix each composition within the context of his specific time and place; namely, mid-nineteenth-century Thanjavur, in the deep Tamil country. When we learn from Subbarama Dikshitar's notations, we travel back in time and rediscover lost melodies. This happened to me when I was learning the "Luminous." Sometimes the changes that have occurred may seem insignificant and minute. But when the composition unfolds and we pass through every one of those recovered accents, loops, turns, bends, and twists, we realize a seamlessness, something that seems to be erased in later versions. One such change is in the first line of the verse (caraṇam), where in the stretch gaṅgā-dharam (Shiva with "the River [Ganga] / in his hair"), the second syllable gā is held on an elongated Madhyama (Ma) note, and the third syllable dha is held on an elongated Gāndhāra (Ga) note. Today when the Kedaram raga is rendered, this musical phrase is almost never heard. But when I discovered it with the help of the notation in the SSP, it felt perfect, almost as if River Ganga had paused within Shiva's locks. Note also that in the very next line, the author, Muttusvami Dikshitar, incorporates the raga's name, Kedaram, in the phrase: śrī-kedārâdi-kṣetrâdhāram.

Niraval is a form of improvisation where the performer chooses a line from a composition and retains its syllabic and rhythmic structure while exploring other melodic contours possible in the raga (in this case Kedaram). In this composition the following caraṇam verse is usually chosen for niraval:

saṅgīta-vādya-vinoda-tāṇḍava-jāta-bahutara-bheda-codyam

But in this recording I have chosen a different line. I am not sure what made me choose this verse from the secondary refrain (bhukti-mukti-prada-daharâkāśam), but exploring a line that describes the subtle, ephemeral, and eternal being beyond the bounds of the line's original melodic framework did seem ideal.

With Muttusvami Dikshitar we can almost always find unexpected hints, connections, and interrelations in compositional construction, and this composition is no exception. For example, the number seven can signify the complete set of seven worlds, and the number fourteen, a multiple of seven, also has a special significance. In Hindu cosmology there is also a fuller set of fourteen worlds that make up the universe. It is said that the letters came into being when Shiva sounded his two-headed drum fourteen times. Thus it is indeed not surprising that Muttusvami Dikshitar's musical meditation on Shiva, "Luminous," is set to a rhythmic cycle of seven beats (the same is true of another composition, "You Took the Form of the King of Dancers in Chidambaram," *Cidambara-naṭarāja-mūrtim*).

Let me end my thoughts on this composition with Shiva's celestial dance that has been most poignantly re-created by Muttusvami Dikshitar in the very musical passage that concludes the composition. There is a conjunction between the words describing Shiva dancing, on the one hand, and the drum-like sound pattern— *ta-dhing-gi-na-tom*—that is almost always used to conclude any purely abstract (*nṛtta*) Bharatanatyam piece, on the other.

"Friend of the Goddesses of Life and Learning". Listening to Eileen Shulman sing the second composition, "Friend of the Goddesses of Life and Learning" (Śrī-sarasvatī-hite) my mind filled with cultural and political questions. Most high-culture stakeholders thrive on ownership and, being insiders, act as the gatekeepers of their tradition. In their minds, there is an innate sense of superiority, even condescension toward other cultures. When outsiders seek entry, they are vetted and forced to undergo a transformation. They must model themselves on the "owners" of the tradition. It is in this way that they can begin to be accepted by insiders.

Is Eileen Shulman an insider or an outsider? What do I hear when I listen to her: her own voice or the sound of my cultural pride. Look! Here is a Jewish musician singing a *kirtana* in praise of Goddess Sarasvati with so much beauty. Do I find myself thinking that she is quasi-Hindu, a convert of sorts in some way? Or that she is a Jewish Sarasvati?

But in her rendition Eileen Shulman does something entirely different than these thoughts of mine suggest. She takes the composition, imbibes its every nuance, and then fills it with her own self. Her performance is what it is, a tender musical outpouring that blurs every political, linguistic, racial, and cultural line that we routinely draw.

Eileen Shulman's unadulterated rendition forces me to reflect on myself as a performing musician. Musicians with a high level of professional proficiency are addicted to their own voice. This leads to a constant need to add, complicate, embellish, and even redraft the compositions of others. Increasing complexity brings us happiness. But as a result, the compositions lose their sheen and become too heavy as they are overlayered with musical ideas. Unable to withstand the weight of musical overindulgence, they fall apart. Eileen Shulman reminds me that being straightforward, simple, honest, and truthful is as essential in art as it is in life. In her rendition every graceful turn (*gamaka*) is clear, and that atypical, rare glide from the *Madhyama* (*Ma*) note to the *Shadja* (*Sa*) note as the secondary refrain connects to the primary refrain is rendered with utmost elegance.

Eileen Shulman's performance does justice to this second composition. Composed in Māñji raga, this Kirtana is a small delicate jewel. Even in this simple, descriptive offering to Goddess Sarasvati, Muttusvami Dikshitar manages to surprise. The composition begins with the word *śrī*, which is sung in the *Shadja* (*Sa*) note in the middle register, even though the intuitive musical reflex would be the note *Ṛṣabha* (*Ri*). I have heard musicians struggle with this playful choice of Muttusvami Dikshitar. But it is also musically ideal for this particular raga. The musical phrase rendered in the first line ("friend of the goddesses") instantaneously brings the melodic identity of the raga to the fore.

Māñji has today become a rare raga. The reason for this marginalization can be largely attributed to the emergence of Bhairavi as a dominant raga. Not only did Bhairavi become a powerful raga in Carnatic music, it also changed in character. When this change happened, Bhairavi absorbed many melodic phrases that were typical of Māñji. As a result musicians have found it hard to render Māñji as an independent individual entity without crossing over into Bhairavi as it is performed today. Nevertheless, compositions like "Friend of the Goddesses" help understand and appreciate Māñji on its own musical terms.

When Muttusvami Dikshitar asks Goddess Sarasvati to "care for me" (the last phrase from Shulman's translation of "Friend of the Goddesses"), he may be also asking for the same from all of us who render his compositions. It is not just his composition that is at stake here, but music itself. He is appealing to all of us to take good care of ragas, *tāla*s, and whole compositions. Every time I render his compositions, he seems to be whispering in my ear: "Allow yourself to be moved; let the music roam in freedom; respect the past but don't chain yourself to history; delve deep into musical creations and find yourself in every note and every word."

READING IS AN ACT OF TRUST

Donald R. Davis, Jr. (Far Reader)

The truth is, I don't much like classical Indian music. Even worse, I have no training in how to listen to or perform it. So, when Charles Hallisey, my friend and mentor, asked me to consider an essay in honor of David Shulman's model as a reader and grounded on two works of Muttusvami Dikshitar by two contemporary performers, I did so out of trust. What I write here is thus a double instance of the trust needed to prompt sensitive reading. Good reading entails friendship and esteem.

Words.   In the composition that begins with the word "joy," themes of friendship, esteem, and trust structure the poet's relationship to the god Shiva. In this way, the poem itself tells us how to read it. The poet cries, "I go to him," or, I take refuge in the lord. In Sanskrit, it's just two words. Everything else builds on, extends, and specifies the word "lord." Taking refuge connotes dependence and yielding to the lord or master. The strong word "lord" suggests distance and difference, but in the characteristic manner of religious devotion, or bhakti, it is a distance that is meant to be bridged through intimacy. More subtly, "joy" exemplifies friendship in the stream of allusions to moments in the biography of Shiva or to his common descriptors. The poet recounts the moments of Shiva's mythological life as though he were there, as though he were an intimate part of the events themselves. Though addressed to Shiva, the many elaborations of who the lord is start to feel like an introduction, a report to a third party about a person the poet knows well. As in all of Dikshitar's work, he puts himself into the poem through his signature as Guruguha. This personalization, too, erodes the distance between the poet and Shiva in order for the words themselves to embody nearness and familiarity.

When Dikshitar put himself into the song, he also put me as the reader into the song. I am reading the poem both because a mentor who became a friend asked me to and because a genius whom we both revere as a master found in it something beautiful. The same distance that Guruguha feels in "taking refuge in the lord" is what I feel toward David Shulman. I've met him a couple of times. When I was a graduate student, I asked him a stupid question once at one of his lectures. Another time, he complimented my Malayalam—such scraps of praise are the stuff of deep memory for academics. But to me, he's mostly a "lord," a kind of distant master, with whom I have a relationship based on his published works. Those works, like Shiva's deeds, make me feel close to Shulman all the same. I think that's what this song is about, too.

The text calls Shiva "the kind father of Guruguha," which Shulman translates "the father of Guruguha, *that is, of me*" (emphasis mine). Dikshitar always signed his poems by referring to himself as Guruguha and Shulman's gloss makes that clear. But, the added clarification here refers less to Dikshitar, in my opinion, than to Shulman himself and, by extension, to me and to you, when we hear the song. "Guruguha, *who is me*" turns in trust to the lord who is "luminous as joy / in his dancing." I want to read this single compound as a string of nouns: "the joy that is dancing that is luminousness." In this reading, the lord is simultaneously joy, dance, and light. When Shiva dances, it means that he is moving in the world and "protects those who are in trouble." That protective movement is joy itself, not a dance *of* joy or one prompted *by* joy. If Shiva stops his dance, then we suffer because the world is not right. Joy ceases when the dance stops. Furthermore, light in our world—perhaps the poet means sunlight—is also Shiva's dance and thus we feel the sunlight to be joy and experience the light as dance, and we turn to these—to him—in dependence. The opening lines of the refrain, therefore, hit me as three nouns all referring to the same thing, to lord Shiva.

The opening phrase also modifies "the lord." In fact, every description in the poem refers simultaneously to the physical spaces and imagery in the

Chidambaram temple and to widespread, often universal, theological epithets of Shiva. Each compound builds on the other and the doubled sense of each compound further complicates the referents and reference of the one lord. So, we are introduced to Shiva as joy, noting that joy here is also a name, the abbreviated name of the vigorous, cosmic dance of joy that is iconographically captured in the famous Nataraja form of Shiva in Chidambaram. But, we also take refuge in "the Lord of the Chamber / that is awareness," which refers to a particular shrine within the temple complex at Chidambaram. Subsequent descriptions layer on new elements or aspects of Shiva's identity. Among the other descriptions or epithets of Shiva, the "infinite space in the heart / that gives both love and freedom" points especially to the "*lingam* of space" in Chidambaram, one of five *lingams*, a standard image of Shiva, in the temple that correspond to each of the cardinal directions plus the invisible *lingam* of space itself. The idea that Shiva is this subtle "infinite space" (a reference to *Chāndogya Upaniṣad*) might also be rendered as the fine spaces in between all things. Shiva exists in all things as the "lord of existent beings" who is also the "god of ghouls" (in Shulman's translation of the same phrase) by permeating the fine spaces. Through such double referents, the words thus teach us that Shiva lives next door to us in Chidambaram and yet he is the god of everything.

One final description seems to draw on a theological principle linking this song of Dikshitar to the other song, "Friend of the Goddesses," which I will consider shortly. When the lord is described as "the one who can be brought very close if you know anything about oneness," the language draws upon the enigmas of the Upanishads (especially *Chāndogya Upaniṣad* 6.1). Later poets searched for ways to communicate that God or Brahman is one, but describable in many ways. In Dikshitar's works, this search manifests poetically as long strings of different descriptions marked with the same grammatical ending. The one-in-many structure of language, therefore, mirrors the ontological structure of the universe. Just as many nouns and adjectives describe the one in different ways, so also does the plurality of our ordinary lives describe or rest upon the one true cause of the phenomenal world. The words are the body of the poem just as the material world is the body of God.

The proliferation of distinct descriptions of God, therefore, is essential and basic for a bhakti-centered poetics in favor of any deity. To learn the true oneness of God, there is no better way than to see how all names, epithets, and descriptions refer back to the singular lord. The shorter second poem, "Friend of the Goddesses," also consists of a long series of compounds, all marked with the repetitive grammatical ending used to address or call people, in this case Goddess Kamakshi (or Kamakoti) of the great temple and monastery at Kanchipuram, two hundred kilometers north of Chidambaram. Then, right near the end, the command "care for me" makes a simple request of the goddess using an archaic verb. To a Sanskrit ear, this plea might sound like "bless me and keep me" would in English—old, but poignant. In Shulman's elegant rendering:

Goddess, friend of the goddesses of life and learning,
you are the thrill of awareness, fused into Shiva,
praised by Indra, king of the gods, and all the others, too,
free from the dark fragrances of the past,
you who live in the shrine of a million desires, in Kanchi,
your wrists decked with jeweled bangles,
your heart softer than anything soft,
the one hope of Guruguha who is me,
who sings this song:
have mercy,
care for me.

The "shrine of a million desires" locates this song in Kanchipuram and the special shrine for this goddess. Dikshitar's self-reference as Guruguha identifies the supplicant as "me," even before the word "me" appears. Apart from the beautiful lyricism in the nearly homophonous secondary refrain "*vāsavādimahite vāsanādirahite*" and the syllabic rhythm of "*[koma]la-ta-ra-hṛdaye gu-ru-gu-hodaye*," the thing that strikes me about the structure of the poem as a written text is the stringing together of simple or compound descriptions in the same grammatical case that we saw in the first song. In fact, both poems exemplify a very common pattern found in the structure of bhakti poems written in a theological context of Vedanta. Long series of epithets in the same grammatical inflection cluster around the singular figure of devotion. That grammatical unity is taken as reflecting an ontological oneness behind reality. Language, specifically nouns and adjectives describing the deity, serves as the bridge to the experience of the deity. The best way to experience God, therefore, is to spin out name after name and description after description until all diversity circles back to the one.

Sounds.   The words of these two songs by Muttusvami Dikshitar contain both beauty and idea, but we know them today not because of their content but because of their sound. What we cannot see in the lyrics by themselves is how they are heard in actual performance; that is, how the words become sounds. In this section, I offer a "reading" of performances of the two songs. I suppose the ear is the organ of reading in this case, not the eye, though it is important to distinguish what the eye can do from what from the ear can do. The first impact of sound concerns the way in which an oral recitation of the poem would sound. Do the words themselves have a beauty and a sense as sounds apart from their meaning? Robert Frost spoke to this poetic power:

> The ear is the only true writer and the only true reader. I have known people who could read without hearing the sentence sounds and they were the fastest readers. Eye readers we call them. They can get the meaning by glances. But they are bad readers because they miss the best part of what a good writer puts into his work. Remember that the sentence sound often says more than the words. . . . To judge a

poem or piece of prose you go the same way to work—apply the one test—greatest test. You listen for the sentence sounds.[1]

Frost speaks here of sounds of the first-order variety, the sound-shapes of the words themselves before they become part of a song. When the words become lyrics and sounds, the arrangement introduces repeats and codas and the singer explores the possibilities of the sounds within the tune and rhythm. Sure, the sound-shapes matter, but, in my opinion, this second-order sound quality is the locus of primary meaning for a song. People like the tune, the beat, or the vibe before they study the lyrics.

Our first performance of a Dikshitar song comes from T.M. Krishna. I have listened to his rendition of "Luminous As Joy" many times, and let's just say he can make someone who has not previously connected (much) with Indian vocal music find something to love. The effect of his voice is alluring and seductive. There's great control and incredibly difficult movement in his voice. That control makes it professional and full of calculated risks, but not emotional abandon. He knows he will get to the notes in the way that he wants. He has a prepared idea of how the song should go and he can execute that idea beautifully, but you can hear the planning, even if the precise execution might vary from one performance to another. And so should it be. He treats Dikshitar's song with as much respect as the poet himself did and puts his professional skill to work accordingly. I do not mean to suggest that T.M. Krishna lacks sincere emotion in his singing here, but rather that his performance properly channels the emotional qualities of the song through a virtuoso's voice. An expert's voice provides structure and intelligibility to the raw emotions of the song.

Krishna opens the refrain in the standard way for male Indian vocalists: a head voice that will reach high tenor notes later begins in a tenor's version of baritone. It is a note that sounds lower than it is (somewhere around D below middle C). The middle range of the opening is a soft point of entry to the high pitches to come in the refrain, secondary refrain, and verses. The ensemble consists of voice, harmonium, tabla, and violin. The congruence of voice and violin in the melody is incredible, especially considering the tonal flourishes that both agree upon. The percussion both breaks up and emphasizes this congruence, moving things forward here and underlining things there. The harmonium, as always, adds an ambience, a constant of sound that unifies the instruments and voice but also seems to bend with them.

The performance repeats the refrain and parts of the refrain several times, then does the same for the secondary refrain. Each verse receives thorough treatment too, though not with the same level of repetition. The first half of the performance offers what seems to be a kind of standard version of the poem in song: multiple refrains and secondary refrains with limited verses. After finishing the second verse, however, Krishna sings the tune with the syllabic sounds of the Indian scale, not the words of the poem. Here the rhythm and pitch matter, not the semantic content of the words. In fact, the drive of the song at this point seems to be exactly the diminution of linguistic meaning in favor of sound. The meaning of the words is respected as such for half of the song, after which the performance begins to tear the words apart and to use them as sounds.

Twelve minutes in, Krishna sings "space" (*ākāśa*) and then "infinite space in the heart" (*daharākāśa*) in repeat. Just when the repetition starts to feel repetitious, he works backward in the compound, adding "gives both love and freedom." It would sound in English like: "space, that space, that infinite space, that infinite space in the heart that gives both love and freedom." The violin sings the same, building and rebuilding the compound in strings. Krishna then builds the compound again from the end to the beginning, breaking the construction by building the compound with syllables of pitch "*ma ga ma ma pa sa ni ni ta . . .*" The embellishments of "space" yield then to repeats and variations on "love and freedom" interspersed with further syllabic flourishes. The song ends on the refrain and the words "I go to him . . . lord of the goddess / who is his passion."

Reading the words of the poem would suggest that the keyword or the main descriptor of Shiva is "lord," since it occurs five times in a short song. Listening to the sounds of the song, however, we realize that the most important word is "space" and the most important phrase is "the infinite space in the heart / that gives both love and freedom." Religious devotion demands specificity and location. God cannot be some distant abstraction, an imaginary reality. Rather, God should have presence and form in a space that we know, can see, and can visit. The song, therefore, is an ode to the *lingam* of "space" within the "chamber that is awareness" (*citsabhā*) of the Chidambaram temple. Such specificity does not deny the universality of Shiva or his power as lord. Rather, it crystallizes his presence in a particular place, thus making him accessible in the tangible, material form of the Chidambaram temple. The lovely paradox in this case is that empty, invisible "space" is not physical at all and yet the song and the temple give it a physical reality. When Krishna utters "space" his voice fleetingly embodies the *lingam* of space at Chidambaram. As devotion makes the universal local, the voice localizes the deity's presence in sound. The devotee and the singer have to initiate the process, however. Each makes the presence of Shiva real for the duration of their worship, attention, and song. For this reason, I, like all others, must take refuge in, call out to, and choose the deity anew in each moment.

The first recording of "Friend of the Goddesses," by Eileen Shulman, had a remarkable and unexpected effect on me. This voice, this singer, has sung this song many times before. Perhaps it sang once for the benefit of others, but now it is self-confidant and self-contained, though not selfish. The song is an offering of the singer to the goddess. It is between the two of them. The voice sings through a memory of a past singing and thus feels distant from the moment of the performance. I feel the memory as much as the song and that is what haunts me: the singing pushes me to the memory and not to the song. The sound asks me to imagine the memory in my mind and to ignore the song in my ears.

To discover more about the song, I also turned to a recording of "Friend" by R.K. Shriramkumar, a violin virtuoso. It is a performance at the Boyer College of Music and Dance at Temple University, Philadelphia, in which Shriramkumar teaches the song to a full auditorium. Since it is not a solo performance but more like a master class, the emphasis on sound is even more pronounced since Shriramkumar will linger on a single syllable and repeat flourishes that are just the vowel sounds: "*hite . . . ite . . . e.*" As he patiently moves the audience through the poem, the units of interest and repetition shift and change. He sings the entire opening address, "*śrī sarasvatīhite,*" then just "*śrī*" with a dip in pitch. After the audience tries it, we hear "*sarasvatīhite*" which they don't quite get. So, then "*sa . . . sa-ra . . . sarasvatī . . . hite . . . hite . . . hite.*" The ornament on "*tī*" (doubled pulse on the same pitch) is tricky for most, hence the repetition. But now it's good enough. Good news for the audience: "*śive*" is the same notes and ornament as "*hite.*" Change the consonants and repeat. We're highish in the vocal register now, so "*cidānande*" has to give us some relief. It moves down the scale from a slight rubato on "*ā*" to a similar ornament on the next "*e*" at the lower pitch and falling off. The final "*śivasahite*" of the refrain loops around the same pitch in quick rhythm. The surprise comes when the initial "*śrī*" is quickly appended to the end of the refrain as a new beginning, a repetition. There's always a slight pause after "*śrī*" whether the sounds stops or not. The end becomes the beginning in fact as the refrain actually ends on "*sarasvatīhite*" with an elongated "*e.*"

Though this version of Dikshitar's poem is a casual teaching of how to sing the song, the place where Shriramkumar wants to arrive throughout is the union of two voices, human and violin. The performance involves no translation of the words. When the audience gets the gist of a section, he then plays the song on his violin along with them, guiding and reminding them with its sharp sound. Shriramkumar's instrument is his violin, not his voice. His voice is pleasant but not as powerful or versatile as Krishna's. In this context, the quality of his voice is not at issue, however, because it is a lesson. Teaching the audience the words and tune of the song is an excuse to get them to experience something of the power of the union between voice and violin. That union is only sustained for short moments of the lesson overall, but it appears vicariously to have its desired effect. The audience nervously giggles here and there when their voices come together nicely or when the violin carries their voices through the end of a phrase. The taste of such unity seems to be the purpose of the lesson.

As I try to make sense of these two very different performances of Dikshitar's "Friend," to read them as sounds, the image that comes to mind is once again from the *Chāndogya Upaniṣad* (6.8.2): "It is like this. Take a bird that is tied with string.

It will fly off in every direction and, when it cannot find a resting place anywhere else, it will alight back upon the very thing to which it is tied."[2] For the Upanishad itself, the bird flies around haphazardly and futilely like the mind in search of an ultimate foundation. The goal is permanent rest and an end to pointless mental flights.

Bhakti poets and singers, however, embrace the flight as a joyful and perhaps necessary means to discover their bond with God. The bond disparaged in the Upanishad is viewed as pleasurable in the devotional context because it is God pulling us back to Himself. The tethered flights in all directions are our human attempts to reach out to God through poetry and song in this case, personal and local variations on a single tether. Ultimately, the bird "alights back upon the very thing to which it is tied" just as "I alight back upon the lord." The same verbal root in both phrases transforms the negative image of bondage into the positive image of relationship. The words and the sounds take us to new heights distant from the source, but the stronger the pull away, the harder the pull back to the source, to God.

It thus seems to me that the message is the same regardless of the medium. The words, the sounds of the words, the lyrical construction of the words as a song, the vocal syllable-notes of those lyrics, and the notes of the violin all communicate the same affection and love for the deity. Various descriptions of the deity in the words themselves lead back to one God. So also do the various musical expressions of the deity lead back to the one God.

To conclude, the reading offered here began in trust and depended on trust up to the end. I connected trust to friendship and esteem and I find the same themes running through the songs of Dikshitar, albeit in the religious trust based on intimacy with and devotion to a deity. Trust conditions the experience of reading. In fact, good reading is part of a chain of trust that links readers to other readers and to authors and performers. Trust first pushed aside my lack of aesthetic appreciation for classical Indian music. Although I knew it intellectually before, trust also forced me to face the truth that my ignorance was my fault. I relied or "alighted upon" on the friendship I have with Charlie to know that this experiment in reading would be worth it to me. The esteem I have for David Shulman and his choice of texts and performances also reassured me and supported my attempt to read them. I trusted that something good would emerge and it did. I overcame my dislike of Indian music and treated it attentively within the limits of my knowledge. More specifically, time spent with the performances revealed a completely different center to the song "Luminous As Joy" in "space" than I had gleaned from the written text and a unity of sounds between voice and instruments that mirrors the unity pointed to by the words. In the end, the words yielded to the sounds by conveying meanings and sentiments that I could not possibly derive from the words.

The Vagaries of Love

EDITORS' NOTE

THE MORE WE READ WORKS OF SOUTH ASIAN LITERATURE in translation, the more we are aware of a generative interplay between what is unfamiliar and what is familiar, between what is recognized and what is not recognized. In the selections in this unit, we see that there may also be a generative interplay between discomfort and comfort.

The two great themes of classical literature from South Asia are love and power. The theme of love has been central to the selections in previous units, and especially so in units 1 and 3. This unit does not contain selections that illustrate the other great theme, power, but they bring the register of power straight into the domain of love, sometimes with quite unsettling, even disturbing, undertones and overtones: In what ways is love like war? And when does love stop being love and becomes coercion and violence?

Like unit 3, with its inclusion of music, this unit expands the circle of consideration for sensitive reading beyond literary texts. It opens with an example of sculpture before turning to two retellings of stories that are also found in the two great Indian epics, the *Ramayana* and the *Mahabharata*, reminding us that these two texts are often the headwaters for the streams of Indian literature. The sculpture of the God of Love and his consort, Desire, is from a Hindu temple for Lord Vishnu. That religious context is shared with the *Ramayana*, whose central hero, Rama, is an incarnation of Vishnu. The selections here are not only about the generative interplay between art and religion in South Asia, as important as that is. Rather, they focus our attention on "moving scenes," to adopt an expression from Tawfiq Daʾadli's essay, moving in every sense of the word: scenes of seen movement, scenes that are better seen by moving, and scenes that ultimately move us.

9

Desire and Passion Ride to War
(Unknown Artist)

SELECTOR'S NOTE

This sculptured pair of the Hindu god of love, Manmatha (or Kamadeva), and his wife, Rati (Desire), is from the Varadaraja temple in Kanchipuram, one of the most important temples dedicated to the god Vishnu in the far south of India. These two lovers adorn the marriage hall where wedding ceremonies for the temple's main deity, Vishnu the King among Boon-Givers (Varadaraja, who lends the temple its name), and his consort, the goddess of wealth, are held as part of annual festivals; marriage halls are a feature of Hindu temples built during the Vijayanagaram period between the fourteenth and sixteenth centuries. The marriage hall of the Varadaraja temple is one of the major repositories of the refined sixteenth-century sculptural style in the Tamil country of south India. I like this sculptured pair because of their boldness, scale, and fierce movement.

FIGURE 1. Rati and Manmatha panel. Photo courtesy of Brigitte Majlis.

FIGURE 2. Rati and Manmatha panel. Photo courtesy of Anna Lise Seastrand.

PILLARS OF LOVE: A DIALOGIC READING
OF TEMPLE SCULPTURE

Anna Lise Seastrand (Near Reader)

This short essay takes inspiration from *anubhava*, a Sanskrit word meaning perception, apprehension, or understanding that occurs through aesthetic experience. It is the word that describes the experience of divine love and enjoyment, and is particularly associated with praise of the god Vishnu in the tradition of Tamil devotional poetry in southeastern India. These ideas are particularly apt for a close reading of the imagery at the Varadaraja temple complex in the city of Kanchipuram, which culminates in the relationship between a pair of sculptural pillars joined together as a dynamic, oppositional couple within the Kalyana Mandapa, a hall of auspicious union that celebrates divine beauty and love.

Kanchipuram, in the far southeast corner of India, is an ancient city crowded with hundreds of temples and royal foundations. It is a beautiful city, situated along the Palar River, which flows out to the Bay of Bengal, some forty-five miles downstream. It is lush with palm trees, fields of bright green paddy, and numerous ponds and lakes. Kanchipuram has long been a cosmopolitan center, a point of contact for traders, scholars, and pilgrims: in the seventh century, the Chinese Buddhist pilgrim Xuanzang reported visiting the court of King Narasimha Pallava and finding more than one hundred Buddhist monasteries and thousands of monks in the region. Buddhists lived alongside others who worshiped Shiva, Vishnu, the Jina, and the Goddess, among other lesser-known deities. The temples built to worship these gods were famed far and wide, as were the luminous silk and gold fabrics woven to adorn them.

Situated in the southeast part of the city on a small hillock is the temple of Varadaraja Perumal, a form of Vishnu. Here he is joined by Perundevi Tayar, a form of the Lakshmi, the Hindu goddess of wealth, fortune, and prosperity. In every south Indian Hindu temple, the god and goddess are at once their distinct individual selves, particular to the place they inhabit, and at the same time universal deities that transcend their local manifestations. There are innumerable forms that Vishnu takes in different times and places. Here he is Varadaraja, the King among Boon-Givers. His temple is ancient but still young: ritually renewed, renovated, and expanded for more than a thousand years.

Today's pilgrims—whether pursuing art or devotion—enter into the temple from the western gateway tower, or *gopura*, which rises eight stories to a height of 160 feet, towering over the temple compound's roughly twenty acres enclosed within high walls. Stepping through the massive structure, the visitor enters into a huge open courtyard. Straight ahead, across the courtyard, is another monumental gateway that leads into the enclosed space of the temple's shrines. But to the left, within the grand expanse of the courtyard, is an open structure, striking for the massive granite-carved figures, warlike horses, and gods and goddesses that extend from the surface of raised foundation and pillars that support the deep eaves and curling roof, in the absence of enclosing walls. The glinting sun, reflected by the temple's pond beyond, illuminates this monumental building from the north. This radiant space is the marriage festival hall (*kalyāṇa-maṇḍapa*).

The hall is approached from the south—but even before entering, the attentive viewer is rewarded with a show of sculptural virtuosity. Along the roofline, stone cats stalk stone pigeons; long open-work chains carved from a single piece of granite hang under graceful ornaments at the roof's corners (see fig. 2). Under the deep eaves are carefully sculpted beams, a *trompe l'oeil* that imitates wooden architecture. Across the front of the building are eight monolithic pillars, four on each side of the center stairway; each features a mounted rider who emerges from the stone at one-third life-size. Walking up the stairs and into this pillared hall, the pilgrim is met by spear- and sword-wielding warriors mounted on rearing horses on both sides of the processional path to the central dais. These rearing animals and riders, caught in mid-action, threaten to emerge from their architectural matrix, so fully are they sculpted in the round. When Vishnu and Lakshmi are present, seated on the raised central platform, these imposing and lifelike figures augment the living presence of the deities.

The dais at the center of the hall is situated on the back of a tortoise, whose shell, legs, and head spread out from under the gods' seat. Cosmologically, the tortoise is the support of the all that is. Separately carved images of demigods are fit into sockets around the base of the dais: traditional temple architecture uses no mortar; instead, all the stone pieces interlock with one another. This architectural feat is even more impressive in the ornate lantern-dome ceiling above, from which an elaborate pendant lotus extends down toward the deities when they are seated during festivals. Altogether, this central space of the hall is a microcosm, where the gods rest above the tortoise, who holds the world aloft, beneath the rising heavens crowned by the pendant lotus that points back to the deities seated below. During the festival of their wedding, the gods are the center of this cosmic scheme, surrounded by the ninety-six monolithic pillars whose sculptural figures situate the gods within the context of their devotees' lives. This is a building literally inseparable from its decorative program, which celebrates *kalyāṇa*—good fortune, prosperity, virtue, joyful celebration, and marriage.

The sculptures invite their viewers into limited communion: a tiger pounces on a rider; an entertainer's disfigurement attracts and repels; dancers make festive a now-silent space. Among the most captivating figures are two pairs of the god and goddess of love, Manmatha and Rati, facing out on the massive pillars on both sides of the hall's southern entrance (see fig. 1). The god of love, Manmatha, seated on his gander, and the goddess of desire, Rati, astride her parrot, ride toward the visitor who approaches the marriage hall, a reminder that this is a space of erotic and auspicious union.

Manmatha means love or desire; he is also known as the love god Kama. *Rati* is desire, longing, and even coition. Manmatha and Rati, Love and Desire, are paired between guardian figures at the front of the building on both the east and west sides. Like the guardian figures, they too are dressed for battle, carrying sugarcane bows and lotus-stalk arrows. Love is, they seem to say, a battlefield. Indeed, the intersubjectivity of love is like that of combat: both are intimate, exhilarating, and potentially devastating. The piercing arrow of desire, like that of battle, abolishes the distance between the self and the other. The dynamic exchange between the lithic manifestations of Manmatha and Rati suggests just such a union. Their coupling is expressed in the paired oppositions in and between Love and Desire's columns: inside and outside, male and female, individual and pair, play and war. The longed-for union of Love and Desire is expressed across the physical space that separates them; the conjugation of figural sculptures that face each other across the two columns enlivens the space between them.

To read these sculptures' figures with sensitivity to their disposition and regard toward one another requires that the viewer linger over their forms, counting each detail as an important part of the whole. Indeed, the sensitivity required of the viewer is like that of the lover who knows intimately each part that makes the whole of his or her beloved, the shades of meaning betrayed by a glance or the shape of the body. This kind of loving, careful description of the form of the beloved is a trope that crosses languages and genres of Indic literature. To *read* the sculptures is to share in an aesthetics of participatory enjoyment and experience—*anubhava*. To read them closely is to savor them as one savors the beloved—a mode of description and devotion closely identified with southeast Indian devotional literature that identifies the beloved as God himself. Devotional poetry in praise of Vishnu draws extensively on tropes of erotic and filial love, as well as visions of martial victory. War, death, love, and union are the extraordinary contexts for the most intimate and transformative acts of human life and intersubjectivity. Perhaps it is precisely the intimacy and transformative possibility that draw both love and war into the heart of the expression of religious experience.

The following description portrays the relationship between each pair of figures, from the top of the columns to the base, to which the mounted figures of Manmatha and Rati are attached, though the columns are not visible in this image. Those on the east face of Rati's pillar are paired with those on the west of Manmatha's.

On the east side of the capital above the figure of Rati (invisible from the eastward-looking perspective of figs. 1 and 2) a female musician holds a veena, an instrument associated with the goddess Sarasvati, patron of learning and knowledge. The veena player faces a male dancer, visible on the capital of Manmatha's column. The figures' bodies each mirror the other's pose. They are mutually attuned—in tune, yet different, poised in counterpoint, in dance and music, facing each other across the space of the columns' distance.

Just below the capital, and inside, at the top of the column to which Rati is attached, a woman speaks to a parrot she holds in her left hand. Parrots are strongly associated with love, and in literature they often serve as messengers between lovers. Parrots are able to repeat what they hear, and as witnesses to lovemaking, also have the capacity to embarrass the lovers or to reignite their passions upon hearing the parrot's repetition. Here, the woman whispers into the ear of her avian companion, hoping the message might reach her lover. In the corresponding sculpture on Manmatha's column, a male figure dances (fig. 2), his body and face turned directly out and across to the woman and her parrot. He holds his right hand aloft, perhaps ready to receive love's messenger.

Seated below this figure and turned in three-quarter profile is Manmatha, mounted on his gander, his feet in the stirrups, his right arm drawn back to launch a devastating weapon: the piercing arrow of love. Complementing this image of imminent yearning is the figure of a woman on the opposite pillar who lifts a mirror to her face with her left hand as she reaches over her head with her right hand to apply an auspicious mark (*pottu*) on her brow. Like the woman holding the parrot, hers is a conventional representation, described in treatises and depicted on temples throughout the Indian subcontinent. She is "the maiden holding a mirror" (*darpaṇa-sundarī*) an auspicious female figure described in an eleventh-century text on temple decoration, where she is said to be beautiful and to give pleasure to people who see her. She is one of the many conventional beauties (*sundarī*) that decorate auspicious buildings and are imbued with meaning in this context. Paired across from an iconographically specific form of Manmatha and integrated into the column of Rati, this figure is polyvalent. She is the conventional *type* of woman, described in typologies of beautiful and auspicious women, and she is an aspect of Rati, the goddess of love and paradigm of both lover and beloved. As one who holds a mirror, she is a metadiscursive figure, alerting us to the mirroring of the themes and poses of the figures depicted on the two columns.

At the lowest level of the pillar is the figure of a woman who holds on to the tender stem of a banana tree, which curves over her body, echoing its sensuous form. She kicks the banana stem with her right foot, causing it to flower and bear fruit—its fruition is evident in the heavy blossom hanging freely on the right side of the figure. She is *śālabhañjikā*, an auspicious female form common to Buddhist, Jain, and Hindu temples from ancient times, who with her laugh or the kick of a foot causes a tree to bear fruit. It is an iconography repeated in art and literature, perhaps most famously in the story of the mother of the Buddha, who grasps the fruiting tree as the Buddha is born from her side. At the hall of marriage, this fructive figure is coupled with another opposing image of Manmatha, who dances, his left hand clutching the sugarcane bow, while held aloft in his right hand is a small fruit—ready, it seems, to be launched in play toward his beloved, a fruit for the one who causes fruition.

This account of the two faces of the Manmatha and Rati columns that face each other suggest a progression from the flirtation of song and dance that attunes one body to another, to the expression of love and desire through the messenger of the parrot. Below, the god of love launches his arrows, while the mirroring Rati adorns her body with signs both auspicious and beautiful. Finally, the fruit of union is portrayed in the physical fruits that both figures bring into being. While one could find such a reading overdetermined, the sensitive reader would no doubt discern the figures' polyvalent potential in the play of literary and visual tropes, symbols, and figures.

The other faces of both pillars retain the themes of pleasure and desire in figures that are both well-known tropes of beauty and love as well as aspects Manmatha and Rati. Those on Manmatha's column include the god in seated and standing positions, holding his sugarcane bow and flower arrow. At the lowest level of the east face, he is an affectionate lover, holding close a woman who cradles his chin in her hand. On the north face, he is a royal figure, a crown on his head, and fine textiles draped over his arm. Rati's pillar also further suggests the theme of the lover: on the north face, female figures are shown holding parrots, the messenger of love and Rati's conveyance and confidant. On the west, women entertain and serve: the middle and upper images show a woman dancing, while the figure on the lowest level is a fly-whisk-bearing attendant. Collectively, the figures show aspects of the paradigmatic lovers. That the figures are meant to do so is reinforced by the separation of gendered depictions: while other pillars depict both female and male figures, these pillars are segregated by gender, save for the single image of a loving couple. The iconic variations on the themes and guises of love, courtly pleasures, and auspicious fecundity are echoed throughout the building, on the exterior and interior, where scenes of battle and images of gods and saints stand cheek by jowl with images of romantic pleasure, sex, and childbearing. Seen in this light, an expansive reading of the figures of Manmatha and Rati places them in the context of the hall of marriage, a place that celebrates auspicious union and the riches and pleasures that follow.

The density of ornament upon every surface of the marriage hall, from the rooftop carvings to the massive pillars atop the narrative bands of the building's plinth, overwhelm any ambition to identify each and every detail, figure, or story. Enjoyment of the sculptor's skilled work and his own loving attention to detail and ornament requires careful, slow, and patient looking on the part of the viewer. The fine details of the figures' costume, the curls of the goose's tail, or the design of his bridle encourage the observer to linger. At the same time, to take in the entirety, to consider the ways in which the particular relates to the whole, requires a different mode of perception. The modes of reading that architecture of this kind invites is perhaps akin to the way one reads an epic. Rarely does one encounter the authoritative text of an epic, or read it cover to cover. Rather, one dips into the story, starting at one place or another, picking out an apt moment or lesson, returning to a favorite episode, or being caught off guard by a detail that had escaped notice. Like the palimpsestic texts of the great Indian epics, architectural representation invites multilayered readings, inflected by the season or occasion of their telling. Taking a wider view of the architectural context of the pillars, they may be read in light of the festival function of the marriage hall, at the center of which is the dais on which the god and goddess are placed during the celebration of their union, set within the ordered cosmos, and among their loving devotees.

Reading these sculptures with sensitivity means moving in and then again away; caressing the details, if only through sight; and taking in the whole, if only through intuition. It means considering the beauty of the individual and the individual's relationship to others. Such looking invites us into the microcosm of the work's aesthetic world and propels us into the macrocosmic order in which it participates. Such a sensitive reader would surely have been struck by the desiring arrow of a passionate love.

SIDE OBSERVATION OF A SMALL PORTION
OF VARADARAJA TEMPLE

Tawfiq Da'adli (Far Reader)

When someone who has become a professional student of art looks at an unfamiliar work, professional habits usually come to the fore as part of the process of analyzing and understanding its meaning. These include itemizing its elements and putting it in a historical and aesthetic context. An expert on Egon Schiele, for instance, will catalog the laundry hung in front of a house and aim to decipher its semiotics. Another alternative is to just stand in front of a painting or a statue, observe it, and enjoy the moment. Such is often the experience when one happens to wander inside an Indian temple: one takes in the icons and sculptured mythological scenes with pleasure, whether or not one has prior knowledge about their background. When professional habits cease to be relevant, then a route to appreciation and enjoyment becomes visible, even though it was always there, accessible to everyone. The key is to observe the surroundings with an open eye and a steady gaze. Works of art are the products of minds that seek to communicate with whomever is willing to participate in this communication. What follows is an exercise in observation leading to appreciation and enjoyment: observing what, for me, is the unknown but reachable in the temple of Varadaraja, King among Boon-Givers.

The Varadaraja temple contains a colonnade supported by no less than ninety-six pillars. Each "tree" in this stone forest is sculptured in a different pattern, but in the main they include figures of warriors and horse-mounted hunters. In front of this massive army of local and some European soldiers are Manmatha and his wife Rati: they welcome visitors into this ornamental pavilion.

Manmatha and Rati's welcome is meant to confer good fortune and prosperity on those approaching the temple. It is no surprise that this ornamental pavilion is used for the annual ceremonial marriage of the god and the goddess. Perhaps the road to prosperity always involves being struck by a love arrow. Indeed, Manmatha is preparing to take a shot: one of his hands holds the bow while the other presses an arrow on the string. Notice that the fingers of his right hand are split sideways in a way that makes the posture look more realistic. As you approach, he is aiming at you, so be prepared: soon the arrow of love will hit you.

Rati and Manmatha ride two massive vehicles, a parrot and a gander, respectively. These winged mounts are the core of their individual shafts; that is, these figures of the gods' vehicles are the bulk of the construction and support the ceiling in addition to the gods themselves. Although they are relatively thick and massive, they do not strike us as such at first blush. Indeed, the rounded breast, thin legs, and feather saddle lend them lightness. Although the birds stand solid and are rooted in the rock, they seem to pierce the space in front of them. They are on the move. Charging forward in a similar manner is the horse to the left of Manmatha. Now what is seen with the eyes joins with what the ear hears, for there is no way to observe its legs, leaping up, without hearing the sounds of the horse's neighing and trotting. The horse has been on the move for quite some time, something we know from the way its lower jaw is hanging down with exhaustion.

Rati, situated closer to us from the perspective of figures 1 and 2, is even more welcoming than Manmatha. Manmatha's leg is bent, and you can see the tenseness in the muscles as the leg presses around the lower part of the gander's breast in full alert. By contrast, Rati's leg seems softer—more flesh than muscle—as it is curved around her parrot's feather saddle. Rati's body is also rounded and curved, especially her breast and hip, and her face is orb-shaped with clear features (wide eyes, bold nose, thick lips) and ornaments (necklace and two rounded earrings). If roundness is what unifies Rati's depiction, being muscular, firm, and erect are Manmatha's characteristics, as can be seen in his elongated hat, powerful thighs, brawny palms, and his thick arrow or cluster of arrows.

Just ahead of this orchestra of round lines, floating figures, and a sweating horse hangs a chain that falls in isolation from the roof. This straight, suspended line, which appears to be falling from the sky, is also carved in stone. It is easy to lose sense of its weight, as the surrounding air dwarfs the links of gray stone. There is more thickness here, but now thick rings appear thin, and the chain ends with the last link attached to a kind of lotus bud, its pointed end facing down, making the line appear even thinner. The tension between the lightness of the line and the mass of the horses and the winged mounts increases the sense of motion.

These Indian-style caryatids, then, both support the ceiling and move the entire temple through space. They do not stand still like the ones at the Acropolis. They are constantly on the move. Motion is key. More specifically, the caryatids are on the move just like almost everything in the typical Indian temple in the Deccan. Vishnu of Three Steps (Trivikrama) is constantly in motion: one leg reaching to conquer heaven, one taking hold of earth, and a third descending down to the nether world. He cannot stand still. Other gods, too, have to hurry: they must act quickly to save their devotees from evil powers or from taking their own life (as in the case of the Srisailam temple mentioned later).

The chariot is also on the go, and chariots and temples are closely linked. Temples are chariots, leading the devotees on their journey to the beyond. In addition, most temples in South India have a chariot to carry the gods on their tours and seasonal processions. Sometimes you see a chariot engraved in stone, like the magnificent one I was fortunate to see in front of the Vitthala temple in Hampi: it is carved from stone but appears as if it might move with the slightest breeze. Every detail of decoration is so finely carved, the sense of motion is so present, yet when you near this Hampi chariot, you realize that the movement is seen by the mind's eye, not the body's. If you are distracted and stop seeing the motion that the mind's eye sees, and begin to see only with the body's eye, you get stuck: when seen with the body's eye alone, the chariot will never move, and god will never make his rounds.

On the move is also the temple visitor, the moving observer. I recall my early morning visit to the temple of Srisailam: I remember circling the compound clockwise, walking around the outer walls to observe the richly carved panels. I had to complete the circle to observe the numerous deities. I had to keep moving, and one simple reason was that the crowd, also in constant motion and absorbed in endless recitation, did not allow me to stand still. As a visitor, you can perhaps only come to a halt once you have come full circle. Only then do you begin to realize the nature of your journey.

Srisailam and Varadaraja are large temple compounds in major pilgrimage sites. But even in the smaller shrines inside each temple, you have to keep moving. If you stop, you may overlook a statue of a god, or a small sanctum that awaits your donation—a coconut, or burning incense. Sometimes the deities hide in a remote corner: without circumambulation, you will miss them, and they will miss you. Better to keep moving. The only thing motionless and stable is the *lingam*, that aniconic image of Shiva at the center of the temple.

Almost no inch of the surface is devoid of motives or figures. The stone leaves behind its hard and frozen nature after being modeled by the chisel. The more the eye wanders with wonder—and this happens naturally, or perhaps it was programed by the artist—the more detail it will see. Dragons supporting the chests of the vehicles, the parrot and the gander, female figures above Manmatha, and more figures above and below the horse in the background. After the body's eye does what it can, the mind's eye will do the rest.

Greek caryatids support the entablature with the classical order composed by the frieze and the cornice. Manmatha and Rati also support an entablature, but in India the order and composition are clearly different. Some sort of order is created by classical vertical and rectangular shapes resting on the deities, but soon the strict lines are replaced with the curves of female figures moving or dancing. At first glance, they seem free; at second, you realize they are part of the column and are also supporting the ceiling.

Unlike their Greek or Roman counterparts, these gods and figures are still active and are thus surrounded by modern facilities. In figure 1 we can see electrical wires hanging from the ceiling, and two of them, one white and the other blue, appear almost wrapped around Manmatha's bow. As we have seen, Manmatha has no need for any external power. However, visitors need artificial light to lead them on their path to the holy of holies, especially at night. Hence the scattered electrical wires and the fluorescent lamps that are crudely attached to the fine reliefs and the works of art. But these too inevitably become part of our observation and, indeed, enjoyment. In popular temples, prayers pulsate with red and orange fluorescent lights. At night you can see the parrot breast with some touches of green flashing from the lighted signs. On the same occasions, you can hear the different gods speaking in some soap opera playing on plasma screens, hanging in the different parts of the temple.

Our brief glimpse of a small portion of the temple's welcome façade is as overwhelming to the senses as it is lasting to the mind and the heart, maybe even the soul. Two stone wheels that threaten to start rolling impose themselves in your line of vision. Then you realize that those wheels are mounted by two figures who seem to be comfortable with the ride. As you observe more and enjoy more, you begin to realize that those figures are Love and Desire embodied. One is the object of male desire; the other is shooting love arrows like Cupid.

Unfortunately, as we are observing the whole moving scene from the side, Love and Desire are passing in front of us—there's little chance we can keep up with them. And at the end, an invitation to a future beginning is heard: better that you come at the time of the festival.

Ravana Visits Sita at Night in the Ashoka Grove, from Kamban's Tamil *Ramayana*

TRANSLATOR'S NOTE AND TEXT

The *Ramayana* is one of India's two great epics; the other is the *Mahabharata*, in which the stories of Nala (told in unit 1) and Girika (told later in this unit) are found. The *Ramayana* tells the story of the war waged by the god Rama (also called Raghava) to regain his wife, Sita (also known as Janaki, the daughter of Janaka), who has been kidnapped by Ravana, a demon king who terrorizes the entire universe. Kamban's Tamil version of the *Ramayana* (Irāmâvatāram) prob- ably belongs to the twelfth century, when the Chola empire, based in the Tamil country, was at its height. Kamban himself is linked to the village of Teralundur in the Kaveri delta, whose verdant landscapes he loves to describe. The selection shows us Ravana's doomed attempt to seduce his prisoner, Sita, as the monkey Hanuman ("Anjana's son"), a divine ally of Rama's, watches from his perch in the tree. Kamban's *Ramayana* is possibly my favorite Tamil book.

KAMBAN'S *RAMAYANA*, VERSES 5.425–51, 5.453–54

> He came—the demon king—sighing
> fierce sighs that scorched the golden garden,
> buds, branches, flowers, roots,
> and turned it black at every step.
> Although he knew exactly where the goddess
> was sitting, his mind was scattered and,
> like a snake of many heads that has lost
> its great jewel, he was looking for her
> in every nook and cranny. (425)

He was powerful, no doubt about it.
Anjana's son could see it clearly, watching
calmly as the demon came near. He thought
to himself: "His crooked nature, his deeds,
and all that has to happen will now
become clear." Reciting the name of Rama
of the chiming anklets, he hid himself nearby. (426)

Now the demon arrived at the spot
where *she*, a lamp to all womanhood,
was staying. The crowd of dancing girls
and others turned aside. And now she
was scared, trembling as if the breath of life
was leaving her, crying like a young doe
about to be eaten by a striped tiger,
raging in fury, eyes blazing smoke. (427)

Hanuman saw it all with his own two
perfect eyes. Saw her, her very life
fleeing in dismay. Saw him, adrift,
befuddled by desire, and soon
to die. His heart swinging back and forth,
the monkey whispered: (428)

"A blessing on Janaki, blessings on Raghava,
blessed be the four Vedas, blessed are the Brahmins,
blessed be the good Way!" No wonder the fame
of this monkey of blessings lives on
age after age. (429)

The monster came near. What he wanted to say
was just this: "When, oh my cuckoo
whose waist is aching under the weight
of your breasts, will you give me your
sweet love?" It was like someone
who mistakes poison
for the nectar of life. (430)

His mind had lost not an ounce
of its self-satisfaction, not even
after Shiva himself had humiliated him.
But now, tormented both by desire
and by diffidence, he shyly started
to speak. (431)

"All our todays are gone,
and our tomorrows too.
Look how you're treating me,
oh my girl with fierce eyes that reach
to your earrings!
Are you going to wait till I'm dead,
till you've killed me,
to join me in bed? (432)

I'm the one who looks after
this singular world and the two others.
There's no limit to my wealth and royal
power. But you, oh my jewel,
apart from the storm you've stirred up
in me, loving you, are you going to give me
anything more than disgrace? (433)

My golden bow, my long-haired beauty,
you've scorned the luxury of long-lived fame.
That lover of yours, sweet to your spirit,
is still alive, wandering through wilderness.
Is the life he lives—that lousy
human business—anything
like living? (434)

Have a look at what great Yogis
and sages of subtle understanding
think is the best they can do,
sweet woman whose breasts
burst their bounds: they want only
the happiness of serving me together
with my other godly slaves. (435)

When you speak, your gentle murmur
drives to distraction
all that has meaning, the music of the lute
and the haunting Vilari raga,
the mumblings of the mynah bird.
The Creator with his four heads must have worked
very hard to fashion your mind
with its odd kindness
and your waist, fleeting
as a flash of lightning. (436)

Your days, your youth
will never come back.
Little by little they're wasting away.
When they're gone, when days
meant for delight are a void,
when will you start to live?
Or will you go on drowning
in this great sorrow? (437)

I may lose the breath of life.
Let it go.
It's all because your mind
is warped, as anyone can see
by your sad face.
But what then? Do you think
you'll ever find a man worthy
of your character and your beauty,
a match for your desire—
a man like me? (438)

Feminine grace and beauty,
firmness of spirit—you've got these
and other virtues. But what about
empathy and generosity rooted in kindness?
Have they died out in Janaka's noble line? (439)

You heard that voice, *his* true voice, crying for help
just before he died.¹ And yet you keep on thinking
you'll see him again. The truth is, my little cuckoo,
that your lucky time has come, but instead of reveling
in it you scorn it. Does that make sense? (440)

Let's say I'll die (because of you). Without delay,
all my wealth will die with me. But no—you, you're one
of a kind. You could have gone along and had
all the wealth and fame in the world. Instead,
you've lost everything. You're left with nothing
but blame. (441)

You could have ruled the three deathless worlds,
gods and goddesses worshiping at your feet.
All this was yours, and you threw it away.
Is there anyone—and I mean *anyone*—
as senseless as you? (442)

Accept me—king over all who live
in all three worlds—as your lowly servant.
Have a heart!" He cupped his hands over his head
and fell full-length at her feet on the ground,
heedless of disgrace. (443)

His words were like iron rods heated in flames.
They scorched her ears even before
she heard them. Her heart wobbled,
her eyes poured blood. She had no mercy
on her own life's breath as she started
to speak, in a way no woman should or could. (444)

She was hoping to move the heart of that brawny,
crooked monster. "You're no more to me
than a blade of grass," she began, burning
with rage. "Your words are rough, unspeakable
in the presence of a married woman.
There's nothing like a woman's loyalty in love
to turn her heart to stone. Now listen. (445)

If you would like to split open Mount Meru,
or to cleave the sky so you can walk beyond it,
or to put an end to all fourteen worlds,
then my noble lord's arrow
can do it. Even you know all this, ignorant
as you are. And still you use these lusterless
words, as if you wanted to cast off
all ten heads. (446)

You were scared to death of my lord, so you waited
till he was away, sent that seductive golden deer
and only then came to me, hiding your true self.
If you want to go on living, you'd better
set me free, because when you face in battle
that one who is poison to your whole clan,
your eyes will no longer see. (447)

Your ten heads and all those arms
will be only too lovely a target, a happy game,
for *him*, skilled archer that he is, with his many
arrows. It seems you still believe
you have the guts to do battle. Remember
Jatayus, who threw you to the ground?[2] (448)

The truth is, you were defeated that day
by a bird. Only with the sword you got from the god
who holds a gushing river on his head did you
manage to win. Without it, you'd have died.
So the long life you were promised because of your
harsh vows and all the wishes you were granted
and all the clever thoughts you've had—
all of them belong, now, to Death. A hero's arrow
has taken aim. (449)

So there's the sword, and the long life, and the strength
you were born with, and all the other things that Brahma
and the others said they would give you. As soon as Rama
strings his bow, you can throw them away, and all that's left
will be to die. That's the truth. Can darkness
stand before light? (450)

When you lifted up his mountain, Lord Shiva squashed you
with his toe. And it was his great bow, made from Mount Meru
to burn the Three Cities with a single arrow, that my husband
snapped in two that day—though it seems that *you*, Sir,
never heard the sound it made that echoed
through the cosmos.[3] (451)

Idiot! My prince—god bless him—knows
where you're hiding. He'll be here soon,
and on that day the ocean and Lanka
will perish. But his rage won't stop at that.
Time itself will change its course
and die, together with your life's breath. (453)

You've chosen a crooked way. His generous fury
won't be satisfied by killing off a few fierce demons.
I'm afraid the whole universe will be wiped out,
obliterated, leaving
no trace, as the God of Goodness
is my witness." (454)

KAMBAN'S TAMIL AS A KIND OF SANSKRIT

Whitney Cox (Near Reader)

One dominant way to understand the relationship between languages in premodern India sees Sanskrit existing in a privileged place. On account of its precocious systematization and its career as a timeless and placeless medium of learned culture, so the argument goes, Sanskrit played a generative role within the Indic language order. As other literary languages began to emerge from the many local speech-forms of the subcontinent beginning in the second half of the first millennium CE, the cosmopolitan standard set by Sanskrit provided a crucial impetus: the resources of Sanskrit's grammar, lexicon, metrics, literary canon, and poetics provided conditions of possibility for these languages' emergence. But these took shape as entities conceptually and ontologically distinct from Sanskrit; typically, this was seen as a matter of declination from Sanskrit's unchanging, purportedly divine prototype.

From this perspective, to claim Kamban's Tamil as a kind of Sanskrit doesn't make much sense. Tamil already presents a historical anomaly within the Sanskrit cosmopolis: by its own antiquity and its dogged independence at the level of grammatical theory and literary practice, Tamil stands outside of (or perhaps alongside) the millennia-long historical arc of cosmopolitan Sanskrit. But here I am less interested in the relation between the languages over the long term, and more in thinking about how Kamban challenges us to radically rethink this relationship. To find Sanskrit within Kamban's Tamil *Ramayana* is not to claim that the northern origins of his narrative make him derivative of a Sanskritic model or source. Nor does it mean that Kamban's poetic idiom is unusually suffused with borrowings, whether lexical or figurative, from a putatively separate tradition. Instead, this long poem enacts an argument about the kind of thing it is. This is never stated outright by the poet, but I think it is worth lingering over for a moment, before turning to the verses that David Shulman has translated.

The idea of Kamban's Tamil as a kind of Sanskrit presents a model of language order that is quite starkly opposed to the usual cosmopolitan language–vernacular language binary. The model of language Kamban's work enacts resonates with, and is indeed an inspiration for, the view of language that Shulman has implicitly argued for throughout his career. Such a view of language leads us to usefully question the supposedly firm boundaries that separate out one speech-form from another. In the conventional view, "Tamil" denotes one such entity, "Sanskrit" another; "Hebrew," "French," "Bahasa Java," and "Wolof" are all further tokens of the type. In historical and sociolinguistic terms, these conventional delimitations of the domain of language prove to be full of crossings and exceptions, with hybrids and creoles (or, in south India, *maṇipravāḷam*s) proliferating everywhere. So there are good empirical reasons to be suspicious of them. But even if we accept these conventions as useful fictions, each language-continuum is itself stretched along a cline, from the simplest communicative act up to language at its most intensified and self-reflexive. The latter is the language of poetry, above all: it might also be said to be the point at which any given language extends into its own kind of Sanskrit: "Intensified" is, after all, a fairly good literal translation of *saṃskṛta*.

If Tamil thus harbors Sanskrit within itself, this is the Sanskrit that Kamban's *Ramayana* presents in such luxuriance. Kamban makes relatively little use of direct borrowings of Sanskrit vocabulary in the excerpted passage: the scattering of nouns and (much less frequently) verbs that are Sanskrit-derived are all domesticated into distinctly Tamil forms. But some of the passage's carefully wrought intensities are direct adaptations from Sanskrit prototypes. The passage actually begins at the tail end of a long verse sequence sharing a single syntax—a *kulakam*—that is an inheritance of the Sanskrit tradition of long poems (*mahākāvya*). The opening words of the first verse ("He came—the demon king") correspond to words actually occurring eighteen and nineteen verses earlier in Kamban's original. This sort of long descriptive parataxis was omnipresent in earlier classical Tamil, but here it is projected across the segments of Kamban's stanzaic *viruttam* verses. This metrical form itself bears a resemblance to its namesake, the *vrtta* meters that form the mainstay of classical Sanskrit literature. But there are more differences than similarities. Where Sanskrit *vrtta* meters are invariant in their scansion, the Tamil *viruttam* allows much more freedom in its patterning. And while the classical Sanskrit long poem usually employs a single meter for each canto, leaving aside a few concluding verses, Kamban is free to shift between different varieties of the *viruttam*, in order to mark significant shifts in the narrated story, or to signal a shift in the poet's or the reader's attention.

Kamban's idiom effortlessly slides along the scale of intensity that marks out the continuum we may call "Tamil." Here is one of the great strengths of vernacular poetry: Kamban's Tamil or Shrinatha's Telugu—or for that matter, Shakespeare's English—can move between the rigorously formal pole of its most intensified diction and the poet's own language of everyday life. In Kamban's case, this is made even more complex by the availability of the old idiom of the Sangam, the morphology and thematic repertoire of which he freely draws upon. This pendulation between distinct registers is very clear from the outset of the passage. Immediately after ramping up the listener's expectation by the long linked series of verses, Kamban turns his attention to Hanuman and his thoughts. The style here is balanced, austere, classicizing, exemplified by the second verse's pivotal third quarter ("He thought / to himself: 'His crooked nature, his deeds, / and all that has to happen will now become clear'"). This is Kamban's Tamil-as-Sanskrit, where every single word in the original is Dravidian in origin. As Ravana draws close to Sita, Kamban continues to frame the hidden monkey hero. The poet shortens his metrical reins with a series of heavy syllables, while sharply simplifying his style—the description of Hanuman reads practically as spoken prose (the translation of 428, "Hanuman saw it all," beautifully captures the shift.)

Ravana's attempted seduction of Sita, which follows over the next thirteen verses, is full of surprises. The barrage of compliments he aggressively pays to Sita—"oh my cuckoo whose waist is aching under the weight of your breasts" (430), "oh my girl with fierce eyes that reach to your earrings" (432), "whose breasts burst their bounds" (435), and so on—is conventional: Rama showers her with much the same praise before her abduction. A leitmotif of Ravana's speech is the theme of worldly transience, which fell within the public (*puṟam*) division of Sangam Tamil literature, and was prominent in the didactic poetry of other late-classical texts. This world-weariness, of course, is here subordinated to Ravana's erotic designs. The ensuing cognitive dissonance—the art of seduction as a lecture that all things must pass—is intended by Kamban: by speaking in the public *puṟam* manner to a private *akam* end, Ravana's effort is doomed from the start. All of this is reminiscent of Sanskrit poetics' category of "false feeling" (*rasābhāsa*) or the semblance of literary emotion, the product of an ethical or ontological mismatch between would-be lover and beloved. For critics writing in Sanskrit, Ravana's love for Sita provides the paradigmatic example of a false feeling; Kamban domesticates this problem of Sanskrit literary theory within the resources of the classical Tamil past, fusing the two registers into something new.

For all his fumbling, Kamban's Ravana possesses considerable powers of eloquence. In one of the long vocative periods he offers to Sita—*pŏruḷum yālum viḷariyum pūvaiyum / maruḷa naḷum maḷalai vaḷuṅkuvāy* (5.436: "When you speak your gentle murmur / drives to distraction / all that has meaning, the music of the lute / and the haunting *vilari* raga, / the mumblings of the mynah bird")—the play of labial and liquid sounds (all those *p*-s, *v*-s, *m*-s, and *l*-s) imitate the sweet voice that Ravana describes. Elsewhere, he is cosmically arrogant, in another instance of Kamban's chaste classicism:

> Have a look at what great Yogis
> and sages of subtle understanding
> think is the best they can do,
> sweet woman whose breasts
> burst their bounds: they want only
> the happiness of serving me together
> with my other godly slaves. (435)

Sita's response to all this is signaled by a shift in the meter. The lines grow longer, with a recurrent rhythmic cadence introduced at the end of each: a final drumbeat, iconizing Sita's rage and resolve. She is not remotely swayed by Ravana's pledge of love. The first of these verses ("They scorched her ears . . . ") lights up Sita with a series of staccato flashes, quickly passing over her ears, her heart, her blood-red eyes, and her inner being before coming to rest on her unwomanly words. The following verse begins with the poet speaking in his own voice, its opening line coolly composed ("She was hoping to move the heart of that brawny, crooked monster"). What follows is a wrenching contrast: what Shulman renders as "You're no more to me than a blade of grass" translates a single word in the Tamil, the final word in Sita's rebuke. This is a totally accurate translation, but English cannot quite capture its connotation: the word possesses a humiliating casteist undertone, and its use by Sita is jarring. She throws Ravana's string of compliments back at him—448 ends with the long vocative phrase: literally, "you who were once cast on the earth by Jatayus." Kamban fuses elements of a perfectly naturalist stream of invective with the intensifications of theme and diction that belong to his long elevated poem. To give only a single example:

> When you lifted up his mountain, Lord Shiva squashed you
> with his toe. And it was his great bow, made from Mount Meru
> to burn the Three Cities with a single arrow, that my husband
> snapped in two that day—though it seems that *you*, Sir,
> never heard the sound it made that echoed
> through the cosmos. (451)

Once again, the sting is in the tail—the ironic *aiya* ("Sir") at verse's end sounds drawn from life; the strong contrast with the verse-opening nonrespectful pronoun *nī* ("When *you* lifted up . . . ") is surely deliberate. Between these poles of dismissal and mock respect, the poet juxtaposes two earlier myths—Ravana's humiliation by Shiva and Rama's breaking of Shiva's bow—into a breathless rush of action. Yet for all its density, the verse is easy to follow. It wasn't even that big a deal, breaking the bow, yet the whole world—except befuddled Ravana—could hear the result.

Sita's words frustrate the dichotomy between the elevated language of poetry (Tamil-as-Sanskrit) and the spoken speech of everyday life. This breakthrough is something that Kamban achieves over and over again: bear in mind that in producing just his monumental *Irāmâvatāram*, he is the most prolific Tamil poet, ever. Tamil's master poet, in his work of astonishing breadth and depth, staged moment after moment where his language is at once close at hand and self-transcending.

CAN DARKNESS STAND BEFORE LIGHT?
ENCOUNTERING AN EPISODE FROM A MEDIEVAL TAMIL MASTERPIECE

Yehoshua Granat (Far Reader)

Thousands of handwritten texts of late antique and medieval Hebrew poetry have survived in the Cairo Genizah, typically fragmented and often barely readable: a great many of them still await identification and evaluation.[4] A philologist dealing with such documents on a daily basis is bound to be haunted by an urge, as well as an obligation, to decipher these long-forgotten, precious pieces of verse as precisely as possible, so that the very text is accurately reconstructed. This is obviously an essential prerequisite for adequately interpreting the often elusive and highly allusive lines of verse, continuously conversing with biblical verses and other writings of old. Hardly could such a philologist avoid a poignant self-doubt, while facing the unusual opportunity to make a comment on a work rooted in a civilization much remote from the one(s) more or less familiar to him or her.

Pondering over David Shulman's English translation of an episode from Kamban's *Ramayana*, the nocturnal scene of Ravana's visit to Sita in the Ashoka Grove, one wonders if any (poetic) justice can indeed be done to this captivating passage through a foreigner's gaze, devoid, alas, of familiarity with the text's cultural milieu. Might such a far reading be likened to Ravana's "fierce sighs" as he approaches the grove, at the very beginning of our episode, scorching "the golden garden, / buds, branches, flowers, roots," and turning it black at every step? Admittedly, the local colors, sounds, and odors, the landscape, its fauna and flora, and the specific timbre of voice and diction are well beyond the reach of such a gaze from the outside, and this lack is surely a significant one. As Shulman himself has put it in a recent journal note written at "the Koneru pond, where we sat reading Telugu poems": "Is there any other place to read them? Only in that light and fragrance can I understand them. A goddess turned up to bless us."[5]

At the same time, such a view from the outside might also bring to mind Hanuman's position in our scene. Though hidden "nearby," distinctly outside of the encounter of Ravana and Sita, their dramatic rendezvous is followed closely and emphatically by "this monkey of blessings," who, in a sense, may be representing here an ideal, deeply alert "sensitive reader" of the encounter. Hanuman sees "her [Sita], her very life fleeing in dismay . . . [sees] him [Ravana], adrift, / befuddled by desire, and soon / to die," while his own heart is "swinging back and forth." Indeed, though situated quite farther, and with no pretension of having "two perfect eyes," such as Hanuman's, I was also drawn into the deeply expressive account of Ravana and Sita's confrontation. And as if in compensation for my lack of familiarity with its original echo chamber, at some points the passage brought to mind, by way of association, some scenes, topoi, and segments of early writings with which I am a little bit more familiar.

The meeting of Sita, "a lamp to all womanhood," with Ravana, the demon king, whom the narrator compares to "a snake of many heads that has lost / its great jewel," takes place at an idyllic "golden garden." To a biblically oriented reader's mind, such a scene is almost bound to recall the fatal encounter that took place, according to the Book of Genesis's third chapter, at the primordial Garden of Eden, between Eve, "the mother of all living" (Gen. 3:20) and the devious serpent, who "was more crafty than any beast of the field" (Gen. 3:1). Mutatis mutandis, of course: the narrative contexts are essentially different. Still, it is interesting to note that, quite unlike Eve, whom the cunning serpent rather easily persuades to disobey God's command, Sita remains unwaveringly faithful to Rama, her absent companion, despite all of Ravana's ceaseless efforts to seduce her ("There's nothing like a woman's loyalty in love / to turn her heart to stone"; 445).

In other instances, specific phrases and motifs evoked comparable utterances. Ravana's address to Sita as "my cuckoo / whose waist is aching under the weight / of your breasts" (430), for example, can bring to one's mind the Lover of the biblical Song of Songs, picturesquely addressing his Beloved as "my dove, that art in the clefts of the rock (Cant. 2:14) . . . thy stature is like to a palm tree, and thy breasts to clusters of grapes" (Cant. 7:8). Perhaps it is even more reminiscent of

Andalusian Hebrew erotic verse (roughly contemporaneous to Kamban's epos) and its typically hyperbolic depictions of the feminine figure.[6] Subsequently, while urging Sita to accept his courtship, Ravana presents her with the argument that the days of youth "will never come back. / Little by little they're wasting away. / When they're gone, when days / meant for delight are a void / when will you start to live?" (437) and so on. Quite unmistakably, this is an expression of the *carpe florem* theme, a prevalent element in the European tradition of love poetry from Greco-Roman Antiquity to the age of Baroque.[7]

Ravana's appeal to Sita indeed appears to overflow with stock phrases and clichés of courtship discourse, some of which may be of cross-cultural prevalence. But the most captivating feature in this passage is probably the paradoxical contradictions of strength and weakness embodied in the figures of both Ravana and Sita. The former is portrayed as "powerful, no doubt about it" (426), "king over all who live in all three worlds" (443), whereas the latter, his helpless captive, as "crying like a young doe / about to be eaten by a striped tiger, / raging in fury, eyes blazing smoke" (427). But the seemingly clear-cut balance of power between omnipotent Ravana and feeble Sita is gradually revealed as intrinsically ambiguous. Addressing Sita, the mighty Ravana is described as "tormented both by desire / and by diffidence" (431). He asks her to accept him, "king over all who live in all three worlds," as her "lowly servant," and then falls "full-length at her feet on the ground, / heedless of disgrace" (443). The frightened Sita, in contrast, replies to her captor most daringly, speaking, as the narrator puts it, "in a way no woman should or could" (444). Referring to Ravana as "no more to me / than a blade of grass" (445), she bluntly refuses to accept any of his offers and declares her total devotion to Rama, her absent husband. Much more than the various details of Rama's deeds that she counts, what is most significant and striking in her address is probably the fervor of her clear moral conviction, so powerful that it turns her inferiority as a vulnerable captive into immense power: "That's the truth. Can darkness / stand before light?" (450).

"Darkness" clearly stands here for the presence of the threatening Ravana, whose fierce sighs "scorched the golden garden, / buds, branches, flowers, roots, / and turned it black at every step" (425). Light represents delicate Sita, whose waist was "fleeting / as a flash of lightning" (436). At the same time, light symbolizes truth, which by its essence defeats falsehood. This may bring to mind the biblical association of light, truth, and righteousness. The Psalmist turns to God, calling "O send out thy light and thy truth, let them lead me" (Ps. 43:3), and in the Book of Proverbs the juxtaposition of light and darkness symbolizes the contrast of the path taken by the righteous, which eventually leads to success, and the way of the wicked, that is doomed to fail: "But the path of the just is as the shining light, that shineth more and more unto the perfect day. / The way of the wicked is as darkness: they know not at what they stumble" (Ps. 4:18–19). Sita's last words in our passage are "the God of Goodness / is my witness" (454). Notably, this declaration can also be paralleled to biblical phrases such as "The Lord is witness against you" (1 Sam 12:5) or "my witness is in heaven, and my record is on high" (Job 16:19). One can detect here remarkably similar manifestations of the human yearning, at crucial moments of crisis, for an undoubtable clarity that can be found only in the realm of the divine.

Beyond betraying the present reader's cultural horizons, specific resemblances of expression, as the ones observed between Kampan's lines and passages from ancient Hebrew sources, may reflect a rather far-reaching truth: boundaries of culture and civilization can be transcended by a universal, deeply humane ideal, such as the aspired victory of moral conviction over tyrannical oppression. Be that as it may, I am genuinely grateful for the poet-translator's resonant passage, for making it possible for me (alongside many other "distant readers") to be enchanted by such masterly verse from afar.

When a Mountain Rapes a River, from Bhattumurti's Telugu *Vasu's Life*

TRANSLATOR'S NOTE AND TEXT

The following are two segments from my favorite Telugu book, which purports to tell the tale of Vasu Uparichara, one of the ancestors of the Pandavas, when he falls in love with Girika, daughter of a mountain and a river. The paternal mountain in question, Kolahala ("Clamor"), fell in love with the Shuktimati River when he happened to see her on a visit to heaven and tried to persuade her to marry him; when she refused, he blocked her path and raped her. Vasu interrupted the assault, kicked the mountain with his toe, and sent him flying far from the river, but not before the river became pregnant and gave birth to Girika ("daughter of the mountain") and her twin brother. This story is briefly told in the *Mahabharata* (Book 1), but it is immensely elaborated by Bhattumurti in verses that are replete with puns and other complex figures as well as near-constant metapoetic reflections. It is a musical work, deeply engaged in the properties and expressive potential of musical sound; less than two centuries ago, scholars in the Godavari region still knew which raga was suited to each verse. This work is included in the canon of major poetic works associated with the Vijayanagara court (in its exilic center of Penugonda, following its decisive defeat in 1565).

In the first section, we hear what Kolahala Mountain says to the river when he first approaches her, and we then hear her response (this section actually appears in the poem in the form of a flashback: it is reported to Vasu's friend by Manjuvani, Girika's maid). The second section describes the moment King Vasu first sets eyes on Girika in the wilderness.

I. *VASU'S LIFE* (2.125, 128–33): A CONVERSATION BETWEEN THE
KOLAHALA MOUNTAIN AND THE SHUKTIMATI RIVER

Kolahala:
"I saw you when you were leaving
after bowing to the god, you and all the other
lovely rivers—saw your limpid way of being,
your good taste, your depth, the way you contain
us all, your flowing fullness. Since that moment,
in my mind I can imagine
only you. (2.125)

Wise people go to any lengths to celebrate—
indeed to immerse themselves in—whoever has
clarity and sweetness and grace. So I, too,
yearning to be close to you, have come here,
despite the distance, for only you
can quench the fire inside me. (2.128)

What more can I say? I want to give my life
to you, like water gushing down
a mountain. I'll never leave you, and I'll learn how
to make you happy, you whose breasts are round
as the ruddy geese on your waves. Please agree.
Bring me into your innermost heart, where goodness
and love are alive. Do away with my sorrow, make me
a river's husband and lord." (2.129)

Shuktimati:
"I belong to the bottom, the very lowest level,
where things trickle and flow. My nature
is slow and sluggish and cold.
Even if I happen to be full, at heart
I'm immeasurably shallow, so I've nothing
to be proud of.
In my innermost place you'll find only slime.
My watery life is mostly bubbles, and my only hope
is for a dark, rainy day.
My movements are twisted and crooked.
At my best I'm nothing
but broken waves.
To say I'm even a little bit stable
is an outright lie, and whenever I do stand still,
I stink. Do you really think it's a good idea

for you, with your grandeur and dignity,
your so-weighty-mind, you who are solid
and sinless as a rock, to get close
to someone like me?

On one side: mountains, the kings
of the earth. On the other: wobbly,
watery streams. Their union
doesn't look very likely. Do you think
my juicy tastes can reach up
to your infinite height?" (2.131–32)

Kolahala:
"Lovely river,
it's all true, but I'm already drowning
in the flood of your beauty. Are you going to be cruel
and sink me in your whirling currents, or will you embrace me,
flow into me, float me on a raft of sheer joy?" (2.133)

II. VASU'S LIFE (2.62–70): VASU SEES GIRIKA FOR THE FIRST TIME

His two eyes were full of desire.
More than the two eyes, his mind
was full of desire in a very strange way.
Even before his mind, his body was flooded: a wonder.
Even more than that change in body, hunger,
agitated and pressing, rushed in. (2.62)

As the king looked at that woman, he wanted never to blink.
He succeeded in this by joyfully surrendering, with all his memories,
to her moonlike face. Then he wanted to be king
of the unblinking gods, with a thousand eyes.
That's how kings are. They're unstable, always striving
for a higher station. (2.63)

First lingering at her feet,
then rising to her thighs,
then reaching the zone of her belt,
his glance longed to climb up to the mountain bastion
of her breasts—which would have made him emperor
of the whole world. (2.64)

Eagerly entering the tunnel of her navel,
grasping the ladder of her three folds of skin,
pulling himself up by the ropes that were the hairs
on her tummy, and finally conquering the high fortress

of her breasts: the king's vision fulfilled
a soldier's mission. Is there anything that can't be achieved
by one who delights in battle? (2.65)

His glance fell upon her face, like a wild garden,
with the fragrant *tilaka* mark on her forehead
(or was he seeing dark *tilaka* trees?),
then it slipped from her cheeks that were glossy
with the fresh honey of her smile
and slipped again, over and over, as if seeking a footing
on smooth moonstones, until, desperate,
it found the vines of her long, thick hair
and held on for dear life. (2.66)

Once more, that royal glance:
it turned her feet into fresh buds,
revealed her thighs, like the stem of the banana plant,
as the site of all happy beginnings,
showed an elephant's back in her buttocks,
caused her nonexistent waist to merge with the sky
and her breasts to touch the mountain peaks,
drew the conch, one of the nine treasures, on her neck,
let him find whatever fruit he desired in her sweet lips,
disclosed the shape of the syllable Shri in her ears,
transformed her lovely face so that it could rule over the moon
(and all other kings), and as for her dark curls—
they were rainclouds, or any other rich
wondrous thing. (2.67)

He was a king all right, even the best of them all,
but he was drowning in dense wonder,
an ocean of driving passion where all
was one, beyond word or mind.
He praised her beauty deep in his heart
that now depended on no
other object. (2.68)

[Now a typical metalinguistic verse (2.69), which allows only for
    prose translation:]
Her dark curls, which we call *bhramaraka*, have given bees their
name and helped them proliferate. Her face, which menaces the lotus, justifies the title we give the moon: *san-mitruḍu*, "a true friend"
(also: friend of the stars). If people call the *dŏṇḍa* fruit *bimba*, that's
because it's a pale reflection (*bimba*) of her sweet lips. Her breasts

are golden mountains, which is why people affectionately call mountains *gotra*—(their) "relatives." Necklaces are so similar to her arms that they are called *sarulu*, "equals." Wheels, being round, are *cakra*—that is, an army subservient to her buttocks. Do you know why lotuses are called *tammulu*, "younger brothers"? It's because they were born as the younger siblings of her feet. As for flowers, named *prasavamulu*, "pupils"—that's because they learned to be flowers by studying her fingernails.

Darkness had a problem. The girl's face
had defeated his enemy, the moon,
using her eyebrows as its bow, and her glances
as arrows. Her smile stole the ambrosia,
her gleaming cheeks took the radiance,
her forehead the moon's slim slices
of loveliness. And Darkness saw it all.
Still afraid, even more frightened,
he took refuge in her full black hair. (2.70)

IRRECONCILABLE DIFFERENCES AND (UN)CONVENTIONAL LOVE IN BHATTUMURTI'S *VASU'S LIFE*

Ilanit Loewy Shacham (Near Reader)

David Shulman calls Bhattumurti's *Vasu's Life* (Vasucaritramu) his "favorite Telugu book." There are many readers of classical Telugu literature who share Shulman's love and appreciation for *Vasu's Life* in general and for Bhattumurti's poetic artistry and mastery in particular. Yet there seem to be different opinions as to just what the text is about. Whereas most readers talk about *Vasu's Life* as a conventional love story between a man (King Vasu) and a woman (Girika), Shulman has argued that, "the real heroine of the work is none other than Nature herself in the infinite varieties of form made manifest to the receptive observer."[1] Taking these views into consideration and using Shulman's selections, I propose that a painful separation between Nature and convention governs the narrative core of *Vasu's Life*.

In South Asian literature, within the domain of love, conventions often signify harmony, order, and compatibility, but for the protagonists of our story, incompatibility is not merely a break from convention. Rather, incompatibility is a force so powerful it brings about natural and personal disasters. Although there is indeed a love story at the center of *Vasu's Life*, conventional it is not.

In the first selection (2.125–33) an infatuated (Mountain) Kolahala is telling (River) Shuktimati about his desire to be with her. His words are heavy with double entendre or *śleṣa* (lit., embrace), a figure of speech used extensively throughout *Vasu's Life*. For example, he begins by praising her as having fine qualities that describe her both as a river and a woman, such as her "limpid way of being," her "good taste," and her "depth" (2.125). His final plea, also couched in double entendre (unpacked into two separate statements in the translation), is a request to "do away with my sorrow" and make him "a river's husband and lord" (*nannu[n] adīnu ceyave*, 2.129). Shuktimati's immediate response is a two-verse rejection in which she articulates their stark incompatibility. In the first verse (2.131), she takes the time to negatively outline various aspects of her physical attributes and nature: as a river, she belongs to the lowest level, and in her there is crookedness and instability, whereas he, the mountain, belongs to lofty domains and in him there is dignity, sinlessness, and stability. In the second verse (2.132), she succinctly concludes that the immeasurable disparity between rivers and mountains makes their union unlikely. Within this short section, Bhattumurti creates layers and textures, all of which highlight his complete control over language: the density and volume of the mountain's punned speech is in stark contrast to the river's light and crisp rejection, which, as if moving away from the implicit "embrace" of *śleṣa*, primarily features a figure of speech that highlights "discrepancy" (*viṣama*), which has incompatibility or incongruity as its core theme.

Somewhat surprising here is that in her initial rejection of Kolahala's advances, Shuktimati does not mention an obvious fact, namely, that she is already married. Indeed, in India all rivers are female (except for one, the Brahmaputra), and they are all married to the ocean as indicated by the numerous epithets for "ocean" which mean "river's husband," or "the husband of rivers." Bearing this in mind, Kolahala's request to become the "river's husband and lord" already encapsulates its own futility: a mountain's request to become the ocean. Yet, Shuktimati does not make that obvious counterargument to Kolahala's advances; instead, she rejects him only on the basis of incompatibility as seen from her own personal perspective. In the last verse given here from Kolahala and Shuktimati's exchange (2.133), Kolahala basically agrees with Shuktimati regarding their incompatibility but states that he is already drowning and asks her to save his life by uniting with him. Shuktimati's second response (2.134–35, not given here) adds depth to the initial claim of incompatibility by invoking physical attributes, character, and marital status. Physically, she explains, they would be an impossible match; a heavy mountain, not to mention his relatives, will not be able to stay afloat in a river such as herself. She then suggests that lofty Kolahala (who is described as "blinded by desire") might be better matched with beautiful heavenly women, if sexual pleasures are what he is after. Utilizing double entendre in Telugu, she describes herself as a river/ascetic that wanders from one holy place to another and dries up in the hot season/grows thin as the result of austerities. She concludes her double speech by describing herself in an epithet that means both an ascetic who "dwells in forests" and as one who is "married to the ocean" (2.135). By using *śleṣa* here, Shuktimati is able to provide a perfectly tailored response to Kolahala's initial double-tongued requests: to the one that she give him pleasure, Shuktimati responds by saying she is an ascetic; to the other, that she make him a river's husband, Shuktimati responds by stating she is already married.

One could argue that the reason that Shuktimati did not mention her marriage to the ocean at first is because, as other examples in South Asian literature show, the union between the ocean and rivers is often not strictly monogamous, and there are precedents of erotic encounters between mountains and rivers (as they flow on land en route to the ocean). Thus if Shuktimati wanted to be with Kolahala, her marriage could conveniently not be a problem, and elsewhere in the text (verse 2.137, not translated here), Kolahala invokes examples in which rivers took on extramarital lovers (such as the case of the river Ganges and the god Shiva). However, Shuktimati is not interested in Kolahala, and this is a focal point in Bhattumurti's text. Thus, the fact that she brings up her marriage last should not be taken lightly. In similar cases of unwanted advances in South Asian texts (such as Ravana's abduction of Sita in the *Ramayana*), marriage and loyalty to the husband are the core vocabulary through which women articulate their rejection of unwelcome suitors.[2] Shuktimati's rejection, however, is articulated from the perspective of an individual. The central reason she rejects Kolahala is that she sees this as a match of two beings whose differences cannot be reconciled. Thus, although Shuktimati eventually mentions her marriage, her being married is secondary to the argument about her and Kolahala's fundamental personal incompatibility.

Further indicating Shuktimati's determination to reject this match in her own terms is that she refrains from discussing her husband—unlike women in other South Asian texts who, in similar circumstances, often compare their husband favorably with the unwanted suitor. Instead, Shuktimati compares herself and Kolahala, initially suggesting that she is just not good enough for him. Yet, as her response unfolds, it is clear that she means the opposite (one of many reversals in the text)—he is not good enough for her. She first highlights her unstable and base nature as set against Kolahala's solidity and grandeur, but then goes on to describe herself as an ascetic, the epitome of steady self-control. Conversely, although she initially describes Kolahala as a lofty, dignified, and stable mountain, it is clear that what she sees in him is uncontrollable desire, and that she wants nothing to do with it.

In her responses, Shuktimati delineates this match as something that goes against her nature and against Nature in general, as implied in her question to Kolahala whether a river can be made to flow up the hill and reach his infinite heights. It should come as no surprise then, that when Kolahala forces himself upon Shuktimati, he dams her flow and brings about a natural disaster in the form of terrible floods; following this, the citizens of the Chedi Kingdom are forced to beg Vasu for help. With one toe, he flicks Kolahala away from Shuktimati, restoring her flow to its natural course. But at this point, she is already pregnant with Girika and her twin brother.

Here I would like to pause for a moment to focus on the *Mahabharata*'s version of this story. In the *Mahabharata*, both the rape of Shuktimati and the love story of Vasu and Girika are narrated in extreme brevity (in chapter 57 of Book One). There Shuktimati presents Vasu with her twins, a boy and a girl, by way of thanking him for freeing her from Kolahala. Vasu makes the son a general in his army and takes the daughter, Girika, as his wife. After the two wed, Vasu goes out to hunt. Thinking about Girika while away, Vasu is overcome with desire and ejaculates. He collects his semen on a leaf and asks a bird to carry it to Girika so that she can conceive through insemination. After a string of somewhat comic events, Vasu's seed ends up in a river, impregnating a fish (who is really a heavenly nymph under a curse) that gives birth to twins—one of whom (Satyavati) later gives birth to Vyasa, the author of the *Mahabharata* and the father of the main protagonists of the epic. Thus, in the *Mahabharata* this entire episode is presented as embedded in the epic heroes' genealogy. Shuktimati's rape explains Girika's birth, and Girika is simply a catalyst who is no longer relevant once her husband ejaculates while thinking of her.

Bhattumurti's *Vasu's Life* presents interesting changes that impact the core of the epic story. Recall that in *Vasu's Life*, the story of Kolahala and Shuktimati is not presented in sequence but rather as a flashback, within the context of Vasu and Girika's own love story. Specifically, we learn about the rape that led to the birth of Girika only *after* Vasu has seen and fallen in love with her, as he learns more about Girika's background. In South Asian narratives, information about one's parentage is often offered as a way of indicating the compatibility of a match (social background is key in determining mutual suitability). Girika's origin is anything but typical, and Bhattumurti does not mute or minimize the terrible story of rape behind her birth. Instead, he takes the time to develop it by elaborating on the victim's rejection, the offender's use of force, and the ways in which Kolahala is acting against nature. In Sanskrit, the birth of a child to a couple in which the mother is of a higher social standing than the father is called "against the grain" (*pratiloma*). Although in *Vasu's Life*, the (mis)match is not determined by social standing but rather by the natural order, the warning against transgressing social order is understood by extension: a match that violates this order has repercussions in the following generations. This narrative thus provides a productive explanatory framework for the later problems that children born into Shuktimati's line have with consummating their marriages, beginning with Girika herself. Thus, if in the *Mahabharata* Shuktimati was simply the mother of Girika, in *Vasu's Life*, her articulation of incompatibility reflects her strong singular voice and also explains the DNA of the lineage. Similarly, this same DNA prevents Girika from being a fully developed love interest in the *Mahabharata*, but in *Vasu's Life*, the story ends with her marriage to Vasu in a way that allows the poet to avoid the entire spilled semen episode. Thus in *Vasu's Life*, Girika is cast as the heroine in her story against all odds.

With the full trajectory of Girika's story in mind, we can now turn to the second selection provided here—an earlier episode in *Vasu's Life* where Vasu gets his first direct glimpse of Girika. Bhattumurti describes Vasu's gaze as it sweeps from Girika's feet to the top of her head. This type of description is extremely common in South Asian literature and generally involves various conventions, such as the direction of the gaze (either bottom-up or top-down), the body parts that can be described (feet, thighs, breasts, face, etc.), and the standards of comparison to which each body part is compared (breasts to geese or mountains; face to the moon, and so on). Such descriptions indicate the heroine's extreme physical beauty but are often utilized for other purposes as well. In the second selection, Bhattumurti uses this depiction to weave in echoes of Girika's past (which has not yet been narrated) and future (which is beyond the narrative of *Vasu's Life*).

For example, consider the first two verses in the second passage that provide the framework for Vasu's gaze. The first (2.62) describes a flood that begins with the king's eyes and takes him over completely. Bhattumurti describes Vasu as one whose "body was flooded" and who was "drowning in dense wonder, an ocean of driving passion." Furthermore, in an epithet not translated here, Bhattumurti refers to Vasu as the "person who defeated the mountain" (Kolahala). The combination of water imagery, flooding, desire, and Kolahala foreshadows Shuktimati's story (as a river whose flow was tampered with as a result of Kolahala's lust), as well as Vasu's future (as a man whose desire resulted in spilled seed and the impregnation of a fish). In the second of the two framing verses (2.63), Bhattumurti describes Vasu as someone who "wanted to be king of the unblinking gods"—a playful way to suggest the notion of a thirst that cannot be satiated (in South Asian literature, gods never blink). He uses the term "unblinking" more than once within the same verse—a clear indication that Vasu's wish to gaze uninterruptedly at Girika is paradoxically interrupted by the torrent of his rushing desire. Now, Vasu doesn't just want to be unblinking like a god; in order to drink up more of Girika's beauty, he wants to be the king of the unblinking (gods), Indra, who has "a thousand eyes." This is a seemingly odd request, given that Indra's thousand eyes were a punishment and a reminder of his inability to control his own desire toward Ahalya, another man's wife (he was initially punished by having one thousand vaginas attached to his body, and only later were these replaced by eyes).

The poet concludes that kings are "unstable" and "always striving for a higher station," even though it is quite clear that when it comes to the domain of desire, being like Indra is perhaps not quite a step up. Indra aside, both of the verses that set up the description of Girika reflect a tension between the dynamic and the static, thereby echoing the clash of the river and the mountain, and are powered by the disfiguring force of desire.

We then witness the physical, mental, and poetic manifestations of desire, as Vasu runs his gaze three full times from Girika's feet to her head. Each time, the quality of his desire changes. First (2.64–66) is a gaze stripped of all embellishments—all the components that make a woman beautiful are there, but his desire prevents Vasu from seeing anything beyond the body parts. Reflected by the vocabulary of military conquest (climbing up mountain bastions, grasping ladders, delighting in battle, etc.), this first gaze not only highlights the physical struggle that such a desire-fueled conquest entails, but also its thrills and joys. The second sweep of the eyes (2.67), "that royal glance," is more refined and involves poetic comparisons between Girika's body parts and various standards of comparison, such as flower buds and the conch. All of the elements in this verse are conventional and found in almost any poetic description of women in South Asian literature. Note, however, that here Vasu's gaze activates these conventions, not the poet. Indeed, the poetic conventions are framed as something revealed, discovered, and transformed by his desire-filled gaze. Between the second and last sweep, Vasu internalizes everything; his desire no longer depends on a gaze, an object, or even on language, which paves the way for one last sweep—a metapoetic contemplation on his love interest, Girika, speech, and the relationship between the two. Bhattumurti's exploration of the mechanics of desire and its unintended results is interesting in its own right but is also an indirect reference to (and even an explanation of) Vasu's spilled seed incident—the water imagery and the fact that his desire is internalized and no longer depends on her physical presence allude to this story, untold in *Vasu's Life*. Although base desire was transformed into something internal, elevated, and refined, its problematic nature remains.

Modern scholars have read *Vasu's Life* as a conventional, archetypal, and even stereotypical love story. However, even from this brief discussion, the limited nature of such readings is clear. Nature and culture are deeply intertwined (and not just in the poetic domains of South Asia), and Kolahala's attack marks the falling apart of the order upon which both rest. Girika's birth, the outcome of this attack, thus marks the end of the familiar and the beginning of the unknown, and Bhattumurti's tale can be seen as an attempt to connect the two in a meaningful way. Indeed, even though Girika and her story stem from an act against nature, Bhattumurti does not try to intervene or change the flow of the story, highlighting instead both its productive and destructive potentials. By subjugating Vasu and Girika's story to the conventions of a love story, Bhattumurti heightens its unnatural aspects. In doing so, he creates a story in which an individuality outside of order is key.

The theme of working with conventions is also suggested in the beginning of *Vasu's Life*, when Bhattumurti (through the words of his patron) tells the readers that invented stories are like "artificial diamonds" whereas old stories are like authentic gemstones in the rough; the former are of little value, but the latter, when "reworked by good poets with their irresistible imagination, are precious gems perfectly cut" (1.19). Finding a balance between the old and new and between reality and imagination is what poets during Bhattumurti's time were seeking—each in radically different ways. For Bhattumurti, the key is located within certain conventions that provide both the raw materials and the tools of the trade; through inspired craftsmanship, conventions then can be meaningfully broken in a way that creates space for the old and the new, for love that brings about pain, and for desire that is both productive and destructive.

DESIRE, PERCEPTION, AND THE POETRY OF DESIRE: A READING OF *VASU'S LIFE*

Deven M. Patel (Far Reader)

In the introduction to these short excerpts from Bhattumurti's *Vasu's Life* (Vasucaritramu), we learn that the story of the mountain, the river, the king, and the daughter of mountain and river comes to us from the immensely long, complicated, and shockingly violent Sanskrit (and Telugu) epic poem *Mahabharata*. The fifteen verses given in this selection undoubtedly intersect with the broader systems of significance in that epic and in Bhattumurti's shorter court epic. These stanzas may also form, however, a system in their own right, especially if we take parts 1 and 2 as homologous to each other, as allied variants of the same meaning-structure, and even as contrasting poles of that same structure.

Upon first reading and, in fact, upon subsequent readings as well, the selected stanzas are scant on narrative action. An amorous mountain sees a diffident river, falls in love, and announces his desire. The river politely declines the mountain's proposal, arguing that they would not make a good couple—he is, after all, lofty and stable, the river says, while she is lowly and erratic. The mountain seems to agree with this analysis but verbally persists in his pursuit, before the six conversational verses of part 1 trail off into the nine verses of part 2. In the first seven of these verses, a narrator describes how the desire-filled King Vasu's glance—imagined as a conquistador scaling a mountain—travels (twice) up the body of an ethereal woman named Girika. The eighth and ninth verse of part 2 paint a startling portrait of Girika not as the otherworldly object of desire, but as the enigmatic standard against which all metaphorical statements about Nature are measured.

Love at First Sight. Part 1, "A Conversation between Kolahala Mountain and Shuktimati River," begins with a familiar type of anthropomorphism. The "clamorous" (Kolahala) mountain seeks to romance a shiny, silvery river (Shuktimati) unluckily caught in the crosshairs of his glance during a pious moment ("I saw you when you were leaving / after bowing to the god"). He follows with a string of double-meaning pearls meant to flatter all rivers—and Shuktimati, in particular—praising her physique and flavor alongside her moral clarity and aesthetic sophistication. He specially notes her "limpid way of being" (transparency?), her "good taste" (or that she tastes good?), and her "depth" (thoughtfulness?). The mountain candidly admires all rivers for their "flowing fullness" (down mountain slopes?) and their inscrutable capacity to "contain" mountains (by forming gorges?). This is all prelude to a gallant declaration, anchored by two "only yous":

> Since that moment, in my mind I can imagine only you.
> . . . for only you can quench the fire inside me. (2.128)

Then comes a proposal, with an outpouring of metaphor ("I want to give my life to you, like water gushing down a mountain . . . you whose breasts are round / as the ruddy geese on your waves") punctuated with a desperate promise (2.129): "I'll never leave you, and I'll learn how / to make you happy." Finally, the rhetorical nod toward submission and fidelity comes with a clinching request rendered in a cold imperative mood: "Please agree. . . . Do away with my sorrow, make me / a river's husband and lord." In between the moments of clarity in this lover's discourse, which began with "What more can I say?" there is cryptic hyperbole (2.129): "Bring me into your innermost heart, where goodness / and love are alive." He just saw her—how does he know about her innermost heart? How is goodness and love alive there? For that matter, how does he judge her "good taste" or her "depth"? He cannot, of course, and admits as much: "Since that moment, in my mind I can imagine / only you" (2.125). Can anything be more mysterious than a lover's imagination?

A one-way mirror, as it were, divides mountain and river. The river sees the reality that faces her from the darker side. The mountain reflects himself, on the brightly lit side of the mirror. He *feels* reality without envisioning anything other than himself. The river, it is clear, feels his words like a coarse, craggy finger brushing against her moist cheek. She senses the subtle violence of the mountain's language, disguised brightly as romantic gesture, and covertly tries to fight back with language, discerning the mountain's true nature. However, what good does language do her? Language gives the illusion, often through praise of itself through itself, that it is powerful. Just as no amount of language in the *Mahabharata* averts the war, nor the violent impulses that prompt it, the river is helpless with her words. Her "It's not you, it's me" tack only buys her time. The mountain, in contrast, arms himself with words, like the god of love (Kamadeva) with his flowery arrows. In the end, the words hardly matter. Do the god of love's arrows really matter? What are the god of love's flowery arrows, after all, but flowery words? Upon further reflection, we anticipate what a dark conversation this will turn out to be, between mountain and river.

Love Is a Battlefield: Love Is Like Climbing a Mountain.   In part 2, we do not have a conversation. It is doubtful if we even have a beloved. We only seem to have a lover and, that too, only the imagined voyeurism of a lover presented to us by a narrator in a frenzy of words and metaphors. Desire still dominates the semantic structure established in part 1, and images of being "flooded" and "drowning" or "yearning" continue to signify a meaningful range of a lover's feelings of surge and excess, suffocation, and hunger. What changes in part 2 is the lover's vision and the discourse around it. Whereas the mountain's perception of the river—buried in his own words—imply a stark optics of domination, Vasu seems robbed of his own perceptions. In compensation for this loss, however, the poet enriches his experience as a lover with a far more wide-ranging and textured sensorium.

Vasu's experience is indeed rich (2.62). The sensory experience ("His two eyes were full of desire"; "his body was flooded") allows him to discriminate, recognize, and appreciate. The mental experience ("his mind was full of desire in a very strange way") intellectualizes, psychologizes, spiritualizes, and ultimately dematerializes. He has a memory-consciousness ("joyfully surrendering, with all his memories") that allows him to recapture, recall, and perhaps access subconscious states (2.63). Above all, he has imagination (2.64–67) that can conceptualize, create, fabricate, and fantasize. Finally, he tastes transcendence ("an ocean of driving passion where all / was one, beyond word or mind") that takes him to the supernatural and the sublime. Both lovers are aware of the inadequacy of language and, in the case of Vasu, even the inadequacy of thought when it comes to being in love.

The mountain places faith in the efficacy and immediacy of straightforward linguistic communicability, even when he seems to articulate an inadequacy of language. When the mountain says, "What more can I say?" he is content that he has made himself clear and, therefore, present in the situation. The account of Vasu's experience, set in a past time, represents the memory and imagination of a feeling already experienced. The very act of representing these feelings suggests, however, that the voice describing Vasu's inner movements cannot withdraw into silence in the face of emotional or imaginative ineffability and must struggle, through every linguistic means available, to confront the impenetrability of the experience. Vasu may be aware of the limitations of ordinary (physical) love, unlike the mountain, but why does he not see the correlative to this proposition: the limitations of *describing* ordinary love? What drives the narrator to verbalize, in Vasu's name, what he knows to be beyond words? Is it an escape into the poetic and the imaginative? We are to assume (from the third-person narration and preterite verbal constructions) that Vasu, the human king, makes no pretense of believing in ordinary communication. He, therefore, takes refuge in a hyperlinguistic communication of feeling through the marshalling of tropes and allusions that do not even seem to map onto his actual reality but emerge rather from an inherited canon of experiences not entirely his own.

With his plain speech and earnest inability to read the signs, the mountain exhibits the appealing confidence of both a childish and mature lover. As a childish lover, he is pathetic in his naïvete and, as an adult, admirable in his persistence. Kolahala recognizes Shuktimati as a unique lover, to match the specific requirements of his desire, and believes her to be the "only" one who can "quench the fire inside." In doing so, he humanizes both himself and Shuktimati the river.

Vasu, by contrast, seems helplessly confused by the upward forces that compel him to climb the mountain of Love while coming to grips with the friction his glance causes as it rubs up against Girika's magical body:

> He was king all right, even the best of them all,
> but he was drowning in dense wonder,
> an ocean of driving passion where all
> was one, beyond word or mind.
> He praised her beauty deep in his heart
> that now depended on no
> other object. (2.68)

In a startling reversal of anthropomorphism, Vasu's voyeuristic impulses, sharpened to extraordinary clarity, root out, in effect, whatever humanity Girika had acquired and returns her to her wild nature:

> Once more, that royal glance:
> it turned her feet into fresh buds,
> revealed her thighs, like the stem of the banana plant,
> as the site of all happy beginnings . . . (2.67)

In not being able to comprehend her, he seeks instead to survey her, as a conqueror would an alien landscape:

> First lingering at her feet,
> then rising to her thighs,
> then reaching the zone of her belt,
> his glance longed to climb up to the mountain bastion
> of her breasts—which would have made him emperor
> of the whole world. (2.64)

And again: " . . . the king's vision fulfilled / a soldier's mission. Is there anything that can't be achieved / by one who delights in battle?" (2.65)

Though the "king's vision fulfilled a soldier's mission," there is no need for Vasu to act out any desire and the need for a lover's language—so central to Kolahala's mission—is altogether absent in part 2, as metaphors stand in for release into an objective domain of literary signs that exclusively operate external to Vasu. Vasu, as subject, has lost agency. Explicitly or implicitly, the second-person pronoun "you" is invoked by Kolahala in his address to Shuktimati some twenty-five times. That she is his object of affection/possession is not in doubt. With the absence of the "you" and, perforce, the "I," with Vasu's ascent to Oneness ("her beauty deep in his heart / that now depended on no / other object"), all trace of human love has dissolved into impersonal, fragmentary memories of personhood: body parts and their flimsy associations (2.68). Vasu himself has encased himself in solitude, and his experience of the beloved Girika is locked up in his heart with the debris of all other lived experiences.

More alarming is Girika's fate. Whereas her mother, even as an object of desire, maintained a tenuous subjectivity, Girika's identity completely vanishes. Kolahala's fantasy—of Shuktimati's potential to transform his life for the better—constructs his desire. Hyperbole in praising the river merely underscores his objectification of her. Vasu does not seem to seek fulfillment in the Other but instead chooses to assimilate the Other into himself. He does this through transforming himself, a human, into his beloved, Nature's child, to achieve his "mission." Though conveyed in third-person narration, we are to understand that Vasu has obliterated the subjectivity of his object of affection/possession, rendered it as either nothingness or as something that is neither cognizable nor uncognizable. Having done this, he has achieved harmony, unanimity, wholeness, and peace, but at what cost? In what sense has he truly attained union with Girika?

Love Is Love Poetry.   The final two verses of part 2—drawing on the extraordinary powers of language to collapse dualities into unities—completes the reabsorption of Girika to her preanthropomorphic state, among the mountains and rivers. These verses also suggest that perhaps whatever it is that Vasu and Kolahala experience (love?) exists in its mimetic representation or in the poetic language that redirects or threatens that representation. In other words, perhaps love exists because love poetry exists. The homology would be with Girika and the natural world (2.69). Her dark curls (*bhramaraka*) name the bees. Her moon face—rival to the lotus in beauty—"justifies" being called, simply, moon and, by extension, a "friend of the stars" (*san-mitruḍu*). The metapoetic transformation of reality—of bees, the moon, mountains—into a *literary* reality, through rhetorical techniques such as double-meaning constructions (*śleṣa*), also mirrors Vasu's ultimate triumph of union with Girika, a singular being where stability and instability harmonize.

Perplexed by the chasm that separates realities and the powers of language to describe them, the reader finds himself in the position of darkness. First, there is confusion. How is it that the girl's face defeats darkness' enemy—the moon—but that the girl's face, in another semantic system, is itself the moon? Does her face defeat itself? Is it that she is both a rival of the moon, in the first place, and then, once defeating it, her face becomes the moon? This is the kind of circularity typical of the literary sign, changing meanings or disappearing altogether as it shifts from one semantic field to the other. Finding ourselves on such uneven ground, what recourse do we have but to seek refuge in the literary imagination, just as the darkness takes refuge in Girika's "full black hair" (1.70)?

Love's Interior Landscapes

Four Selections from Tamil Sangam Poetry

EDITORS' NOTE

ALL OF THE SELECTIONS IN THIS UNIT are drawn from the corpus of the earliest Tamil poetry known as Sangam literature. The Sangam corpus dates to the first centuries CE (although the dates remain subject to considerable debate). The imprint of Sangam literature, however, is not limited to that corpus. Its aesthetic conventions, especially its division of poetry into "public" (*puṟam*) and "inner" (*akam*) modes, each with its own conventions and subdivisions, can often be seen in subsequent Tamil literature as, for example, in *Chivakan's Gem* in unit 3 and Nammalvar's *A Hundred Measures of Time* in unit 6. Indeed, the corpus occasionally serves as a reference point for modern Tamil poetry, as, for example, in the essay by the contemporary poet, R. Cheran, who hails from Sri Lanka and composes in Tamil while living in Canada. In short, Sangam poetry possesses both antiquity and contemporaneity to a striking degree, as A.K. Ramanujan famously noted.[1]

E.M. Forster's injunction "Only Connect" is key to experiencing the pleasures of Sangam poetry, whether one is connecting individual poems to their ancient aesthetic and cultural contexts or to the manifold contexts of the present.[2] Another injunction might be profitably added to Forster's: "Only Select." The examples in this unit bear witness to the power of selection—whether the selection of a single verse or of a discrete unit (like that of a decad in "Ten on the Wild Boar")—to open up the fullness of poems, to illuminate the text in its many appearances in the world, and, above all, to allow them to become the conditions for ever-new pleasures for readers. Reading these Sangam poems reminds us especially that as we take pleasure in them, we ourselves are changed in the process. As Archana Venkatesan says in her essay, "through our reading, mediated through Shulman's finely grained translation, much like the hero [of 'Ten on the Wild Boar'] who learns to be sensitive, we too will form ourselves into readers of sympathy."

"Ten on the Wild Boar"

TRANSLATOR'S NOTE AND TEXT

These selections from the earliest strata of Tamil poetry include relatively concise individual love poems, in what is called "the inner mode" or "inner landscape" (*akam*)—that is, the world of imagination and feeling, always correlated to the external environment with its flora and fauna. Within the four classical anthologies of *akam* poems, the *Collection of Five Hundred Poems* (Aiṅkuṟunūṟu) has two distinctive features: first, each century of poems is attributed to a single poet and describes one of the five prototypical landscapes; second, the basic unit of composition is a decad of very short, haiku-like verses meant to be read as a whole. The decad translated here, "Ten on the Wild Boar," is situated in the mountain region, where, according to the conventions of the inner mode, the young lovers have met, fallen in love, and consummated their love. However, this happy moment is very soon encumbered with the emotional complexities, loneliness, and frustration of any real love relationship.

"TEN ON THE WILD BOAR" (FROM THE *COLLECTION OF FIVE HUNDRED POEMS*)

A fierce boar who feeds on soft millet
sleeps on the lower slopes littered
with heavy stones in the land
of that man. Is it because he's afraid
of what our father knows that he
doesn't come? (1, verse 261)

A fierce boar who feeds on tiny shoots of millet
lives with his mate on the rocky slopes—
there, in the land of that man.
He wants me. His desire

will come back. But, my friend,
does he know
what would truly heal? (2)

A black touchstone, a boar
feeds on ripe golden millet
in the hills of that land.
He's come back, my friend—
and with him, my beauty
has come again. (3)

In the hills, gleaming with water,
of *your* land, a boar, tusks
curved like the crescent moon,
makes love to his mate, dark
as carissa fruits.[1] You'd better look hard
at the eyes, all too pale, of this woman
who has loved you. (4)

So he forgot—the man from the hills
where a boar with crooked tusks guards
young piglets, striped and tender,
after their mother was killed by a tiger.
He has left me behind—me and his
golden son. (5)

A boar with small eyes
and big rage
fights a big short-legged tiger
in your land. As for us,
we're embarrassed.
In the eyes of the woman you love:
frozen tears. (6)

A boar with small eyes
and big rage
eludes the bowmen on the rocky slopes
and grabs the growing rice
in the land of this man
who once cared for this girl,
her hair heavy with bees.
Now he speaks treacherous words, certain
she'll believe them. (7)

The striped piglet holding tight,
the mother dead, a boar

feeds with him on sparse millet
on the rich mountainside where hunters go
and sleeps on the high peak
in the fine land of that man.
What good will come
if he goes away, leaving us
behind? (8)

Reeds rooted up by a boar in the wasteland
are as close as you get
to paddy growing in a field
in the land of that man
who hasn't come. If he stays there,
taking his own time,
while you weep, girl,
with bangles on your wrists and oil
in your hair, I'm sure
to lose a friend.
Not only that, it's my own
stupid fault. (9)

On the slopes where boars
dig up roots, the forest folk
have harvested the young millet
and moved on. If she just looks
at that mountain, shorn of beauty,
lonely as lament, her eyes
fill with tears. And he noticed.
He's come, the one
we love. (10)

READING "TEN ON THE WILD BOAR"

Archana Venkatesan (Near Reader)

The *Collection of Five Hundred Poems* (Aiṅkuṟunūṟu) is a garland of five hundred
short compositions. Unlike other compilations of classical Tamil poetry, in which
poems and poets have a somewhat autonomous existence, the *Collection of Five
Hundred Poems* has a multitiered structure that destabilizes our notions of what
constitutes a poem. At first glance, it presents itself as a single work of five hundred
brief verses. It was composed by five male poets, each deliberating in a cycle of one
hundred songs, on one of the five landscapes (aintiṇai) of classical Tamil poetics.
Each of the five sections, the work of a single poet, is itself a poem—his com-
prehensive exploration of a specific landscape (tiṇai) and the particularity of love
on which it comments. The poet further divides his hundred songs into smaller

sets of ten verses (*patikam*), held together by themes and tropes specific to that landscape. The titles of these subdivisions—"Ten on Spring," "Ten on Monkeys," "Ten on the Wild Boar," and so on—alert us to the possibility that these tens can themselves function as self-contained poems, even while the *Collection of Five Hundred Poems'* structure demands that we read them as parts of a whole. Finally, at the molecular level, every one of the five hundred verses is also a poem, where its meaning does not need to be linked to its position within the ever-widening cycles of tens and hundreds. The brilliance of the *Collection of Five Hundred Poems* resides in its deliberate challenge to how we understand a poem, and in its ability to take the principles implicit in other classical Tamil collections to their inevitable conclusion.

So, what would it take to read a work like the *Collection of Five Hundred Poems* sensitively? The entire apparatus of Tamil poetics, a heady concoction of delicate suggestion and bold imagery, is no doubt important to imbibing the poems on their own terms. Yet, one can drink deeply, and even become intoxicated, absent such particularized knowledge. I frame my response to the "Ten on the Wild Boar" (Kēḻar-pattu) by following the text's by-the-numbers-organization—from five hundred to hundred to ten to one. Attention to the poem's organizing principles is a demand to sensitivity, to how subtle alterations reshape poetic texture, feeling, and meaning. David Shulman's translations draw our eye and ear to this startling feature of the *Collection of Five Hundred Poems* (exemplified in this decad), where repetition, iteration, and variation are used both to bind the verses together and to enable them to exist apart.

Just consider the decad's first three verses, which juxtapose two elements—millet and the wild boar—and guide us to what is important in these verses. Both occur in the opening line, and again in two subsequent verses (2 and 3), with minor but significant alteration. "Ten on the Wild Boar" begins with a reference to the "soft millet." The wild boar is introduced next—as hungry and fierce-eyed. In the following verse (2), the boar remains fierce-eyed and insatiable, but the millet has become something else; it is now "tiny shoots of millet." In the third verse, the millet has ripened to gold, and the boar is now a glistening black touchstone. Through all these tiny alterations, one thing remains unchanged: the boar's relationship to the millet, which exists only as a source to sate the boar's hunger. The millet disappears for the next several verses, reappearing in the eighth verse, and tellingly again, in the tenth verse. Its absence only emphasizes the intimacy and interdependence of these two natural elements, which index cultivation and wildness respectively, and by extension, the heroine and hero.

Tamil poetics provides us with an edifice of resources to help us unpack this suggestive, evocative relationship between flora (millet) and fauna (boar) that ushers us into the "Ten on the Wild Boar." Suggestion may be the arterial pulse of classical Tamil poetics, one that demands a sensitive reader, but attention to obvious rhetorical moves, such as the ones that open the "Ten on the Wild Boar," is what *makes* the sensitive reader. And through our reading, mediated through Shulman's finely grained translation, much like the hero who learns to be sensitive, we too will form ourselves into readers of sympathy.

The defining conceit of the *Collection of Five Hundred Poems* is the principle of the "five landscapes," each indexed to a specific stage of a love affair that begins in disruptive secret desire and ends in the ephemeral stability of marriage. The "Ten on the Wild Boar" upends this conventional order. It picks up the story media-res, in the agricultural tracts (*marutam*), where desire has already matured to love, and the exhilaration of new love has given way to the wounds of betrayal and infidelity. The poem begins in quarrel and disruption, but it ends auspiciously with the patient waiting characteristic of the pastoral lands, signified by the jasmine (*mullai*) and the principal characters reunited. As Martha Selby notes, "In the [*Collection of Five Hundred Poems*], the landscapes move from poems about fracture, jealousy, and infidelity and settle finally into verses describing and celebrating trusting domestic romance."[2] Even as this decad traverses a familiar path, from separation to union, it defies adherence to narrative linearity. Instead, the first bloom of love, always secret and illicit, is itself hidden within the heart of the *Collection of Five Hundred Poems*, producing an effect of concentric yet intersecting circles of poetic force: everything radiates out and collapses into the untamed mountains of the landscape of *kuṟiñci* and the wild love it signifies, which is seeded at the text's very center. The *kuṟiñci*-hundred—where the "Ten on the Wild Boar" is embedded—is the *Collection's* womb, for it births the furtive love that radiates simultaneously and paradoxically in opposite directions, toward lonely waiting and happy union. This is one of the defining features of not just the *Collection of Five Hundred Poems*, but of all classical Tamil poems: the interplay of linearity and recurrence, where even when love bends toward marriage, it is always overlaid by the inexorable oscillations of separation and union.

The cycle of "Ten on the Wild Boar" (verses 261–70), located almost at the midpoint of the *kuṟiñci*-hundred (that is, verses 61–70 out of 100) and just past the halfway point of the *Collection of Five Hundred Poems*, miniaturizes the collection's long meditation on the endless experience of the loss and recuperation of love. For those who seek a narrative in the "Ten on the Wild Boar," it is easy to find. The set unfolds iteratively, dwelling on particular phrases (as seen in the opening triad of the "Ten on the Wild Boar") to develop a theme and a narrative arc that like the *Collection of Five Hundred Poems* itself begins in separation and ends in (ephemeral) union. In the very first verse, we are told that the hero has failed to arrive for an assignation, perhaps because their secret love—the domain of the landscape of wild love—has been discovered by her father. By the final verse (10), the hero has returned, brought back by the force of his lover's tears. The narrative progress is indexed by the boar, which starts out snuffling millet (1) only to find itself eating roots in the end, while people reap the first harvest of millet (10). Like the millet that goes from tender shoot to golden grain by the cycle's conclusion, these ten verses offer us glimpses of the buds of early love, its gradual ripening, and its final maturation. This is the heroine's version of love. The hero has his story, too; it is a story of a reckless, perhaps even faithless man (i.e., the wild boar) learning something of himself, awakening to awareness.

The key to this decad rests in the boar's relationship to its environment, of which the opening trio of verses with their pointed but subtly altered repetition leave us in no doubt. Though a wild boar, the animal constantly finds itself connected to cultivation: the millet it feeds on (1–3, 8) and the carefully nurtured paddy that it steals (7, 9). In the opening verses, the boar *is* wild—it eats, sleeps, and mates—motivated only by these most primal impulses. Meanwhile, the heroine, delicate and tender, her love nourishing as millet, simply waits, hoping to domesticate all that wildness. Then, halfway through the decad, the poem changes to become a fight between the impulse to remain free, happily roaming the hills, and to surrender to the relentless gravitational pull of domesticity. In the fifth verse, the boar nurtures piglets orphaned by a tiger, in the sixth, it fights off a tiger, in the seventh, it evades archers who try to catch it for stealing rice, and in the eighth, despite its best efforts to go on its merry way, it is described comforting another orphaned hogling. These four verses (5–8), the most abstract in the decad, offer an important counterpoint to its opening triad. Here in the cycle's center, we confront the inherent instability of the natural world, and by extension, the instability of a stolen love that exists outside boundaries. It suggests that marriage, the public covenant of love, is what stabilizes desire. It tells a tale of a hero from the mountains who awakens the heroine to desire, but who must himself be awakened to love in all its forms.

If we only follow the trajectory of the boar, this is the story that emerges. However, every verse in the series of ten, like all classical Tamil poems, has a second, human part. These offer a very different narrative. It is the civilized counterpart to the boar's uninhibited urges. In these sections, the heroine simply waits, a passive, reactive figure. Her beauty returns temporarily when he comes back (3), but she is then reduced to tears (4, 5, 9) and gullibility (7). It is only in the tenth verse that the position reverses, with the hero's return in response to her quiet, silent tears. Despite this happy-for-now ending, the dominant theme of the decad is that neither public knowledge nor marriage is a reliable failsafe against betrayal, infidelity, or separation. Lest we miss the point, the fifth verse makes this explicit: the heroine tells us that the hero has left her and her son. In the context of classical Tamil poetry, the presence of the child signals to us that the verse describes a situation postmarriage. Marriage is an unusual topic for the *kuṟiñci* landscape with its ethos of spontaneous, stolen love, and its very presence in this decad, and placed at the center no less, tells us to be sensitive to what it might evoke.

These dense themes flourish in the compact, yet suggestive format of individual verses, which each follow a formula: the opening lines describe the boar—a proxy for the hero—and its relationship to the world it inhabits, while the concluding lines center on the heroine, her fears, her loneliness, and her all-consuming love for him. One way to approach this dual architecture is to read the verses' two parts along two parallel trajectories. If we follow the path of the boar, it is the hero's story—a story of self-awakening and self-understanding. If we stay with the heroine—who significantly does not move—it is a tale of love as loss, and of the futility of domesticating something that is fundamentally wild—be it desire or the hero. Put the two parts together, and we get a series of verses that explore desire-love as it exists in the infinitesimal space between public and private, between union and separation, between loss and recovery.

Much like the rest of the *Collection of Five Hundred Poems*, the "Ten on the Wild Boar" presents a picture of love that is uncomfortable. In "Ten on the Wild Boar," love emerges as savage, capricious, and disruptive, as both nourishment and illness; it is such love that needs to be both tamed and contained. The wild boar and the millet function not only as surrogates for the hero and the heroine, respectively, but as metaphors for the twinned sides of love. Equally, the decad offers a commentary on what happens when a private, secret affair becomes a matter of public knowledge. The answer comes to us in the cycle's two framing verses and with the two male figures who dominate the heroine's little world. In the first verse, the speaker (who could be either the heroine or her friend) speculates that the hero stays away because of the father. The word used, *entai*, can be taken to mean either *my/your* father or *our* father—Shulman has chosen to emphasize the latter in his translation. There is no such ambiguity in the decad's final verse, which ends with the phrase: "the one *we* love." The hero who begins the decad owned only by the land to which he belongs is now possessed not just by the heroine and her love, but by all ("we"). As the two verses of the piglets imply, this new possession means not just the care of the heroine and their child (a duty he will fail, as the fifth verse foreshadows), but of her kin. Like the boar, he too is no longer just of the land. And she, a millet perhaps growing untended on the mountain slopes to be rooted out by a foraging boar, is now to be carefully nurtured, harvested, and nourished. Their love, first unbound by desire and lust, and now circumscribed by kinship, is in the final analysis, a thing to be shared. Then, the cycle starts again in some future-past—with him the father and another girl with frozen tears awaiting her lover's return.

It is certainly possible to read the "Ten on the Wild Boar" as a cohesive whole, bound not just by the motif of the boar, but by the many themes on which it touches, some of which I have explored. Nevertheless, this cohesion is not total. There are fissures as the hero and heroine part (1, 2, 4, 6, 7, 9), reunite (3, 10), marry (5), and elope (8). The poem does not simply take us from separation (1) to union (10), as the decad's framing would suggest, or of a love that transforms easily from private to public. Certainly, we can read this decad as a poetry of interruption, one that understands that the shadow of separation always looms over union, just as the promise of union gilds the starkest of separations. Nevertheless, I would suggest that these breaks within the "Ten on the Wild Boar" are deliberate, drawing our attention to the artificiality of the *Collection of Five Hundred Poems'* structure, and pointing us to the possibility of a single verse to carry within it the whole of love.

Let us take as an example the eighth verse in this decad. In the first half, the boar cares for an orphaned piglet as they feed on millet. In the second half, the speaker wonders if the hero can be trusted—will he leave us behind? The verse is rich with possibility, even without the cumulative power that gathers around the boar or the millet. Taken on its own terms as an autonomous entity, the poem is not about the domestication of desire, about a private love that has become public. Instead, it is a quintessential *kuṟiñci* poem, about a dangerous, secret, stolen love. Their love therefore still remains theirs alone. Yet it also anticipates that separation always borders union—there is nothing to hold the hero, and the heroine and her friend know that he *will* leave: "What good will come / if he goes away, leaving us / behind?" Here is a verse that condenses the curious circular spatial-temporality of the five-landscape scheme into its compact structure and stands as a poem in its own right.

In the *Collection of Five Hundred Poems*, each set of hundred and each cycle of ten within it is a crucible of individual virtuosic poetic ability. Simultaneously, each plays its part through an exponential intertextuality to unfold a story that begins with quarrel in the fields, where the *marutam* flower blossoms, and ends with hilly lands of longing, marked by the jasmine (*mullai*). The *Collection of Five Hundred Poems* approaches this poetic experiment not in mixing landscapes and moods, but in enforcing boundaries, by giving us one hundred verses on each of the landscapes. Yet, it defies, in small ways as we have seen in the "Ten on the Wild Boar," those very boundaries. The fifth verse of the "Ten on the Wild Boar" nods in this direction, even if it does not violate the grammar of the landscapes; all the flora and fauna are as they should be (hills, boars, piglets, tigers), except the content is not (marriage).

The five landscapes form the bedrock of Tamil classical love poetry that begins in illicit love (*kuṟiñci*) and ends with the domestication of that love through the public institution of marriage (*marutam*). Thus, part of the trick of reading classical Tamil poetry is having the ability to decipher the clues within a poem—the time of day, the flora and fauna—to determine the particularity of love of which it tries to speak. Seen in this way, poems are self-contained things, hermetically sealed, each its own universe, concerned with commenting on a stage of love—waiting, more waiting, separation, infidelity—and inaccessible to those who cannot speak this special language. Yet, each is also ever echoing both the past and present of love, for a poem about love, private life, and intimacy (*akam*) also participates in an intricate web of storytelling, each landscape building on the other—waiting making way for elopement making way for infidelity making way for the quiet stasis of marital contentment. Poems that breach the boundaries of landscape (called *tiṇai mayakkam*) suggest that the ancient Tamil poets were not only well aware of this ouroboric character of the poetry they created but actively sought to push the boundaries of what constituted a poem. The *Collection of Five Hundred Poems* may well be the terminal point of these experiments, with its embrace of the improvisational possibilities presented by a bounded landscape and a bounded poem, and the "Ten on the Wild Boar" the pinnacle of that achievement.

Three Poems about Love's Inner Modes

These three standalone Tamil Sangam poems are taken from the following classical anthologies: *The Short Collection* (Kuṟuntokai), *Excellent Landscapes* (Naṟṟiṇai), and *Four Hundred in the Inner Mode* (Akanāṉūṟu). The first manages to evoke in a few lines the all-too familiar feeling that at least one of the lovers is never in the right place at the right time. In the second, we have a somewhat surprising farewell scene: the man is on the verge of leaving his beloved behind as he sets off in order to seek his fortune. Things don't quite work out as he had planned. The last poem, a longer statement like others in *Four Hundred in the Inner Mode*, brings the man's not-so-secret lover, a courtesan, into contact with his wife (once his true love, before marriage). The presence of a child generates an unexpected solidarity between the two rival women.

A POEM BY PARANAR FROM *THE SHORT SELECTION*
(KUṞUNTOKAI 128)

You're like a wingless old heron on the waves of the eastern sea
trying to fish for minnows on the shores
of the western sea, near Tondi, where the Chera king
drives his fine chariot. All you can think about,
my heart, is that distant woman, utterly
beyond reach. You're in pain, or rather:
pain is who you are.

A POEM BY EYINANTAIMAKAN ILANKIRANAR FROM *EXCELLENT LANDSCAPES* (NAṞṞIṆAI 308)

She heard the bustle of leaving.
Cold tears came to her eyes, dark with mascara,
like dew on flowers. When I called her, she came,

shyly, reluctant, very slowly. She didn't ask me
anything, or try to stop me, but like a finely painted doll smudged,
coming unstuck, her fragrant hair glistening,
she was shaken, lost in thought, and then she sank
onto my chest, and my heart, still thinking about money,
saw it and, like an unbaked clay pot drenched by rain,[1]
took her in and was happy.

A POEM BY CHAKALASANAR FROM *FOUR HUNDRED IN THE INNER MODE*
(AKANĀNŪRU 16)

Perfect hands
like petals enfolding
pollen-soaked filaments of lotus in the ancient otter pond,

mouth red as coral that
murmurs sweet wordless words
that make you smile,

gold bracelets that everyone envies . . .

It was just our son
driving his toy chariot in the street,
alone. She saw him and,
teeth flashing, thinking no one
was watching, drew near,
took him between her young breasts heavy
with gold. "Come, my life," she said,
very happy. She'd noticed
the resemblance.

I saw her standing there. I did not
move away. "Why so confused,
young lady?" I said. "You, too,
are this one's mother." Quickly
I came and embraced her.
Like lovers taken by surprise, she looked down,
scraped the ground with her toe,
ashamed. That is how I saw her—and,
husband,
even I could have loved her then, you know?
She's like the distant goddess in the sky,
perhaps rightly compared
to your son's mother.

BETWEEN US: READING TAMIL *AKAM* POEMS

Jennifer Clare (Near Reader)

When we read these beautiful translations of a few early Tamil poems, we are confronted with the most fundamental questions shaping what it means to be a sensitive reader of these traditions. On the one hand, Shulman's wielding of language, from vocabulary to syntax to rhythm, has produced poems that seize us with their exquisite beauty, love poems of the highest order. On the other hand, references throughout the poems, as well as their placement in this volume, remind us that these verses draw on conventions unfamiliar to most of us. As poems deeply embedded in a distant time and place, any interpretation that ignores these conventions seems deprived and wanting. Furthermore, these poems are of course translations from Tamil to English, with the full sense of loss and absence present in that word. How do we sensitively read poetry that speaks to us so intimately and also suggests such impenetrable distance? What is our relationship to these verses and the traditions—ancient, modern, Tamil, English, among many others—that inform them? There is, of course, no one answer to these questions, but the Tamil poems themselves offer models for thinking about our relationship to these verses in terms of the paradox inherent in relationship more generally, and the displacement that haunts all experiences of emotional connection. The models of relationship at work in the Tamil poems enrich and enliven our understanding of not only these individual verses, but also the experience—joyful, maddening, transformative—of deeply reading them.

At first glance, these poems seem to be about a very different kind of relationship than the one between a reader and a text. These are love poems, identified as interior (*akam*) by the Tamil poetic tradition, in which a fixed set of characters react to and comment on a series of highly codified stages of romantic love between an anonymous hero and heroine. The resulting vignettes, expressed in direct speech to an imagined addressee, share concerns with love poetry throughout South Asia and beyond: the joys and sufferings that come with navigating the emotional terrain of premarital and marital love.

Paranar's poem from *The Short Selection* (Kuṟuntokai 128) centers on one common conventional scenario: the hero berates his heart for yearning for a distant woman. Here, as in all *akam* poems, human relationship is the subject of the short verse. What primarily strikes the reader of this poem, however, is not the description of the relationship itself, but the way in which relationship structures the choice of literary figures for expressing this scenario. Specifically, in this poem, the relationship becomes visible through the figures of simile and identification. In the simile, the hero's heart is likened to a grounded old heron, looking for prey in the wrong place. Lost, flightless, pathetic—the specificity of the image of this feeble being draws us into a vivid, imagined landscape that generates a variety of complementary and contradictory feelings ranging from compassion to disgust to humor. On its own, this opening image creates a complex emotional palette that colors the questions that quickly follow: How did the bird become so lost? What is the Chera king doing here? These questions stay with us, evocative and open ended.

As the first part of an extended simile, this image of the frail and aged heron does not stand alone; it has an intimate connection to the second part of the poem, in which the hero berates his heart for dwelling on his distant beloved. By the end of the poem, the two—heron and heart—are entwined in our minds; one can no longer think of one without the other.

What is before us is a figure of identification, not just a simile, and the intensity of the identification denies the individual characteristics of heron and heart. Our interpretive work is to understand how this identification happens, and ultimately, to answer the question: how is the heart no different from the heron? However, like similes do, the literary figure of identification makes for an excess that it cannot erase; heart and heron may be the same, but they are also distinct, inevitably separate. The tension inherent in the figures of simile and identification—what is the same? what is different?—introduces an ambiguity in how we understand the relationship between heron and heart that is central to our reading of this poem.

This may all seem like much ado about literary figuration, but in fact the tension that structures these figures—between sameness and difference, union and separation—enacts the tension at the heart of the relationship depicted by the poem, that is, between the hero and his beloved. The experience of union leaves our hero intimately entwined with his lover, his heart and body no longer distinct from hers. At the same time, this union is haunted by the separation inherent in any relationship—how can we ever completely abandon the self (body, mind, heart) that distinguishes us from others? The literary figures of simile and identification are apt choices to express the paradox of relationship at the heart of this type of poetry.

So far the use of literary figures in the Tamil poems resonates with the use of simile and identification in love poetry throughout the world, especially in poems that describe love in separation. When we look at the *akam* poems in the context of their poetic tradition, we deepen our understanding and appreciation of how relationship functions in these poems. The form of Tamil poems of the interior is shaped by the conventions of a signifying system that ties the emotional worlds of the protagonists—the "interior landscapes"—to the exterior landscapes of South India. These systematic conventions are so strong that the mere mention of natural components (such as plants and animals—in our case, the heron) or cultural aspects (such as music or artisanal professions) associated with each exterior landscape is enough to bring into play an entire interior world. Moreover, through these conventions, every individual poem is simultaneously infused with the similar experiences found in other poems of the *akam* corpus.

This is certainly the case with Paranar's poem. Per the conventions, the exterior landscape of the seascape in which this poem is set is a signal that the second part of the poem explores an interior landscape of anxious waiting. The landscape of anxious waiting includes the emotions associated with the hero's leaving the heroine before marriage to pursue his education or his career, but with the intent to return as a more eligible husband. It is a scenario that the readers of Tamil *akam* poetry would have encountered many times before.

In this poem, however, the central image of this exterior landscape is not a crab or crocodile, creatures typical of the seashore by convention, but a heron, conventionally associated with the exterior landscape of the delta, that is linked, equally by convention, with the interior landscape of marital infidelity and constant jealousy. How are we to understand this apparent breach of convention? Is our hero an ambitious young man suffering to better himself for his beloved, or is he a regretful old cheat? Tamil commentators on this poem took this ambiguity as a problem to redress and provided two contradictory readings that depend on committing the poem to one external and interior landscape or the other.

However, committing to one reading or the other misses the richness of the ambiguity produced by this mixing of conventions. We can read the contradictory readings as explicitly informing each other; after all, the lovesick young man may one day be the cheating husband, and the exiled two-timer may experience anxious waiting as he waits for his wife to let him return. We can also read the break with conventions as a reminder that these poems are both deeply connected to the conventional system and independent of it. On the one hand, the poem's deep connections with other poems in the tradition generates an intertextual web of signification from which an individual verse cannot be extricated. At the same time the verse stands as a distinct utterance, both in its unique wielding of literary linguistic conventions, and in its living history, whether sung at a royal court, used as examples for medieval grammars, or included here in a volume of South Asian literature in modern English translation.

Again the poems offer a model for thinking about this paradox, in which the verse and the tradition are simultaneously inseparable and distinct. As a poem about a young hero and/or a cheating husband, Paranar's is a poem about displacement, that liminal state that suggests the participant's belonging to something, as well as his or her exile from that state. Displacement infuses the image that begins Paranar's poem. While the poem doesn't reveal the reasons for the lost heron's displacement from delta to seashore, the contrast between its location on the east and the fish on the west suggests its frustration and inability. The heron's pathos in exile is juxtaposed with a brief description of the Chera king, whose movement, in contrast to the heron's, suggests purpose and ability. This dense, highly evocative image quickly becomes an analogy for the displacement in the second part of the poem: that of the hero's heart. Like the heron, the hero's heart searches for something beyond reach. Like the heron, the hero's heart is stuck in a limbo of exile, separated both from the beloved as well as from the hero himself, whose second-person admonishment of his heart further alienates it in a double exile.

Displacement, at once transformative and revelatory, is central to the logic of the corpus to which this poem belongs. For the protagonists of these poems, the experiences of love they navigate are closely bound up with separation from each other. The reasons for this separation vary from the hero's leaving the heroine to accumulate wealth, or to serve a king, to his spending time at the homes of beautiful courtesans. Many times, the reason for the separation remains unexpressed in the poem, but nonetheless it provides the contours for the complex emotions experienced by all the characters affected by the love dramas. As such, these characters themselves exist, like the heron and the heart of Paranar's poem, in a perpetual state of in-between, in which they are neither wholly united with their loved ones, nor wholly absent, as their inner worlds are consumed by the yearning, frustration, and occasional hope that are part and parcel of the experience of separation.

Just as the lovers exist in a liminal state between union and separation, the poems also mediate between two worlds: that of the interior lives of the protagonists, in whose voices the poems are set, and the exterior landscape of the seashore. The relationship between the interior and exterior landscape is both iconic—the exterior landscape occasionally, but not always, provides the location for the love scenes—and symbolic, providing a language for exploring the complexity of human emotion. Regardless of how strictly we apply the symbolic vocabulary, we as readers nonetheless find ourselves suspended between two landscapes—exterior and interior—that are, like the separated protagonists of the poem, simultaneously interdependent and distinct, simultaneously particular and generic.

Returning to the identification of the heron and the heart, we encounter another profound dislocation. As parts of a simile, hero and heart are neither discretely intact, nor wholly consumed by the figurative union. As sensitive readers of the simile, we too are always in between. The resulting interpretive ambiguity can never be resolved or erased; rather, it is in acknowledging the disorientation of displacement, at the level of character, landscape, or figure of speech, that we understand the nature of relationship as expressed by the *akam* poems.

If Paranar's poem enacts relationship through the use of simile and the poetics of the interior landscape, the second poem, by Eyinantaimakan Ilankiranar, gives us a rich narrative of the transformations that come to be in displacement. The poem begins with "the bustle of leaving," that threshold moment of departure in between presence and separation. The next few lines depict the heroine's physical response to this moment. The changes brought about to her body and mind are both transformative and revelatory: she is changed by her knowledge of the new emotional landscape she has already begun to inhabit, but the bleakness of this landscape (identified as wasteland by the tradition) is offset by the luminosity of her love that this moment reveals. She becomes "smudged," "unstuck," "shaken," as the lines around her blur and who she is becomes unrecognizable. Similarly, the hero, whose heart was "still thinking of money" is transformed by the power of this love, and becomes undone, melting "like an unbaked clay pot drenched in rain," a state that allows him to take her in and be happy.

This is the powerful beauty of the liminal state of relationship expressed by the *akam* poems. We as readers, like the lovers, feel the intensity of this moment precisely because of the imminent separation: the undoing of the hero's heart that is the source of such poignant joy in this poem will condemn him to an even more awful exile. This experience is not narrated here but, as we know from the hero of Paranar's poem, it will be one of great pain. It will be a pain haunted by the fact that this suffering is proof of the hero's capacity for great love, for the kind of love that unmoors a heart from itself and leaves it forever transformed. And we too, as sensitive readers, might feel the intensity of this moment, like the lovers, for the lovers, finding our own hearts unmoored and even forever transformed.

The final poem by Chakalasanar presents us with yet another model for how the complexity of human relationship helps us think about sensitive reading. The central theme here is deceit: a wife confronts her two-timing husband about the woman with whom he has been cheating. This is no simple spousal scolding or sulking, but a display of deceit's power to twist, transform, reveal, and even create. But I'm getting ahead of myself for readers new to the poem, who may not recognize the scope of deception on first reading. The poem begins, after all, with a charming portrait of an intimate encounter between a young boy playing in the street and an unidentified woman, who recognizes something in the boy that compels her to embrace him. Unbeknownst to her, this private moment is witnessed by the boy's mother, who interrupts the couple, alleviating any possible embarrassment by assuring the lovely young stranger that both women have a right to the boy's love.

All seems well between the two women, if a bit awkward, united in their love for a healthy little boy. But the poem then shifts to reveal the deceit that underlies the entire verse. What appears to be a woman's story about an exhibition of maternal warmth by a lovely stranger turns out to be a revelation of her husband's adultery, as the boy's mother informs her husband, by means of the story of her encounter with the lovely interloper, that she now knows all about his lover. As her speech comes to an end, we realize, along with the faithless husband, that we too have been subjected to a sleight of hand, in which what appeared simple and innocent is in fact full of deceptions.

In fact, deception has structured the entire poem, beginning with the ambiguity of the opening description. Metaphors that appear to describe the beauty of a woman—her body, her sweet innocence, her jewelry objects of envy—in fact refer to a child, whose role in the poem is not yet clear. A strange woman clutches to her breast a boy who is not her own, because he reminds her of another man and his chariot who is no longer there. The boy's mother embraces the female stranger and comforts this woman who has stolen her husband, both in silent acknowledgment of the deception that binds them together. Once we become aware of the deception that underlies the verse, these interactions demand a different reading.

Throughout the poem, the verse harnesses deception to reveal and explore truths of human relationship. These truths include, of course, the awareness of the affair, but they are more than that. Deception reveals the singular status of wife and mother, singular both in her incomparability and in her loneliness. Deception allows for a complex and unexpected intimacy between two women who love someone whose heart and body does not belong to them. Deception allows for the wife to play with her husband's feelings, evoking the beauty and sweet character of his lover while simultaneously contrasting the shame and barrenness that accompany the "other woman" with the goddess at home that he has neglected. Deception establishes the truths of their fractured marriage, but also reveals the potential for closeness between them as parents who share a beautiful child.

Of the three selected poems, this one requires the most careful attention, especially for readers unfamiliar with the tradition. Without sensitive reading, we might be deceived by the innocence of the interaction on the street, or, more likely, confused about the relationship between the characters. However, this disorientation is not particular to this poem or to this subject matter. Sensitive reading requires that we acknowledge the deception that lies between us and all language. Surely, context helps, just as our understanding of this poem becomes deeper once we situate the characters and subject matter. As in the earlier verses, the poetics of interior landscape provide interpretive guideposts in this poem. The reference to the lotus growing in the otter pond, for instance, situates this poem in the emotional world of married life, and thus helps identify the characters within that world. Even after identifying guideposts, however, we are never sure of where we stand, and it is in this ambiguity, this contradiction, this inability to be paraphrased, that truth lies.

THE UNBAKED CLAY POT IN POURING RAIN: READING SANGAM POETRY TODAY

R. Cheran (Far Reader)

> *In Canada,*
> *There is a body of water unknown to Tamils.*
> *It is called:*
> *Red earth and pouring rain.*
> R. CHERAN, *THINAI MAYAKKAM*

A few days after I finished writing the one hundredth poem for my new collection in Tamil, quoted in the epigraph, I received this selection of a few translated Sangam poems from the editors of this volume.[2] I was still rereading some of my new poems at the time and wondering whether a few minor changes, such as reordering individual poems or adding spaces between stanzas, were warranted. Then I began reading David Shulman's translations. His selections included shorter poems in the *akam* or inner mode from *The Short Collection* (Kuṟuntokai), *Excellent Landscapes* (Naṟṟiṇai), and *Four Hundred in the Inner Mode* (Akanāṉūṟu) collections, as well as an entire decad from the *Collection of Five Hundred Poems* (Aiṅkuṟuṉūṟu), Kapilar's "Ten on the Wild Boar," which was, as Shulman says in his note, "meant to be read as a unit, the individual variations adding up to a powerful whole."

It was a sweet surprise for me that Shulman included both Kapilar and Paranar in his selection. These are two of the greatest and perhaps most famous Sangam poets, and I adore both of them. As I read these poems again in Tamil and in Shulman's English translation together with my new poems, I was struck by the magical continuity of metaphors, metonymy, and the modes of poetic contemplation in Tamil literature across millennia. This perhaps is in contrast to a tendency in contemporary Tamil poetry to eschew the gentle musicality and metaphors of older poetry. This current tendency, as I have noted elsewhere, often prefers to rely on everyday speech, prosaic discourse, and events that can even be characterized as "anti-poetry," as inspired by Nicanor Parra.[3] However, in contemporary Tamil poetry the structures and tone of the Sangam poems still appear occasionally. Whether it is ingrained or intentional is a different question altogether.

I am one of the thousands of witnesses and victims of the genocidal war in Sri Lanka, which ended on May 19, 2009. It may not be an exaggeration to note that after the Sangam period, this was the first time Tamils were engaged in a large-scale war that lasted for thirty years. The Liberation Tigers of Tamil Eelam (LTTE), widely known as the Tigers, were at the forefront of the war on the Tamil side. While fighting for a separate state for Tamils in Sri Lanka, the Tigers also drastically changed contemporary Tamil cultural and historic imagery and rituals to reflect certain Sangam era values and practices. They introduced burial instead of cremation for their war dead. Burial sites became "places where great heroes sleep," and the Sangam practice of erecting memorial stones for the dead warriors was reintroduced. Several songs linking the Sangam and the contemporary periods were composed and sung by popular Tamil Nadu artists, and these circulated widely. Prabhakaran, the leader of the LTTE, was hailed as a "Warrior King" in poetry and songs. In one popular song celebrating the birth of Prabhakaran, the poet says:

> Sing, the dawn has bloomed;
> Dance, the Sangam era has arrived.[4]

Inspired by Shulman's translations, what I intend to do in this essay is to reflect on Sangam poems and modern Tamil poems that speak of war. This will not be an exhaustive survey of war and poetry in either period. Rather, I will attempt to relate my own poetic self and poetics to some examples of classical and modern war poetry in Tamil.

Among the numerous powerful and evocative images from Sangam poetry, the mingling of "red earth and pouring rain" is well known, and in a sense, stands as an apt symbol for this early Tamil poetry's visceral linkages between nature, landscapes, and love in all its varieties, licit, illicit, stolen, and many others:

> What could my mother be
> to yours? what kin is my father
> to yours anyway? And how
> did you and I meet ever?
> But in love
> our hearts have mingled
> like red earth and pouring rain.[5]

The poet is now named after his famous line. His name means "the one who belongs to the mingled red earth and pouring rain." What he emphasizes in his subtle and poetic way is the possibility and reality of two people falling in love irrespective of or ignoring the kind of divisions such as caste, landscape, region, economic status, and so on.

Another poem by poet Kaniyan Pungudranar in *Four Hundred in the Public Mode* (Puṟanāṉūṟu) is equally evocative and is also widely quoted. Amid this century of "public" (puṟam) poems that extoll battlefields, bravery, and valor, this poem stands alone: it is a calmly eloquent verse that says, "Every town our hometown, / every man a kinsman."[6] This line and the poem itself have often been cited as an expression of Tamil cosmopolitanism and migratory attitude of Tamils in an ancient context, but it became especially vivid during and after the thirty years of civil war in Sri Lanka.

Shulman's translation from *Excellent Landscapes* (308) takes us to another powerful earth and rain metaphor—not in the context of love and union, but to the moment of separation, anguish, and the quintessential dilemma of whether to leave behind a beloved because of circumstances beyond one's control:

> She heard the bustle of leaving.
> Cold tears came to her eyes, dark with mascara,
> like dew on flowers. When I called her, she came,
> shyly, reluctant, very slowly. She didn't ask me
> anything, or try to stop me, but like a finely painted doll
> smudged, coming unstuck, her fragrant hair glistening,
> she was shaken, lost in thought, and then she sank
> onto my chest, and my heart, still thinking about money,
> saw it and, like an unbaked clay pot drenched by rain,
> took her in and was happy.

The unbaked clay pot dissolving in pouring rain is in stark contrast to the previous poem of the mingling of rain and red earth creating a union across divisions. The landscape simultaneously symbolizes both union and separation.

Prompted by reading Shulman's translations, I began rereading other Sangam poems in my own context of exile, war, displacement, and modern Tamil poetry. The decades of war in Sri Lanka have produced a huge corpus of modern Tamil poetry. In my reading, I was looking for instances of communities in exile, of mass displacement due to war, of deep sufferings, and of the consequent individual and collective trauma. Aside from the poem attributed to Pari's daughters, lamenting the loss of their father and their home in the Parampu hills, there are not very many poems about defeated people leaving their land.[7] Burning of enemy villages, destruction of paddy fields, and looting are more commonly depicted as heroic acts befitting powerful kings. For example:

> You march into the alien territories and play havoc on their guarded groves;
> You set vast paddy fields on fire, which are ignorant of losing their uberty.
> By your invasion, fertile plains turn into woods;
> . . . the places where villages flourished
> Are now scenes of great ruin.[8]

In a sense it was not surprising. Tamil kings and chieftains commissioned the compilation of poems into anthologies. The relationship between poets and hero-kings was mostly symbiotic. There are poems providing good counsel to the kings and in a few cases admonishing the kings for their moral failures. In one such instance, a certain Chola king, victorious in his battle against his enemy, imprisons that enemy's children along with others and brings them to his country only to kill them cruelly. In a public place, where hundreds of people have gathered, he buries them alive, leaving only their heads above the ground, and then has elephants trample them under foot. Coming to know about this imminent inhumane action, the poet Kovoor Kilar rushes to the site. Here are his wise words of counsel:

> You come from the line of a Chola king
> who gave his flesh
> for a pigeon in danger,
> and for others besides,
>
> and these children also come
> from a line of kings
> who in their cool shade
> share all they have
>
> lest poets,
> those tillers of nothing
> but wisdom,
> should suffer hardships.

Look at these children,
the crowns of their heads are still soft.

As they watch the elephants
they even forget to cry,

stare dumbstruck at the crowd
in some new terror
of things unknown.

Now that you've heard me out,
do what you will.[9]

It is not surprising to find many poems depicting the horrendous suffering of ordinary people in war and mass displacement. The uneven nature of economic development in various regions and poetic landscapes always exacerbates suffering and loss. My rereading of Sangam poems "from below" pointed above all to certain absences and silences.

I will now return to the poem in the epigraph at the beginning of this essay and to my two new anthologies that are all largely centered on sea, rivers, and lakes, and focus on exile, mass displacement, genocide, and trauma. The first anthology is entitled *Tiṇai mayakkam allatu neñcōṭu kiḷartal* ("Blurred Tiṇais or excited and extended conversations with the heart"). The one hundred short poems included in this collection are close to Sangam poems in tone and style. They are partly autobiographical, partly historical, and partly metaphors in search of a moral compass that lies outside the traditions of faith and religion and can be adequate to the context of war and the context subsequent to war.

My second anthology, *Añar*, consists of several elegies for my friends who disappeared or were killed in the war, and fellow poets and writers who passed away or committed suicide in the years that followed.[10] After more than thirty years of writing war poetry, the elegies collected in this anthology now seem to me to be some of my best. The word *añar* in Tamil connotes irreparable grief, continuous grief, mental wounds, as well as individual and collective trauma. There are several references in Sangam poetry describing *añar*.

Those poems are also deeply embedded in the violence that spanned the past forty years in Sri Lanka, during both the war and its aftermath. The landscapes and mindscapes were scarred, tortured, and mutilated. They have literally become "minescapes"—lands littered with thousands of land mines and unexploded ordinances (UEOs).

The confusion and intermingling of the classical Sangam landscapes (*tiṇai*) in the context of war, displacement, and separation of people and families, eternal waiting, and searching for people who have disappeared have all added extra dimensions to Tamil poetry composed after the Sangam period. One such addition, as I have noted in an essay on theorizing Tamil diasporicity, is a possibility of conceptualizing exile, mass displacement, and asylum as a new land/mindscape (*tiṇai*).[11] The experiences and trauma of forced migration, Tamil diasporic life with its complexities of multiple belongings and deterritorialized landscapes and mindscapes have been a painful yet powerful source for a new Tamil literature. It is possible to conceptualize this as a new *tiṇai*.

The concepts of landscape (*tiṇai*) and theme (*turai*) in classical Tamil poetry are an important part of our intellectual and literary tradition. They are unique in their creative blending of cultural, economic, ecological, musical, emotional, and poetic attributes. *Tiṇai* can be used simultaneously as a taxonomical tool for literary criticism and to encapsulate a Tamil eco-poetics of the human-nature relationship while equally expanding our understanding of Tamil-ness and Tamil identities and their relations to landscapes, spaces, and memory. As several Tamil poets in the diaspora have articulated, there is now a transnational Tamil poetics at work. This poetics and its social, political, and cultural contexts become crucial in rearticulating Tamil identity. Memory and memorialization, heritage and politics, simultaneously belonging to more than one nation and history are currently the major preoccupations of Tamil transnationalism. As Amrit Lal says, in the title of his review of the book *In Our Translated World*, "Today's Sangam explores grief, trauma, and exile."[12] However, Tamil transnationalism is not free from its old nationalist moorings. The continuation of casteism among some sections of the second and third generation Tamils is another aspect that cannot be missed. A good example comes from many online postings of young Tamils in Germany and Switzerland. They are using a white dot in their Instagram postings to indicate that they are Vellala Tamils. They are proud of their heritage, and as one of the parents said, "we tell them all about our heritage, and they can choose what aspects of our tradition and culture they prefer to maintain and articulate."[13]

The Sangam metaphor of red earth and pouring rain has immortalized love above all human divisions. This is perhaps the best that Tamil has contributed to human civilization. The unbaked clay pot dissolves and creates a messy, muddy body of water. In Canada, as the poem I quoted in the beginning testifies, red earth and pouring rain is the only body of water that no Tamils, Tamil-Canadians, or Canadian Tamils would go to.

How a new *tiṇai* in the diaspora shapes and captures the nuances of transnational Tamil identities, poetics, and politics is a very pertinent question. But that is for another occasion.

Who Am I When I'm Reading You?

EDITORS' NOTE

IN THIS FINAL UNIT, we return to materials similar to the devotional music of unit 3: songs people have sung out of love to their God (here just the lyrics, though these were no doubt also performed). There are such poems in many parts of the world and in different languages and historical periods. Indeed, the first selection here is a Tamil work from south India, written by Nammalvar in the first millennium CE; the second, a *ghazal* by Hafez, was written in fourteenth-century Iran (from whence it reached India, like *The Story of the Four Dervishes* in unit 2); and the third is in Urdu, and was composed in north India during the nineteenth century, when that region was already under colonial rule. One thing common to all three works, however, is their intentional mixture of genres, topoi, and identities. Is the addressee a beloved or God? Is the speaker a heartbroken lover or a pious servant? Is the wine in the *ghazal* ever just wine, and the basil in Nammalvar's poems only basil? And finally, who are the "I" and "you" in these works, and to what extent they are really different? As Rajeev Kinra notes in his reading of Hafez, and as is true to all the works in this unit, "much of the pleasure . . . derives from this intentional hyper-ambiguity . . . that the 'meaning' of the couplet remains suspended in a state of play—always a both/and rather than an either/or."

Nammalvar's Tamil *A Hundred Measures of Time*

TRANSLATOR'S NOTE AND TEXT

The hundred verses of *A Hundred Measures of Time* (as Archana Venkatesan has named the *Tiruviruttam*) adumbrate the medieval genre of *kovai*—literally, a chain or necklace—in which poems ostensibly suited to the old interior (*akam*) grammar of love and its landscapes, including the progression from the moment of falling in love in the mountains to the inevitably dissonant marriage of the couple in the plains, actually celebrate a deity mentioned obliquely in each verse. In *A Hundred Measures of Time*, these two heroes—the lover of the *akam* tradition and Lord Vishnu, here called Kannan (Tamil for Krishna), with the entire repertoire of his divine exploits—are largely merged. The landscape is that of Venkatam mountain (Tirupati), thus suited to the phase of stolen premarital union in the *akam* grammar; but most of the poems are suffused with the sorrow of longing and absence. In terms of style, metrics, and language, *A Hundred Measures of Time* comprise a new departure for classical Tamil. Nammalvar, probably an eighth-century poet from the far south of the Tamil country, is the central figure among the series of twelve Alvars—poet-devotees who created the canon of Tamil Vishnu bhakti. Here I offer the six opening verses of Nammalvar's poem, as well as verse 11.

A HUNDRED MEASURES OF TIME BY NAMMALVAR (VERSES 1–6, 11)

> Knowledge that is a lie,
> bad living,
> foul body—
>
> to give us breath
> so we won't have to suffer all this
> you've been born
> in this womb and that.

Lord of the gods,
hold fast to your body,
listen, now,
to your servant's prayer. (1)

Like fish flashing in a deep pool,
her eyes, streaked with red,
well up with dizzy tears.

Blessings on her and her dark curls
that weave a garland of love
for two feet the ancient
gods revere: his, Kannan's,
black as a cloud bursting
with rain. (2)

It has followed after the great bird
aflame with anger
that he rides, as the gods bow low,
that lord of cool sweet basil
and a fiery discus,

but now, when my lonely heart
sees the gentle girl of the cowherds[1]
with their bamboo flutes,
and Earth, and Splendor,
these goddesses who follow him
as a shadow,

it might just stop and stay with them.
Then again
it might come home
to me. (3)

My lonely heart was lost
once before—to *his*
great bird.

Soon this heart will be lost again
to his cool and fragrant basil.

We, in any case,
are without it.

As for you, frigid wind
poisoned with basil from his crown

after he savored the nipples
of the false and angry demoness,

is it natural that you steal inside
to freeze our very breath? (4)

The freezing north wind that makes us shiver
has put aside its frigid nature
and now, here,
rages with fire,

as this wide-eyed girl
in her sorrow
weeps cold tears, cold
as sweet basil.

For the sake of her black beauty,
the brilliant scepter in the hands
of the lord dark as freezing rain
today
has twisted and bent. (5)

Sinuous vine bearing darts
deadlier than arrows and bent bows,
she is Death, lurking in ambush
to strike down with love

this slayer of demons as he comes riding
his swift bird.

And you: look at her, look
to your own lives
inside this world. (6)

Rare is that vision,
Oh you who are radiant
as the heaven of Kannan, yet
he has gone away, gone many miles
in search of wealth,
or so it seems, though the whole world
was there in your eyes, wide as fish,
as the palm of a hand,
dripping tears rare as pearl,
fugitive as gold. (11)

"YOU CAME SO THAT WE MAY LIVE"

Anand Venkatkrishnan (Near Reader)

The subject of this chapter is seven stanzas David Shulman has translated from *A Hundred Measures of Time*, a collection of one hundred poems by the Tamil Vaishnava poet Nammalvar. My task is not to provide the full context of Nammalvar's poem, but instead to read Shulman's Nammalvar: first his saint-poet (Alvar), and then only ours. Of course, one does not simply read Nammalvar. One hears, absorbs, drowns. To hear the Alvar's poems is to be suffused with a sense of God's simultaneous presence and absence; he is here, in the innermost heart, and yet hidden. The only way to recapture him is to sing together, in a community of lovers. Shulman's translation offers a version of this community, now one of readers. At the same time, it succeeds in disorienting the reader, leaving open the puzzles in Nammalvar's own jagged, searching poems. By revealing that wonder, that strangeness, Shulman's translation urges us to find our own Alvar.

In the first line of the first stanza, Nammalvar's opening words can also be translated as "false knowledge." Instead of the adjective "false," Shulman places the noun "knowledge" in apposition with the word "lie," a more literal translation of the Tamil substantive. Why has he made this choice? Everyday life in a physical body involves learning, from birth onward, but the lessons are a lie: that loved ones will not be lost, that suffering will not touch us, that we will never die. For the fragile, foul body only makes for bad living. The Lord, however, takes on precisely such bodies, incarnating again and again, to give us the breath of life. So, in Shulman's rendering, we pray: come, keep your body, so that we may truly live.

Singing the body of God is not exclusively Nammalvar's concern. Shulman, too, has given much attention to the process. In his studies of the eighteenth-century South Indian musician Muthuswami Dikshitar, Shulman explores the techniques of "auralization" in Dikshitar's compositions. As an initiate of the Srividya ritual and cosmological tradition, which reconstructed the body of the goddess through complex syllabic utterances, Muttuswami Dikshitar attempted to turn incantation into notation, the phonic into the symphonic. In other words, he made music the method by which the goddess could be invoked. Be it Dikshitar's goddess Abhayamba, invoked in the interstices of language and melody, or Nammalvar's Vishnu, visualized by a community of extravagant beholders, Shulman translates their manifestation for us into his own rhythmic writing.

This first stanza also captures the classic Alvar tension of embodied life: as devotees, their experience of Vishnu supersedes all, but as human beings they cannot escape their own mortality. What Nammalvar does in this stanza, as Shulman reads it, is to praise God for refusing to let humans suffer alone. He encourages God to keep at it: take this, our body, in memory of us. You've done it in the past, in the stories we tell about you, why not now? Shulman's subtle switch to the imperative mood toward the end ("hold fast to your body"), before the prayer itself ("listen"), brings out the implicit content of that prayer.

The next six stanzas rush breathlessly through a startling tableau of love: visible, elusive, throbbing, severe. In his brief introduction, Shulman remarks that the two lovers of the classical Tamil love poem merge here. In places one can detect a third voice, not fully omniscient, a shadow over our lovers, like Vishnu's consorts in the third stanza. The heart, too, is its own subject, not completely belonging to the speaker who claims it. This instability of the self, the porous boundary between self and other, is another of Shulman's classic preoccupations. Here, as in many of his translations, he exemplifies that ambiguity.

Stanzas two and three oscillate between a detached, sympathetic observer, and a more emotional, jealous one. Both are witnesses to women's love for the dark one, Kannan; one blesses it, the other curses it. Perhaps, in the second stanza, we are being introduced to the speaker in the third: the woman whose eyes "well up with dizzy tears." In the third she addresses her lonely heart, but in Shulman's version she is not sure if it belongs to her anymore. What will the heart, this thing outside of me, do now? It has already chased after one who is alternately cool and hot and has to watch while he makes love to his goddess girlfriends, stuck to him like a shadow. Will it join them, or will it come back? And who am I, now, to whom it would return?

In keeping with the poem's formal constraints, Shulman begins the next stanza with the compound word that ends the previous, that "lonely heart." It's done this before, the speaker says, running behind Vishnu's great bird Garuda. The slightest whiff of his basil, and I won't have a heart left to be stolen. Shulman deftly redeploys this verb of thieving as the forlorn speaker addresses the cool breeze: as for you (in Tamil, the accusation is direct and sharp), you "steal inside" and freeze our breath with the poisonous fragrance you carry. The fragrance is poisonous, of course, for two reasons: first, it wafts from the head of Krishna as he sucks the poison from the demoness Putana's breasts; second, it embitters and mocks an already empty heart.

In the fifth stanza, the tempest of love's emotions is once again reflected in the elements, as they not only shuttle rapidly between extreme heat and extreme frigidity, but exchange properties as well. The motif of contradictory properties is an old one in South Asian art. In Kalidasa's *Recognition of Shakuntala* (3.11), the infatuated king Dushyanta lashes out at both the god of love and the moon, for their supposedly soothing qualities:

That your arrows should be flowers,
and the moon have cooling rays:
both are patently false for those
in my sort of condition.

The moon ejects fire
with every icy beam,
and as for you, your flower power
becomes a thunderbolt!

The motif is long-lasting, too; a famous song from the Hindi film *Manzil* (1979) begins: "The monsoon rain pours down / kindling a flame in the heart. / In this season, so drenched with rain / how can such a fire blaze?" To return to the fifth stanza, the north wind from the previous stanza discards its coolness and "rages with fire." At the same time, the lonely woman "weeps cold tears." While tears of love are generally hot, in the poem her tears match the complexion of the lord, "dark as freezing rain." This is not an accidental connection; South Asian poetry frequently maps the body onto the world and vice versa. In the poems of the sixteenth-century Braj poet Surdas, for example, the tears of the forlorn Radha, as she mourns the absence of her lover Krishna, generate a landscape all their own. Radha's tears are intended to melt Krishna's hard heart. In Nammalvar's verse, however, it is not his heart, but his scepter that has "twisted and bent." The dark, unsettling imagery here is carried into what is undoubtedly the most striking of Shulman's translations, in stanza 6.

Undaunted in her efforts to win back her capricious beloved, the unnamed woman is now called "Death," wielding the scepter not of final judgment, but of the god of love. She is a "sinuous vine," more dangerous than scattered arrows and broken bows. Her elasticity allows her to coil up and whip out, as she lies in wait for a different killer, the slayer of demons. Suddenly, we are the ones being addressed: "Look at her," says the chorus-like observer, and "look to your own lives inside this world." The shift in modality jolts the listener. We have until now been voyeurs of a fairly common vignette in the context of Tamil love poetry: a lonely heart pines for a majestic beloved, teasing, heroic, beautiful. Her longing, like Radha's tears, is mapped onto certain key words and spaces. Shulman has already called attention to the hills as the landscape of premarital love. However, the emotional storm that has been building since the second bursts into a violent conclusion in the sixth, signaled immediately by Shulman's brilliant use of the word "sinuous" and its sinister sense. It is a shocking scene, the woman no longer pining alone but "lurking in ambush," ready "to strike down with love" the object of her affection. And as we survey the grisly portrait, the speaker sidles up behind us, whispering "And you," expertly marked off by Shulman in a separate stanza. You may think this is about someone else, but watch out: God has a way of pulling you out of yourself.

There is plenty to say about the style, metrics, and language of the *Hundred Measures of Time* that marks a departure for classical Tamil. I confine myself to the arresting content of these stanzas in Shulman's rendering. No longer are we suffused with the anticipation and excitement of union. No longer is the affair innocent, playful, optimistic. Love is deadly, eerie, disorienting. So disorienting, in fact, that by stanza 7, in Shulman's translation, we see language itself disassembling, self-destructing. Initially the subject is a rare vision—of whom?—addressed to a radiant unknown. There is an abrupt shift to Kannan, the Tamil name for Krishna, traveling in search of wealth. Just as quickly, the poem returns to the unknown addressee. The last few lines zoom into the speaker's wide-open eyes, dripping priceless jewels. Through the mist of tears we might discern the following scene: a woman wonders why Krishna, like some everyday merchant, would go anywhere else to find what is right in front of him, "though the whole world," in Shulman's moving translation, "was there in your eyes." These are tears not of longing but of desperation. If he will not stay put even when we are together, then what is the point of love?

Nammalvar's poems, Shulman says, are meant to take our breath away. This breath is precious, precarious, dependent. God breathes into us, and love pumps the bellows. Being a person the Tamil way, as it appears in these poems, is to live in love. This is a frightening prospect, but the reward is unsurpassed. Whether or not we can experience Nammalvar's breathlessness, thanks to this translation, we can follow him some way into the depths.

TAKING THE MEASURE OF *A HUNDRED MEASURES*

Andrew Ollett (Far Reader)

I admit to being at a complete loss when I first tried to respond to these verses from *A Hundred Measures of Time*. It was not just that they come from a world with which I am quite unacquainted, or that they appeared to deal with topics from which I have, for a long time, kept my distance. It was the feeling that whenever an image, conceit, or narrative began to emerge, it immediately slipped away, "like fish flashing in a deep pool." Was it really the case that texts like this stood silent and unyielding before any reader who was not initiated into the protocols of reading in the tradition to which it belonged? I decided to try reading it as if it were a Sanskrit text—which meant only that I would ask of it the kinds of questions that I had learned to ask from scholars and critics of Sanskrit literature, from Abhinavagupta to Shulman. It is incidental that the target poem, and the interpretive techniques, are both connected to South Asia: it is not as if, by asking these kinds of questions, I had somehow bridged the distance "between the text and the present."[2] It is simply that I thought the techniques were powerful enough to address any text, and the text was capable of speaking back in any language in which it was thoughtfully addressed. What surprised me, although it should not surprise anyone who has read David Shulman's work, was this: upon exchanging myself, as a reader, for a cantankerous Sanskrit scholar of my own creation, Nammalvar suddenly opened up to me, as if to scoldingly remind me that the person reading his poem was not prior to imagination but constituted by it.

"Knowledge that is a lie." Can such a thing even exist? If something is a lie, it is not knowledge. Whoever speaks this short phrase must have once considered something to be true knowledge that he or she now considers to be false. And people generally only revise their beliefs in this way on the basis of new information. Thus, this phrase is a "narrative sentence": it hints that the speaker has undergone a profound change in belief as a result of some new circumstance.[3] This first line leads us to read "bad living" and "foul body" in the same way: not just as negative evaluations, but as contradictions, and corrections, of a more positive evaluation of life and embodiment. What the addressee is asked to save us from is "all this"— not just the epistemic, practical, and physical aspects of existence just referred to, but the kinds of painful experiences that have led the speaker to speak of them as being totally devoid of any redeeming qualities. Even before the addressee is identified as "Lord of the gods," we are told of two incredible things about him. First, it is with a certain purpose that he has been "born in this womb and that." The fact that he takes birth with purpose distinguishes him from all other beings, who are "born just to die, and die just to be born again."[4] Second, that purpose is to save us from having to "suffer all this." The fact that he can save beings from the fate to which they are destined distinguishes him not just from all other beings, but all other gods as well. These opening lines thus show that the speaker's chosen deity deserves his title of "Lord of the gods."

We might expect the beginning of a composition to begin with an auspicious word or phrase. And, provided we stop after the word "knowledge," the beginning seems auspicious enough. But why, we might ask, would the speaker begin with three things that no reasonable person would want? The beginning of a poem often announces its theme. Lies, faithlessness, and physical torment—these are indeed thematic in the poem, not in themselves, but as consequences of love for Kannan. And if they necessarily accompany devotion to the "Lord of the gods," then perhaps it is not so inauspicious to begin with them. But it is not only the devotee who experiences these three things. In being born again and again, Kannan experiences them as well. And we have a clue that, among these three things, it is the "foul body" that is actually most important, in the speaker's request for Kannan to "hold fast to your body." It is the only word that is repeated in this first stanza. Embodiment is the condition of suffering, both ours and his, but it is also the condition of love—not the abstract love of the philosophers, but an experience that fills all of the domains of existence with which the poem begins, like blood returning painfully to the limbs after they have been battered numb by a cold and wet wind.

One more observation about the first stanza. What knowledge, specifically, is a lie? The speaker hints that for us, too, what had previously appeared as absolutely secure—the distinction between subject and object, and indeed the stable identity of the subject—will be undermined and eventually annihilated by what follows.

What the speaker had introduced as his "prayer" begins in the second stanza, where the speaker refers to a certain girl as "she" and "her." Those expressions, in general, are only used when their referent has previously been evoked in the discourse.[5] In fact, she has not already been evoked. The speaker either presumes we know who she is already, or is deliberately keeping us in the dark. Well, who is she?

The characters of love poetry are often anonymous—he and she. Perhaps she is "she," the archetypal woman who despairs of her husband's return. There are certain indications the she lives in the world of literary conventions, such as the gathering rainclouds evoked as a standard of comparison at the end of the stanza. The monsoon, which makes travel impossible, will inevitably prolong her separation from her husband. And toward the end of the selection, the speaker comes very close to identifying her husband with him, the archetypal husband who "has gone away, gone many miles in search of wealth." But the speaker disavows this identification immediately after suggesting it by saying "or so it seems." We must find some other world, apart from or in addition to the world of literary conventions, in which the girl and her lover must be located.

Another possibility is that she is simply the poet, who is casting himself as a lovelorn woman in order to depict more sharply the nature of his devotion. But who is the poet anyway? All we can say is: there is a speaker; first-person pronouns are used. The use of "my" and "me" is exactly like that of "her" and "she": their referent ought to have already been evoked, but in fact it is not. Consider the third stanza, in which "my lonely heart" is separated from "me" both textually, through the intervention of several phrases, and narratively, since the final line presupposes that the speaker's heart is *not* within the speaker. If the speaker's heart sees something, does the speaker see it? And those women that the speaker's heart sees as external to itself—Earth, Splendor, "the gentle girl of the cowherds"—isn't it possible that one of these is the speaker, whose heart no longer knows how to recognize her? Identities are withheld, taken apart, made indistinct.

What remains distinct, however, is the way in which one relates to Kannan. We are told that that gods "bow low" to him, and that Earth and Splendor "follow him as a shadow." There is something special about this latter relation. A shadow cannot exist apart from that of which it is the shadow. The goddesses therefore have an existential dependency on Kannan. A shadow is also a fitting comparison because it is just there, independently of any will or desire. This prefigures Kannan's cruel indifference toward those who are devoted to him. But a third aspect of this comparison tends toward a very different conclusion. Gods, it is said, do not cast shadows. The fact that Kannan is said, even in a comparison, to have a shadow suggests the power of devotion to turn the "Lord of the gods" himself, whom we have just seen coursing the sky on the back of his bird, into a corporeal being.

Let us leave the girl with the dark curls in the second stanza for now. The poem itself has shifted from a third-person to a first-person perspective, as if the speaker's heart—disembodied at the beginning of the third stanza—has indeed made its way "home" to the speaker's body. Accordingly the subject shifts from observation to embodied experience. In the third stanza, the "cool sweet basil" and the "fiery discus" appeared more or less as ornamental epithets of Kannan. In the fourth and fifth, they take over the speaker's entire sensorium. From this point, Kannan's basil appears three times. First it stands in for the god himself, who assumes its "cool and fragrant," and thus ostensibly pleasant, qualities. Soon, however, the speaker describes being assaulted by a freezing wind, and hints that the reason for its coldness is that it has been "poisoned" by Kannan's basil. It is not merely that the speaker's evaluation of Kannan's qualities has changed. It is that the god is always described in terms of secondary qualities; that is, those whose character depends on the perceiving subject.[6] Such qualities can be reaffirmed and redetermined on the basis of ongoing experience. And the experience described here is that of the sharp wind of rainy nights in mountain village, the kind that "steal[s] inside," gets inside one's clothes and bones, and makes one's breath as cold as the wind outside. By the time of the basil's third appearance, this time in the standard of a comparison, its coldness has stolen inside completely: for while the freezing wind has been transformed into a raging fire, the tears that the girl now cries are "cold as sweet basil." The speaker thus describes coldness as inhering in three things: first in Kannan's basil, its proper locus, then in the freezing wind, and finally in the girl's tears. This has a cumulative effect, suggesting that a frozen universe is inevitably closing in on the speaker, threatening to dissolve the boundaries of the self.

What underlies these transferences, the dynamic of externalization and internalization? Obviously, it is Kannan's solicitation of "the false and angry demoness." Once again, this phrase is used as if its referent has already been evoked. Perhaps it is well-known that Kannan consorts with a particular demoness. Perhaps this phrase simply designates some other woman, motivated by the speaker's jealousy of Kannan's attentions. Other women, of course, have already been mentioned in connection with Kannan: Earth, Splendor, "the gentle girl of the cowherds." But as we have already observed, the fact that they follow Kannan as a shadow hints at his passivity and indifference to them. Not so with the demoness. Kannan is said to actively "savor [her] nipples." Such an image of infidelity is guaranteed to steal inside and torture anyone who loves him. And it is the freezing wind that carries this image and forms a physical connection between the speaker, shivering in the mountains, with her faithless Kannan.

The jealousy that emerges from these lines, the "cold tears" that the girl weeps—they make sense so long as Kannan and the girl play the conventional roles of lover and beloved, her and him. But isn't he the "Lord of the gods"? Isn't it a mistake for the girl to feel such possessiveness over him? Doesn't the salvation of the world, in some sense, depend on Kannan's promiscuity, his ability to "give breath" to anyone who loves him? The poem has a clear answer here, which is hinted first by the shift from the first-person singular ("my lonely heart") to the first-person plural ("to freeze our very breath") over the course of the fourth stanza. The speaker's singularity, defined first in relation to the aloof Kannan, is deliberately eroded in the process of her being made aware, through the icy wind, of Kannan's presence—with another woman. And we, as readers, are implicated in this process, if only momentarily. For the poem then turns, once again, to the relationship between two individuals. The third-person perspective adopted in the fifth stanza has its customary omniscience: we can see the "wide-eyed girl" weeping, as we can never see ourselves, and we can see "the lord dark as freezing rain," whom the speakers of the previous stanza, suffering separation from Kannan, were not able to see. And hence we can see something else that those speakers could not: the twisting of Kannan's scepter, sure evidence of his betrayal.

"Look at her, look to your own lives inside this world." This statement not only punctures the third-person perspective cultivated in the previous stanza and forces us to see the girl as an externalization of ourselves. It also uses the form "this," indicating a world to which the speaker and the addressee both belong. Does "this world" exclude the world of literary convention, of her and him? Or does it inform us that our world is, in fact, the world we have been speaking of thus far, with icy windstorms that explode into flames? It is, in any case, the world in which we experience what the girl experiences. And what is that experience exactly? The coldness that has been alluded to again and again throughout the poem engenders a certain temporality. Anyone who experiences this kind of cold wants to escape from it, and therefore wishes for time to pass rapidly, while experiencing its passage as excruciatingly slow. This is the characteristic temporality of love-in-separation, a temporality that is nothing other than the theft of the present by the future.

This is the sense in which we should probably read the identification "she is Death": for death, too, is a future that robs the present. It is not that the girl is actually planning to seek revenge by killing Kannan, since he is not subject to death. The idea, rather, must be that the girl's prospective union with Kannan has the qualities of a death by ambush—its inevitability, its finality, and its rapidity and violence. These qualities contrast with the calm and domestic union that the speaker had previously envisioned with her own heart ("it might come home to me"). The girl does not, at this moment, follow Kannan "as a shadow." It is not, then, that we pass our time in the rainy season of existence waiting passively for Kannan to "give us breath." If we cry tears "cold as basil" after enduring Kannan's indifference, if that despair drives us to active and violent rage, then we might surprise the god, confront him with his misdeeds, and make him our own—not in the sense that he belongs to no others, but in the sense that he no longer escapes us.

A Persian Ghazal by Hafez and an Urdu Ghazal by Ghalib

TRANSLATOR'S NOTE AND TEXT

A ghazal is formally and metrically an integrated series of rhyming couplets, usually concerned with introspective states and frustrated desire; the final couplet almost invariably includes an apostrophe by the poet to him or herself. The genre dominates the classical canon of Arabic, Persian, and Urdu (sometimes combining two of these languages in a single ghazal). The introductory ghazal in Hafez-e Shirazi's *Diwan*—that is, his complete collection of poems—begins and ends in Arabic half-lines; in between we have a collage of dark and lush Persian lines painting images of the poet's infinite loneliness and agony. As always, wine is both itself and far more than itself, and the Saqi, who pours the wine, to whom the poet speaks, holds out the hope of a still deeper and ever more painful intoxication. Hafez (my favorite poet) belongs to fourteenth-century Shiraz. Ghalib's Urdu ghazals, composed in eighteenth- and nineteenth-century Delhi, extend the Indo-Persian literary tradition to a South Asian mode haunted by the transient and idiosyncratic images of a poet who is mordant, witty, and fascinated by the infinite possibilities of refined despair. Ghazals are structured to explode any English translation that seeks to preserve the line-final refrain, which tends to sound mechanical outside of Persian-Urdu. I have attempted to capture something of the dense expressivity of Ghalib's refrain *mere āge*, "in front of, before, beside me, or in my eyes" by varying the adverbs and prepositions just a little.

GHAZAL 1 FROM HAFEZ'S *DIWAN*

Turn the cup, Saqi, and pour the wine,
for love once seemed so easy.
Not anymore.[1] (1)

Morning: the soft breeze
tugs at a black curl.
Dark musk bursts in flame.
One drop of blood falls,
no more. (2)

At home in me, in the stations of love,
nothing is sure, when every moment
the bell cries out: "Pack up.
Stay no more." (3)

Or the master speaks: "Pour wine
on the carpet and stain it dark.
This road belongs only to those
who know its lure." (4)

Black night, the violent waves, the whirlpools
of the sea. How can they know how I feel
who stand, unburdened,
on the shore? (5)

It all started when I tried to satisfy
myself. Then it turned bad.
They sing of us at parties. Secret
no more. (6)

If you seek that particular presence, Hafez:
don't disappear.
When you can't find what you're after,
release the world
once more. (7)

GHAZAL 208 FROM GHALIB'S *BĀZĪCHAH-E AṬFĀL*

A child's toy is this world, placed next to me.
Night and day parade without end—before me. (1)

Solomon's throne is my plaything,
that marvel of a Messiah, only one word—to me. (2)

No more than a name, this world has no shape I can see.
Nothing real, a wild thought moving—in me. (3)

In the dust I kick up, a desert hides.
The sea bows its head to the dust—before me. (4)

Don't ask what state I'm in after you.
Ask yourself what you're feeling when you're—around me. (5)

You're right. I'm self-seeing, self-delighting. Why wouldn't I be?
An idol whose face is a mirror sits here—before me. (6)

Then look well to the words, redolent as roses.
if someone would place a goblet of wine—near me. (7)

I've gone through aversion, gone beyond envy.
So how could I ask that you not speak her name—before me? (8)

Faith holds me back, heresy pulls me forward,
the Ka'aba behind, a church—beyond me. (9)

I'm a lover. My work: to trick the one I love.
Laila maligns crazy Majnun—and then me. (10)

Be happy we don't die for nothing when we meet.
Say a prayer for the night you're not there—before me. (11)

Wave upon wave of this sea of blood sweeps me away.
See what comes next, getting closer and closer—to me. (12)

My hand won't move, but my eyes still breathe.
Leave goblet and bottle right here—for me. (13)

He's my colleague, my drinking partner. He shares my secret.
So why speak badly of Ghalib—before me? (14)

THE LAYERED THOUGHT-WORLD OF THE GHAZAL

Rajeev Kinra (Near Reader)

To observe that it is virtually impossible to reproduce the sonic effects and pulsating bundles of meaning characteristic of the Indo-Persian ghazal in English amounts to little more than a truism. This is especially so with a poet such as Hafez, the celebrated author of the first selection here, who is renowned not only for his elegant lyrical flourishes but also for his ability to manipulate language for intense (and often playfully ambiguous) semantic effect. And the challenge is only compounded in the case of the very first couplet when we realize—as all readers or hearers of the original text immediately do—that the poem's first line is actually in Arabic, not Persian: a rather jarring linguistic feature of the original that is impossible to reproduce in English: it must, almost by necessity, be erased entirely by the act of translating two source languages into one target.

And yet, despite these caveats, one may nevertheless contend rather confidently that just about anyone who has ever suffered in love and turned to drink for solace can relate to this opening couplet of Hafez's *Diwan* of collected verse. *Love seemed so easy at first* . . . and yet, inevitably, there were problems. The poet does not specify precisely what the problem is with his lover, however, remaining content with a certain productive ambiguity. In fact—and here we have our first glimpse into the layered thought-world of the ghazal as a form—he does not even convince us that he or she is a real person. Nor does he intend to; for the ghazal beloved is, to borrow a phrase, *more than real*—not just in the mundane sense captured by the English idiom "larger than life" (though that too is often true of the object of one's fervent romantic desire), but rather in the sense that he or she might actually be "He" or "She" (i.e., God), with whom the believer (especially the mystically inclined believer) so desperately desires metaphysical union, only to be frustrated by the cage of physical existence, trapped in a mundane material world that the mystic (and of course the poet) knows to be really just something like a dream.

In this reading, then, the poet is expressing not so much a crisis of romantic desire, but rather a crisis of spiritual faith—the difficulty of sustaining one's love and devotion to the Divine while inescapably mired in material existence—wherein Belief takes the form of Love (*'ishq*). But it is important to note that neither reading is the "correct" one. Rather, perhaps we should say that love, in the ghazal, is always a double entendre, never meaning just one thing ("real" worldly love) or another (real metaphysical Love), but often—one might even be bold enough to say always—available to be read both ways at once. Much of the pleasure, therefore, for both poets and connoisseurs, derives from this intentional hyperambiguity (what the Indo-Persian poets themselves refer to as *īhām*), that the "meaning" of the couplet remains suspended in a state of play—always a both/and rather than an either/or.

Where, exactly, is this drama unfolding? It would appear to be a tavern of some sort, which, as a refuge from the travails of life, love, and devotion (whether real or more than real), had already become a canonical topos in the Indo-Persian literary tradition long before Hafez came along, with the bartender (Saqi) as an associated stock character and the wine, the jug, and the cup as standard accoutrements. By revisiting this topos, and combining and recombining these conventional elements, or in some cases merely alluding to them, poets throughout the centuries could express any number of emotional and metaphysical states relating not only to love, loss, despair, and social alienation, but also to hope, anticipation, excitement, and the thrill of desire. Of course, Hafez's stature as one of the most (if not *the* most) towering figures of this lyrical tradition has always given this particular couplet—which is, after all, just one among countless others playing on the same trope(s)—a certain quotability, an almost proverbial or maybe aphoristic quality that is difficult to adequately explain to anyone unfamiliar with the literary cultures of the Persianate world. Indeed, one is hard pressed to find anything comparable in the Western literary tradition—perhaps some famous line of Shakespeare would come close, but even that doesn't feel quite right.

If the travails of L/love, generally speaking, are the subject of the first couplet, the next couplet moves us into the realm of a more specific problem: namely, the pain of separation from the B/beloved, one of the most common themes in ghazal poetry (as well as in the poetry and song of many other traditions). In this case, the lover is alone, pining for his absent beloved, but he is in luck (or is he?)—the gentle morning breeze (*ṣabā*) has loosened the beloved's curly locks, and, like a kind messenger, brought him a whiff (*bū*; which can also mean "hope" or "expectation") of their perfumed scent. So far, so good. But what is happening in the second line? The musky scent of the beloved's hair, brought by the morning breeze, has caused his heart to fill with blood, thus only further inflaming his passionate agony. And we may detect an even further possible layer of meaning when we note that in the original Persian the term Hafez uses is actually *dilhā*: "hearts," plural. Does this multiplicity of hearts mean that our poet is not the only lover suffering the pangs of separation from this particular beloved? It would appear so—which would imply, too, that he has rivals for the beloved's affection, which can only increase his anxiety over not being with him/her.

But there's more. For if the breeze "tugs" at the beloved's twisty curls (*tāb*), unlocking their scent, it is their radiance (also *tāb*, in a brilliant pun) that heats the hearts of the lovers, causing them to burst into flames. Indeed, as a number of commentators both classical and modern have noted, Hafez is playing here on a very complex physiological parallel between the musk sac (i.e., the source of the perfume) and the lover's heart. Typically, the musk used in creating perfume was harvested from a specific gland, a sac close to the musk deer's navel, which fills with blood when the deer's body becomes heated and eventually falls off, whereupon it can be collected and processed. The blood swelling in the hearts of longing lovers in the second line of the couplet thus mirrors the (implied) blood of the excited deer engorging the musk sac, which is itself a condition of possibility for the scent that perfumes the beloved's curly locks and in turn creates such heartsick agony all over town.

The pain of separation from the beloved is also a theme of the next couplet (3), albeit from a slightly different, one might say anticipatory, perspective. In this case the lover is actually *with* his beloved, but cannot bear the excruciating transitoriness of the encounter—the knowledge that this moment will soon pass, and they will inevitably be separated once again. It is a meditation on the ephemerality of worldly experiences, and the key image here is that of the caravan, which serves both as a literal setting for the verse and as a larger metaphor for life's journey. On the one hand, then, it can be read as a meditation on a specific rendezvous with a specific beloved; but we might also read the verse as a lament over the more general problem of the fleeting nature of life's pleasures, goals, and objectives. At an even more technical level, the word Hafez uses for "station" (*manzil*) here is also used in a Sufi context to refer to a stage along the mystic's path (*tarīqa*) of spiritual awareness (*'irfān*) toward annihilation of the self (*fanā*). Thus, a mystical reading of the verse could be something like: how can I feel satisfied with achieving a new stage of awareness—i.e., closeness to the true Beloved, God—when I know that there is so far to go before I achieve true insight?

Again, none of these is the "correct" reading, as such. Indeed, so much of the pleasure of ghazal poetry lies precisely in the jostling of these multiple interpretations—as well as other potential readings—bouncing off one another, always in a state of suspended animation.

If the setting for the previous couplet was the caravan (of life), here Hafez has returned us to the tavern with a striking imperative: "Stain the prayer carpet red with wine, if the master [of the tavern] tells you!" On the face of it, this instruction is about as blasphemous as it gets. Not only does it imply that one is drinking wine (which is technically forbidden, of course), but it adds the insouciant insult of telling the listener to be so sloppy as to spill wine not just anywhere, but on the prayer carpet. Whether it is because he has gotten so drunk that he just can't help himself, or because he is intentionally pouring the wine out onto the carpet is not immediately clear. Nor, for that matter, is it clear which would actually be worse from the standpoint of the moralist. But either way, here we have returned to the topos of wine drinking, not necessarily as a solace for love gone wrong as in the first couplet, but as a more general escape from social and religious orthodoxies.

The "master" invoked here is the so-called Magian elder (*pīr-i mughān*), who appears as a conventional stock character in a lot of Persianate poetry representing Christian or sometimes Zoroastrian wine sellers or tavern keepers, since, as non-Muslims, they were allowed to engage in such professions without running afoul of injunctions against the sale and consumption of alcohol by Muslims. If we take the Magian elder in this sense, then the second line becomes a straightforward elaboration on the drunk and disorderly command issued in the first: "this road belongs only to those who know its [wine's] lure"—that is, hedonists. Such hedonists were also very common stock characters in the ghazal universe (and in Hafez's society, for that matter). But we should note, too, that in the original Persian the setting for this encounter between the "master" and the rowdy "traveler" (*sālik*) is not the road itself—although the "road" to decadence is certainly implied—but rather a particular station (*manzil*) along the way. Here *manzil*, in its worldly sense, refers to some kind of inn or tavern; and the "ways and customs" of the *manzil* are those of the drinking establishment—the "house rules," if you will, or, in Shulman's rendering, the "rules of the road." But while it is true that Christians and Zoroastrians were often associated with worldly wine selling in Persianate societies, they were also (especially the Zoroastrians) associated with ancient mysteries from the pre-Islamic era, and thus, with hidden esoteric knowledge. And the term *sālik*, although it does simply mean "traveler" in the mundane sense, was also very commonly used in Sufi parlance to refer to those who traveled the mystical path. The master's injunction to stain the prayer carpet with wine, in other words, however seemingly blasphemous, can also be read as an invitation to partake of the cosmic mysteries that are only available to those who are willing to transcend the usual orthodoxies in search of a higher truth, no matter the cost to their reputation or social standing. "This road," in other words, is not the path for any ordinary believer; it is only for those who are in on the secret, who "know its lure" of spiritual mysteries.

In the next couplet (5), we have suddenly left behind all the caravans, waystations, and taverns that have occupied our poet thus far, and been transported not just to another land, but in fact beyond the land altogether. It is the proverbial dark and stormy night, and we are, quite literally, lost at sea—suffering in fear of the churning waves and such frightful swirling eddies. Are we on a boat that is sinking? Or has the boat already gone down, and we are alone floating on the terrible ocean, just waiting until the waters rise up to finally claim us? The poet doesn't specify. But either way, what were we thinking? What on earth could have provoked us to embark on this foolhardy voyage in the first place? Such ambition, such vanity, such folly to think that we were strong enough to overcome nature's awesome power. And yet, at the same time, such vision and commitment—the sea may indeed claim us in the end, but at least we did not sit idly on the shore, wondering what could have been, or worse still, not even bothering to wonder about new horizons at all. They are the true fools, those "who stand, unburdened, on the shore" (*sabuk-bārān-i sāḥil-hā*); how could they possibly know *our* true condition (*ḥāl-i mā*)? It is a sentiment that can apply to any number of situations, most obviously the romantic ("how can those who play by the ordinary social conventions possibly understand the depths—and dangers—of my love for the unattainable beloved?") or even the spiritual ("how can those who play by the ordinary rules of religion possibly understand the enormous depths of my piety, which are forever threatening to drown me in oblivion"—which is not even necessarily a bad thing in the Sufi context!).

But if the fifth couplet explored the potential opportunity cost to any bold venture—it may wind up drowning you—in the next stanza Hafez suggests that there is also an opportunity cost to being the life of the party. The "party" in question is known in Persian as a *maḥfil*, and it can refer variously to a literary salon, a musical assembly, a Sufi spiritual gathering, or some combination of the three. Thus the exact "secret" that the poet is worried about being revealed publicly is not immediately clear, but the verse hinges on the tension between the speaker's compulsive delight in whatever goes on in the *maḥfil* (perhaps drinking, dancing, the recitation of risqué poetry, expressions of heterodox spirituality, etc.) and the moral hazards involved, not to mention the possibility—indeed the virtual inevitability—of his behavior becoming fodder for local gossip, and the ignominy that will surely follow when it is "secret no more."

Though the couplets we have discussed thus far have all been multilayered and complex in their own ways, none is arguably as cryptic as the final verse of the ghazal. Indeed, even expert commentators have disagreed for centuries as to its exact meaning and figurative intent. But perhaps the first thing we should note here, for the general reader, is that from a linguistic standpoint it is a perfect symmetrical bookend to the first couplet, in that the first line is in Persian while the second is in Arabic—an important part of the texture of the original that is inevitably smoothed over, as it were, by any attempt to translate it. At a deeper level, though, the difficulty with this couplet is not so much that we can't figure out what the poet is saying—the syntax is perfectly clear—but that it is not entirely clear what he *means*.

The question before us is what, exactly, Hafez means by the duality of "presence" and "disappearance" to which this verse calls our attention. *Whose* presence does the poet seek that is currently (at least by implication) absent from him? Is it the beloved, to whom he must continue to present himself in order to have any hope of success, despite his/her indifference? Is it a king or some other patron? Is it God? Is it the art of poetry itself, as the noted modern scholar Julie Meissami has argued? Is it some other "particular presence," as Shulman has translated it here with just the right touch of elegant ambiguity?

In the end, the exact meaning remains an elusive mystery. But it is precisely Hafez's ability to create such mysterious yet enthralling poetic effects that prompted a later poet, the celebrated ʿAbd al-Rahman Jami (d. 1492), to famously dub him the "tongue of the unseen" (*lisān al-ghaib*)—using a term, perhaps not coincidentally, that is etymologically related to the very word for invisibility/absence (*ghāʾib*) that Hafez employs in this last couplet. And over the centuries, Hafez's reputation as the "translator of secrets" (*tarjumān al-asrār*) has hardly diminished. Indeed, it is exactly this feature of his poetry that has led people across the Persianate world to use his *dīwān* for the purposes of divination in times of trouble, distress, or worry. This was true in Persopone India as well, but interestingly enough, in the nineteenth century another figure would emerge from the world of classical Urdu literature whose work would also come to be used on occasion for such popular bibliomancy: Ghalib, the poet to whom we turn next.

Ghalib.   For our next selection, we move forward in time by roughly half a millennium, and also move into an entirely different language, now commonly known as Urdu, which began to replace Persian as the preferred literary medium of the urbane courtly intelligentsia in Mughal northern India over the course of the eighteenth and nineteenth centuries. The poet, Mirza Asadullah Khan "Ghalib" (1797–1869), was one of the towering figures of this relatively new classical Urdu tradition, though he was also a prolific Persian poet as well. In purely literary historical terms, then, Ghalib was an important transitional figure: a man born into the elite society of the late Mughal courtly world, and thus still deeply (some might even say stubbornly) imprinted by the established traditions of classical Indo-Persian language, literature, culture, and manners, but also one whose own career and fame in many ways embodied the crest of the new Hindi-Urdu vernacular wave from which Indian Persian language and literature would arguably never recover. He began his life as the scion of an elite family of Mughal aristocrats, and ended it as a subject of Queen Victoria, even going so far as to pen lofty panegyrics to her in hopes of securing the patronage of the British government. He was a man of awesome literary ego (indeed arrogance, in the eyes of more than a few of his contemporaries), who expected a certain amount of deference from most he interacted with; and yet also a man of tremendous wit, and one of the more colorful *bons vivants* of nineteenth-century Delhi—a habitual tippler, gambler (for which he was jailed on at least one occasion), ladies' man (reportedly), and general man about town. He had some notoriously acerbic feuds with poetic rivals, and yet, especially in his letters, could also display remarkable warmth, empathy, affection, and kindness, especially for the downtrodden and down on their luck. He was, needless to say, one of the most fascinating and contradictory figures in all of nineteenth-century Indian cultural life.

A great many of these personality traits are reflected in the ghazal translated here, which Ghalib composed for the royal Mughal salon in Delhi, in May 1853. Overall, it is twice as long (fourteen couplets) as the selection from Hafez, and one of the things that stand out immediately upon reading the original Urdu is the striking emphasis on the self—on the "I" (or rather "my") of the poetic voice.

For a ghazal poet to adopt such a first-person speaking voice is not unusual, per se, but to do so this consistently in a single poem, and with such repeated emphasis, is relatively rare. Another somewhat quirky feature of this ghazal, beyond its intense projection of the poet's own self (or some version of it), is that it begins with what appears to be intended as a four-couplet "set"—something that is also rather unusual in the ghazal tradition, in which each couplet is typically treated as an independent poetic utterance. The ghazal's unity, in fact, insofar as it has any, is in most cases purely formal: the poem must conform to the correct meter and rhyme throughout, but beyond that there are few imaginative constraints on each individual couplet. This is why, as we saw with Hafez, it can be quite difficult to write about a whole ghazal without breaking it up into its constituent parts, its sequence of various "poems two lines long," as the noted Urdu literary scholar Frances Pritchett once described them (or, if you prefer, "orient pearls at random strung," as Sir William Jones famously put it all the way back in 1771). Ghalib, however, sometimes had a sly way of using his ghazals to explore variations on a theme, and this is a perfect example.

One way to read this opening set of four couplets is as an expression of Ghalib's personal sense of confidence and grandeur. But there are other possibilities, the most obvious being a mystical reading: these things, these trappings of material life are all just a show (*tamāshā*), not the ultimate Reality. If we take this approach, then we are suddenly dealing less with the megalomaniacal musings of a self-absorbed aristocrat than with a deeper meditation on the ephemerality of worldly existence as such. Yet another possibility is to think of the speaker neither as Ghalib himself, nor as Ghalib adopting the persona of a visionary Sufi mystic, but rather as Ghalib *in his capacity as a poet*, that is, as a poet-creator. One could even read these verses as a meditation on aging, and the ennui that comes with too much experience of the world. The speaker is so weary of life that he is able to discern the essential flimsiness of material existence in a way that younger, more optimistic, more passionate, and less jaded souls cannot yet appreciate. Ghalib himself was nearly sixty years old when this ghazal was written, so it is certainly not out of the question. Again, one of the great delights of the ghazal as a form—which is also precisely what can make them so agonizing to translate and explicate—is that we are not required to choose which of these is the "correct" reading of these verses. They can all linger in a state of play, and remain so, each potential interpretation more or less equally valid all at once.

All of the grand pronouncements of the first four couplets suddenly give way, however, to the far more common poet-lover's lament over his abasement at the hands of a cruel beloved in the fifth couplet. In fact, in addition to this rather abrupt thematic shift, for the next three couplets the mode of address adopted by the speaker has shifted as well, from general statements about the world as he sees it to second-person statements addressed directly to a specific interlocutor. "Don't even ask about my condition," he complains at the beginning of the fifth couplet—ironically enough, after spending the previous four couplets boasting bombastically about exactly that!—"now that you have left me behind." He is speaking, presumably, to the beloved who has jilted him; and given the ghazal universe's conventional emphasis on—indeed, celebration of—the poet-lover's subjugation to the capricious and cruel whims of the beloved, one might have expected the second line to delve further into his tortured state. But in this case Ghalib chooses defiance instead, telling the beloved, essentially, to take a good look at him-/herself first and see what the effect of his/her cruelty has been on his/her own self. Thematically, then, the verse crackles with a somewhat unexpected insolence on the part of the poet-lover; instead of wallowing in his sorrow as we might expect, he has turned the tables on the cruel beloved and implied that s/he is the one who should truly be sorry.

The next couplet also addresses the beloved directly, but here Ghalib dispenses with the unexpectedly confrontational attitude of the previous verse in favor of a lighter, more playful, and even admiring touch. The first line has the speaker, seemingly defensive, strangely confessing to what might ordinarily be seen as the rather narcissistic character flaws of "self-seeing" and "self-delighting." But then in the second line we learn that the speaker is not infatuated with his own beauty, but rather his *reflection* in the beloved's face, which is so radiant, so shiny, that it acts like a mirror. Mesmerized by his own image reflected in that "mirror-faced idol" (*but-i ā'ina-sīmā*), he appears arrogant, vain, narcissistic, and preening, but he is in fact merely overawed by its reflective power.

In the next couplet (7), however, it is the poet's interlocutor who will do the seeing. "Then look well," the speaker insists in the first line, "to the words, redolent as roses." Here Ghalib appears to be referencing his own poetry (literally, his "rose-scattering style of expression"; *andāz-i gul-afshānī-yi guftār*), telling his interlocutor—perhaps a sympathetic bartender, or perhaps his rival poet(s) in the *mahfil*—that while they may have been impressed with what they had heard so far (whether Ghalib's own verse or that of some other poet), there is much better yet to come, poems of such style and grace that they will be like flowers spread far and wide, as they are recited and repeated all over town by lovers of good poetry. But there is just one thing lacking: a goblet of wine to fuel his inspiration.

As we have seen, the ghazal universe is one that is populated by numerous stock characters such as the poet-lover, the beloved, the bartender, the annoying moralist, the friendly advisor, and the romantic or literary rival, as well as multiple stock topoi associated with them such as the tavern, the garden, the literary gathering, the house of worship, and the bazaar. These and other archetypal characters and physical settings are well known to connoisseurs of the tradition, and one of the things this allows poets to do is to say a lot with an extreme economy of actual words. They are able to *suggest* the presence of certain types of characters in certain situations without having to be explicit, and as we have seen, good poets like Hafez and Ghalib could even exploit this power of suggestion to toy with our expectations and generate intense, and often multiple, meaning(s)—a process that Indo-Persian literary critics refer to as "meaning creation" (*ma'nī-āfrīnī*) or sometimes "theme creation" (*mazmūn-āfrīnī*), depending on the exact features of the verse.

Thus, in three of the next four couplets, Ghalib explores a range of emotive states related to the travails of romantic love, from sorrow and regret to irrational exuberance. There is a seemingly jilted lover (*'āshiq*) who is trying to get over the one-time object of his affections, and can't bear even to hear his/her name (8). This is followed by an apparently scheming *'āshiq* who invokes the classic doomed archetypal lovers Laila and Majnun to proclaim, somewhat mysteriously, that he makes it his business "to trick the one I love" (10)—a strange sort of admission in a literary universe that typically (and often literally) idolizes the beloved, and celebrates the *'āshiq*'s willingness, even eagerness, to endure incredible suffering in her absence and cruel indignities in her presence.[2] Finally, there is an encounter in which the *'āshiq*'s longed-for union with the beloved feels so intense that he literally dies of happiness—and yet, ironically enough, it is in that very moment of blissful self-sacrifice, so often compared in Indo-Persian lyrics to the moth burning up in the irresistible flame, that this particular lover recalls with nostalgia the longing he felt on an earlier night of separation (*shab-i hijrān*) from the beloved, when he so desperately *wanted* to die of grief, even as he is *actually* dying of joy (11). The latter is one of the great "agony of separation" couplets in Ghalib's oeuvre, one that also harkens back to the topos explored in Hafez (in which the poet-lover cannot even truly enjoy the moment of union with the beloved, for all he can think of is the fact that they will soon inevitably be separated once again; couplet 3).

There is also a long tradition in Indo-Persian literature of the ghazal being used to express dissent, particularly against religious orthodoxy. The flouting of social norms and Qur'anic injunctions such as the prohibition against wine, for instance, was probably the most routine form of such dissident expression. Indeed, as we saw earlier with Hafez (4), these paeans to inebriation could sometimes intensify into something more, even verging on outright blasphemy, albeit usually modulated with a mystical sensibility that made such poetry not so much irreligious, per se, but rather a kind of orthogonal piety that was thought to transcend "mere" orthodoxy. What we have in Ghalib (9), however, is a classic example of yet another variation on the theme: not a protest against orthodoxy as such—at least not directly—but rather a *cri de coeur* bemoaning the individual believer's crisis of faith, or existential angst more generally. Ambivalent about faith (*īmān*), and drawn by the allure of infidelity (*kufr*), Ghalib here nevertheless expresses an arguably even greater existential dilemma than Hafez's drunken injunction to simply abandon conventional piety and "stain the prayer carpet red with wine"—namely, that he *cannot* be so cavalier because a part of him still believes, even if he has doubts, and even if he is enticed by the potential truth of other religious traditions.

The theme of existential unease continues in the next couplet (12), which evokes a dread of "wave upon wave" threatening to drown the poet that is similar to Hafez (5), only this time it is even worse—a "sea of blood," with no end in sight. The speaker's only hope is that the storm abates, but how can he be sure that it will? Indeed, it might even get worse. And thus, we are left to wonder about the poor man's fate. But we are also left to wonder: what exactly is this "sea of blood"? Some commentators have interpreted it historically, perhaps as a reference to political turmoil of the nineteenth century generally, or even more specifically to the bloody reprisals that the British visited upon Delhi following the mutiny of 1857. In fact, Ghalib himself even cited the verse in a post-1857 letter to a friend about the devastation he witnessed. And yet, we know for a fact that this particular ghazal was composed before the rebellion, in May 1853 (something we rarely know with such specificity). Another possibility is that the "sea of blood" is actually a deluge of the poet-lover's own tears, which are "bloody" from his grief-stricken bloodshot eyes. Ghalib has a number of other famous couplets in which such "tears of blood" are central to the imagery, as well as a whole host of other verses that play on the trope of the solitary lover crying torrents of tears in grief over his separation from the beloved. The "sea of blood" could even be a metaphor for worldly existence as such—a reading that could be corroborated by other verses by Ghalib that draw on similar imagery, such as the famous one in which he laments: "existence has drowned me, so what matter if I never existed?"

These kinds of intertextual resonances are probably of more interest to connoisseurs than the general reader, but I flag them nevertheless, because they are such an important part of the economy of literary and emotive pleasure associated with the ghazal as a form. Another is the performance setting in which such verses were often recited, sung, and heard, which encouraged poets to tease the audience by extending the ambiguity of the couplet's meaning, and deferring as long as possible the utterance of the key word or phrase that will, in turn, disclose the overall couplet's real meaning(s) and theme(s). The penultimate couplet of this ghazal (13) is a perfect illustration. After the end of the first line, we have no idea what is actually going on. The speaker can barely move, but he still has enough life left that "[his] eyes still breathe." Is he dying? Perhaps! The second line begins with an injunction to "leave" something be, without immediately specifying its object, which creates a suspense that does not carry over to the translation, but might be exploited by anyone singing or reciting the couplet to heighten the effect even further. Is it the shovel they will use to bury him, now that he has died for love? Is it his own body, which, despite all appearances, he protests still has life left in it (at least in the eyes)? Is he trying to be left alone to die a peaceful death and "go gentle into that good night," or is he rather desperate, à la Dylan Thomas, to "rage, rage against the dying of the light"? We still don't know! Until, at last, we hear the key words "goblet and bottle" (*sāghar-o-mīnā*) and it all snaps resoundingly, amusingly, into focus: he's merely been dead drunk all along.

Finally, another feature of the ghazal that poets often exploited for effect is the traditional expectation that the last couplet of the poem (known as the *maqṭa'*) would include some reference to the poet's own pen name, or *takhallus*. This is why, in Hafez (7), the verse is addressed directly to someone named "Hafez," while the actual speaker of the couplet remains ambiguous—it could be Hafez admonishing himself, or it could be Hafez the poet assuming the guise of some other person in order to offer advice to an imaginary version of himself named Hafez. And here in Ghalib (12) we encounter a similar dynamic. The speaker, it would appear, is not Ghalib himself but someone speaking *about* Ghalib to an unidentified third party, one who is apparently speaking ill of the poet. "He is my colleague, my drinking partner," and "he shares my secret," the speaker protests; "so why do you speak badly of Ghalib," and that too right in front of me?

To whom is this complaint addressed? One immediate possibility is that it is the beloved—that is, *Ghalib's* beloved, with whom the speaker is conversing. This reading is supported nicely by the wording of line two, which, in the original Urdu, is almost identical to that of the tenth couplet in which the speaker was either complaining or boasting that Laila was bad-mouthing Majnun, depending on how we interpret it. Perhaps it is one of Ghalib's literary rivals denigrating his poetic talents, or some other prominent person around town denouncing his dodgy morals. Perhaps he is speaking to some religious scold—the irritating orthodox *mullah* also being a common stock character of the ghazal universe—and chiding the latter for being so uptight. Or maybe, just maybe, the speaker actually *is* Ghalib, and he has somehow found himself in a situation where people are bad-mouthing him, or his poetry, or his character, or whatever the case may be, without knowing that they are speaking to the man himself—and this is his cheeky way of telling them off—by continuing the pretense that he is someone else, some other disinterested observer coming to his own defense, but deep down reveling in the irony as if to say: "how funny that you would stand there insulting my good friend Ghalib, in front of me of all people!"—and letting all of us in on the secret.

THE GHAZAL OF WHAT'S MORE THAN REAL

Peter Cole (Far Reader)

FOR D. S.

And now words reach us as Persian meets Urdu,
making ours real, and then some, like David's do

in an English he's always leaving behind
and returning to, as it happens, like dew

on grass or a vine's blue grapes—even a glass
left out in a garden his poets imbue

with powers. Still, he'd be the first to tell you—
it's a mirage. Meaning's mortgage. Maybe true.

True and not true. Glistening, as we see it—
a kind of beloved. Something desire drew,

drawing us too. Again lines are leading him
beyond himself, and soon he's bidding adieu

to ease, with ease, in every way. It pleases
him, who'll share his secrets, as though they were new,

so they will be. So leaning and learning meet
along a mind's mirror, coupling there, a clue.

Residue . . . of a slow knowing—as fog stops
the brown mountain: *I imagine, therefore you*

are. Therefore, imagine, so that I might be
with you, wandering friend, when these debts come due.

Afterword

Wendy Doniger

I have the honor of saying the last word about David Shulman here; the ending, because I was there at the beginning of his mature academic career and so have known David longer than any of the other contributors to this volume. I met him in London in 1972 when he was newly married to Eileen, before his first son Eviatar (Tari) was born in 1973. David was twenty-four, and I was thirty-two. (My own son, Mike, born in late 1971, always delighted in calling Tari, barely two years his junior, "Baby Tari"). I met David just four years after I had received my Harvard PhD in 1968; he received his PhD from SOAS in 1976. He had come to London from Israel and didn't like cold, wet, dark, aloof England at all for some reason; he was impatient to get back to the land "wo die Citronen blühn." Iowa, Israel, India, the places he loves all have to begin with an "I" and tend to be warm or at least sunny.

So he became my first PhD student. Of course, I was not his first teacher. He had already studied in Jerusalem with scholars who remained important to him all his life. And in London, I shared him with John Ralston Marr, his official dissertation advisor, who taught him Tamil and Carnatic music and much else. His other great teacher was Velcheru Narayana Rao, who invited David, in 1982, to study Telugu with him in Madison. That partnership has yielded some of David's and Narayana Rao's greatest books.

And David had other teachers too. When we were together on Gorée Island, Senegal, in 2004, while I was desultorily brushing up my high school French, David set out to learn Wolof, the native language of Senegal. He found a little book, and then he found a woman who made jewelry and who taught him to speak quite well. When he introduced me to her and said I was his teacher, she brightly replied, "I am his teacher too," and indeed she was.

I once asked him why he referred to me as his teacher, and he said, "because you taught me to love the myths." He certainly does love them, and that is his primary way of reading, to see the beauty in them, and the wisdom, and the humor. But he didn't stop there. He went on to learn and to teach that myths are historically embedded, philosophically tangled, that they have political meanings as well as religious, and that some of those meanings are cruel and bigoted. And yet, the main reason to read them is because they are beautiful, and to render that beauty in any translations that you try to make. This is all the more true of his reading of poetry, where his passion for Carnatic music guides him to hear the singing voices inside the poetry and brings that music into the English approximation of the meaning. His very personal method of reading other literary texts differs from text to text, as he bonds with individual authors and seems to be able to imagine himself coming up, all by himself, with the ideas in the texts he is reading. And so he waxes philosophical, or psychoanalytic, or romantic, or tragical-comical-historical, or even pious, as he weaves through so many texts, in so many languages and genres.

When I first met David, I didn't realize how extraordinary he was. True, he already knew Arabic and Persian and Sanskrit, and Greek and Latin, and French and German, and Russian. (And Hebrew: though it is often an invisible thread, a great influence on his unique way of thinking is the fact that Hebrew is his second first language; his poetry in Hebrew has won several awards.) True, he soon began to present me with chapter after chapter of his dissertation, abounding in original ideas, each documented by numerous perfectly translated Sanskrit and Tamil texts, in flawlessly expressed and punctuated English. But I just thought, "Oh, teaching graduate students is going to be so easy!"

So that was how it began. After he left London, David went places I could never follow, to learn things that I myself not only had never taught him but could never learn as he knew them. He became my teacher. From *Tamil Temple Myths: Sacrifice and Divine Marriage in the South Indian Śaiva Tradition* (1980, his revised dissertation) and *The King and the Clown in South Indian Myth and Poetry* (1985), I learned how fascinating the link between Sanskrit and Tamil mythologies was. From *When God is a Customer: Telugu Courtesan Songs by Kṣetrayya and Others* (1993, with Narayana Rao and A. K. Ramanujan), I learned how much more subtle the sexual mythology of Shiva was than I had realized from my work on the Puranas. The subjectivity of *Spring, Heat, Rains: A South Indian Diary* (2008) inspired me to find a more personal voice in my own writing. *More than Real: A History of the Imagination in South India* (2012) made me see a text I thought I knew well, the *Yogavasiṣṭha*, as part of a far more complex mythology of the real and unreal than I had understood. And on and on.

Nor was I alone in this trajectory of constant intellectual revolution that David inspired. *Tamil Temple Myths* and *The King and the Clown* established a new field within the study of Indian religions, the study of local temple myths, particularly local Tamil myths, where previously the field had been dominated by the study of pan-Indian stories and Sanskrit texts. With *When God is a Customer*, he and his coauthors seeded another entirely new field in another linguistic area, Telugu, establishing what was in effect a new body of literature and history in English translation. Narayana Rao and David (for Ramanujan died tragically that same year, 1993) went on to produce many studies of Telugu literature and history and superb translations, such as Peddana's *The Story of Manu* for the Murty Classical Library of India (2015), and there is more in the pipeline. More recently he has immersed himself in Malayalam. There is no end to it.

And so David has encouraged a whole generation of scholars to find new meanings in the poetry and folk traditions of south India, blasting open the Orientalist bubble. It was as if scholars of European literature had studied only the French—Flaubert and the Chanson de Roland—and suddenly someone said, "Look, here's Dante and Boccaccio!" ("And Rilke!" "And Lermontov!"). His books have changed the way Indologists go about their own work and educate their students. Scholars throughout the world greet him with reverence, gratitude, and affection.

His work with Sanjay Subrahmanyam and Narayana Rao (in *Symbols of Substance: Court and State in Nayaka-Period Tamil Nadu* [1992] and *Textures of Time: Writing History in South India* [2002]) has had resonances far beyond the bounds of Indian studies, for they have invented a new model of interdisciplinary scholarship, combining history, literary studies, religious studies, and anthropology in a seamless integration. Often they wrote each sentence together, rather than resorting to the patched-together piecemeal collaborations, with one chapter by one person and another by another, that are usually produced by such enterprises. David also published books of this genre in collaboration with Don Handelman and Yigal Bronner, and edited books with S.N. Eisenstadt and Reuven Kahane; with Shaul Shaked and Guy Stroumsa; and with Galit Hasan-Rokem, Debbie Thiagarajan, Shalva Weil, Yigal Bronner, and Gary Tubb. As director of the Institute for Advanced Studies, in Jerusalem, from 1992 to 1998, he inspired many scholars to join him in a series of wide-ranging international seminars (which he continued to run even after stepping down from his position). Those who have been fortunate enough to work within his great circle have dared to reach out into areas that they had not ventured to before, producing new, original work.

David's list of publications is not only unusually long but amazingly varied in genres and disciplines, including literature, religion, history, politics, folklore, ritual, myth, translation, exegesis, art history, comparative studies, anthropology, performance studies, poetry, and music. *The Hungry God* (1993), for instance, is a model for the right way to do comparative religion, a stunning comparison of the story of Abraham and Isaac and the story of the Hindu god who demands that a couple kill and cook their son for him. At the time I am writing now, David is going around the world introducing unsuspecting audiences to troops of dancers/actors trained in Kudiyattam, Kerala's living tradition of performance of Sanskrit dramas.

How does he do it all? People joke about the MacArthur awards being genius awards, but I do truly think that David Shulman, who won one of those, is a genius, and not merely because of his uncanny knack for learning languages and memorizing whole bodies of literature, which is just the obvious part of his brilliance. He has the sweetness and generosity of a true genius, a love of life that inspires all who come in contact with him, and a confident modesty about his own achievements that immediately relaxes the awe with which most people generally first approach him. This spirit pervades his academic work; it is the quality of a man who is more mensch than saint, though a good bit of both. His *Menschlichkeit* as well as his saintliness are tempered by his scholarly rigor and his poetic gifts, and both are grounded, like everything he does, in his passionate love of human beings, a love whose center is his family, Eileen and their three boys and the ever-expanding roster of allegedly uniquely talented grandchildren.

His scholarship and his activism combined in an extraordinary book that he published in 2007: *Dark Hope: Working for Peace in Israel and Palestine*, a chronicle of his work as a peace activist, a founding member of the joint Israeli-Palestinian movement Ta'ayush. Ta'ayush, which takes its name from the Arabic for "living together," works actively to try to prevent Israeli "settlers" from taking away the land that belongs to Palestinian farmers and shepherds; its members deliver food and medical supplies to Palestinian villages and accompany the farmers to their lands, often clashing with police and armed settlers. When David won the Israel Prize in 2016, he donated his NIS 75,000 prize money to Ta'ayush, a fact that was known to Netanyahu as he obligatorily shook David's hand. The great success of *Dark Hope*, and that of the series of articles on the same subject that he has published in the *New York Review of Books*, has inspired a second volume, *Freedom and Despair: Notes from South Hebron Hills* (2018). This work ranks high in the list of the myriad things that David has done in his life that will surely grant him instant access to heaven.

Like everything else that he has written, *Dark Hope* and *Freedom and Despair* were driven by a deep compassion for another culture and a brilliant gift for making his readers share that compassion. David has always managed somehow, in both his person and his work, to erase the imaginary line between work and person, more precisely between the solitary, solipsistic academic life in which we scholars spend so much time alone with our texts, and the world in which we interact with human beings—our students, our colleagues, and, if we're David Shulman, the Palestinian farmers and the forces threatening them.

He pours his understanding as a student and lover of Indian literature into every report he writes on the terrible events transpiring in the West Bank. And he brings his experience of the world and that conflict into everything he writes about Indian texts and history. Where we mortals experience a boundary, however permeable, between the silent, peaceful communion of the archive and the difficult, often tragic world of interactions with other human beings—for him there is no divide. This is his greatness.

ACKNOWLEDGMENTS

We want to express our appreciation and gratitude to each of the contributors to this volume. They accepted a task that we knew would prove unusual, were agreeable when assigned selections without consultation, and had faith in the project, even before it was clear what it would be. There is a special spirit to their efforts that bears witness to their deep appreciation of and friendship with David Shulman.

We are also grateful to T.M. Krishna and Eileen Shulman for sharing with us the recordings of their musical performances, and to Charsur Digital Workstation for allowing us to use the recording of T.M. Krishna here. Thanks also to Anna Lise Seastrand and Brigitte Majlis for sharing their photographs of the Varadarajasvami temple with us.

We were extremely fortunate to work with Reed Malcolm as an editor, who had faith in the project from the start, and we wish to thank the entire staff at the University of California Press for all their help. We also thank Paige MacKay and the staff at Ubiquity Press for their care in preparing the volume for open access publication. We are grateful to Katherine Ulrich for preparing the index of *Sensitive Reading*. Finally, we wish to express our gratitude to the anonymous readers, whose reviews helped us to improve the volume.

Above all, we wish to thank David Shulman: we know that he had no idea what he was in for when he first agreed to sign up for this project. We kept getting back to him with new demands, and he kept obliging, no questions asked and no complaints. His generosity with this volume is but a token of the generosity he has shown us ever since we met him. If it's not already obvious, this book is for him.

NOTES

INTRODUCTION

1. Toni Morrison, "The Dancing Mind," National Book Award Acceptance Speech, November 1996, www.nationalbook.org/tag/the-dancing-mind.

2. Robert Scholes, *Protocols of Reading* (New Haven: Yale University Press, 1989), 59.

3. Scholes, *Protocols of Reading*, x.

4. Cited in Charles Hallisey, trans., *Therigatha: Poems of the First Buddhist Women* (Cambridge, MA: Harvard University Press, 2015), xi–xii.

5. Archana Venkatesan, *A Hundred Measures of Time: Tiruviruttam* (New York: Penguin, 2014).

1. SHRIHARSHA'S SANSKRIT *LIFE OF NAISHADHA*

1. The external senses (*bahir-indriya*) are nominally gods according to statements in the *Brāhmaṇa*s, some of the earliest Sanskrit commentaries on the Hindu scriptures, the Vedas. But their divinity has to be actualized, as indeed it has been—so the goose says—because Nala's senses are starved of normal objects ever since his mind has locked onto Damayanti as its only object; such ongoing self-mortification and withdrawal from external sense-objects normally produce deathlessness and joy, which is the state his senses have indeed achieved by being saturated with Damayanti.

2. Love is bodiless ever since Lord Shiva burnt him to ashes with a glance from his third eye. In this passage I use *Love* and *Desire* interchangeably as epithets of the god of love.

3. The tenth and terminal stage is death from frustrated desire. The flower in the sky (*khapuṣpa*) is the standard emblem for some unlikely or impossible event.

4. Several verbal features in the poet's use of Sanskrit strengthen the verse's dual focus and the topic of double dealing or treachery. This extends beyond the use of words with two

applications involving similar shades of meaning (ally/kindred friend, enemy/antagonist) to the repetition of words in rather different meanings. The Sanskrit word *mukha* means both "face" and "mouth" and is used twice in the verse, once in each meaning; in its act of treason Nala's face becomes a speaker. And the verb *mantrayate* is repeated in the same metrical position in two different lines, first by itself in the technical meaning of engaging in secret strategy consideration, and then with the prefix *ā-*, which changes the meaning to that of speaking openly. That these differences in meaning are intended is guaranteed by the convention that no good poet will use the same word twice in the same meaning within a single verse.

5. The translation is mine.

6. The translation is mine.

2. ATIVIRARAMA PANDYAN'S TAMIL *LIFE OF NAIDATHA*

1. A modern commentator in Tamil: blue sapphire for the woman's eyes, pearls for her teeth, coral for her lips, and so on.

2. David Shulman, *More than Real: A History of the Imagination in South India* (Cambridge, MA: Harvard University Press, 2012), 186.

3. David Shulman, *Tamil: A Biography* (Cambridge, MA: Harvard University Press, 2016), 33.

4. E. Valentine Daniel, *Fluid Signs: Being a Person the Tamil Way* (Berkeley: University of California Press, 1984), 234.

5. George Hart, *The Poems of Ancient Tamil: Their Milieu and Their Sanskrit Counterparts* (New Delhi: Oxford University Press, 2003), 98.

6. Alexander M. Dubianski, *Ritual and Mythological Sources of the Early Tamil Poetry* (Groningen, The Netherlands: Egbert Forsten, 2000), 12.

7. Dave Eggers, *The Circle* (New York: Alfred A. Knopf, 2013), x.

8. William Butler Yeats, "A Drinking Song."

9. William Butler Yeats, "For Anne Gregory."

3. MALAMANGALA KAVI'S MALAYALAM *NAISHADHA IN OUR LANGUAGE*

1. The phrase used by the commentator (*sākṣān manmatha-manmatha*) is borrowed from *Bhāgavata Purāṇa* 10.32.2, where it refers to Krishna in his dance with the cowherd girls.

2. Like most quotations from the play, this is from Cyril Birch, trans., *The Peony Pavilion* (Bloomington: Indiana University Press, 2002), 49.

3. Birch, trans., *Peony Pavilion*, 46.

4. This is from David Hawkes, trans., *The Story of the Stone* (Middlesex: Penguin Books, 1977), 2:38–39. *The Story of the Stone* (Chinese: *Shitou ji*) is an alternate title of the work *Honglou meng*.

5. David Shulman, *More than Real: A History of the Imagination in South India* (Cambridge, MA: Harvard University Press, 2012).

6. Birch, trans., *Peony Pavilion*, 49.

7. Tang Xianzu's preface to *Mudan Ting* (Beijing: Renmin, 1997); my translation.

8. See the Song of Solomon's translation in *The New Oxford Annotated Bible with the Apocrypha* (New York: Oxford University Press, 1973), 815–21.

4. "KHWAJA THE DOG-WORSHIPER" FROM *THE STORY OF THE FOUR DERVISHES*

1. A.K. Ramanujan, "Repetition in the *Mahābhārata*," in *The Collected Essays of A.K. Ramanujan* (New Delhi: Oxford University Press, 1999), 161–83.

2. I thank Sanjukta Poddar for her help in the preparation of this piece. An English translation of the whole of Mir Amman Dehlavi's *Bāgh-o-Bahār* can be found in Mir Amman, *A Tale of the Four Dervishes*, trans. Mohammed Zakir (London: Penguin, 1994).

3. Ibid., 1.

4. Ibid., xiv.

5. Ibid., 15.

6. Ibid., 17.

7. Ibid., 95.

8. Ibid., 78.

9. Ibid., 111.

5. "TOUCH" BY ABBURI CHAYADEVI

1. Saul Friedländer, *Franz Kafka: The Poet of Shame and Guilt* (New Haven: Yale University Press, 2013), 23.

2. Vladimir Nabokov, *Lectures on Literature*, ed. Fredson Bowers (New York: Harcourt, Brace and Jovanovich, 1980), 250–83.

6. "A STREET PUMP IN ANANTAPURAM" AND FIVE OTHER POEMS BY MOHAMMAD ISMAIL

1. The following poems were translated in collaboration with Karri Ramacandra Reddy.

2. Mohammad Ismail, *Karuna Mukhyam (Ismail Sahitya Vyasalu)* (Kakinada: Kusuma Prachuranalu, 1996), 111.

3. Alistair Hornes, *Seven Ages of Paris* (London: Macmillan, 2002), 14.

4. Mohammad Ismail, "Sixty Years of Telugu Poetry," in *Karuna Mukhyam*, 147.

5. David Shulman, *Spring, Heat, Rains: A South Indian Diary* (Chicago: University of Chicago Press, 2009), 8.

6. Victor Segalen, *Essay on Exoticism: An Aesthetics of Diversity*, trans. and ed. Yaël Rachel Schlick (Durham: Duke University Press, 2002), 20.

7. Shulman, *Spring, Heat, Rains*, 19.

8. Velcheru Narayana Rao and David Shulman, *A Poem at the Right Moment: Remembered Verses from Premodern South India* (Berkeley: University of California Press, 1999), 13.

9. David Shulman, *Tamil: A Biography* (Cambridge, MA: Harvard University Press, 2016), 283.

10. Rainer Maria Rilke, "Archaic Torso of Apollo," in *The Selected Poetry of Rainer Maria Rilke*, ed. and trans. Stephen Mitchell (New York: Vintage, 1984), 61.

11. Shulman, *Spring, Heat, Rains*, 134–35.

12. Ibid.

13. Ibid., 121.

14. John Berger, *Portraits* (London: Verso, 2015), 143.

15. William Carlos Williams, *Selected Essays* (New York: New Directions, 1954), 28.

16. Shulman, *Spring, Heat, Rains*, 128.

7. THE MUSIC CONTEST FROM TIRUTTAKKATEVAR'S TAMIL *CHIVAKAN'S GEM*

1. The following verses are ostensibly spoken, in the Sangam style, by the girlfriend of the heroine, who is overwhelmed by desire.

2. I wish to thank Professor E. Annamalai, my teacher at the University of Chicago, who has read and discussed the Tamil verses with me, and generously commented on a draft of this essay.

8. TWO SONGS BY MUTTUSWAMI DIKSHITAR, PERFORMED BY T. M. KRISHNA AND EILEEN SHULMAN

1. Frost, Letter to John Bartlett, 22 Feb. 1914, in *The Letters of Robert Frost*, vol. 1, *1886–1920*, ed. Donald Sheehy, Mark Richardson, and Robert Faggen (Cambridge, MA: Harvard University Press, 2014), 176.

2. Patrick Olivelle, *The Early Upaniṣads: Annotated Text and Translation* (New York: Oxford University Press, 1998), 251.

10. RAVANA VISITS SITA AT NIGHT IN THE ASHOKA GROVE, FROM KAMBAN'S TAMIL *RAMAYANA*

1. At the time Ravana kidnapped Sita, he sent the demon Maricha in the form of a golden deer to lure Rama away from her; Maricha, pierced by Rama's arrow, imitated Rama's voice calling for help.

2. During Ravana's kidnapping of Sita, the great eagle, Jatayus, tried valiantly to stop him and was killed by Ravana. He is also the "bird" mentioned in the next verse.

3. It's likely that the deafening noise of the great bow split by the boy Rama is meant to call to mind Ravana's roar when Shiva crushed him under Mount Kailasa. It was this roar that gave the demon his name.

4. See Adina Hoffman and Peter Cole, *Sacred Trash: The Lost and Found World of the Cairo Geniza* (New York: Schocken, 2011).

5. David Shulman, personal communication, July 2, 2019.

6. See, e.g., Peter Cole, *The Dream of the Poem: Hebrew Poetry from Muslim and Christian Spain, 950–1492* (Princeton: Princeton University Press, 2007), 146–47.

7. See, e.g., J.B. Leishman, *Themes and Variations in Shakespeare's Sonnets*, 2nd ed. (London: Hutchinson, 1961), 95–101.

11. WHEN A MOUNTAIN RAPES A RIVER, FROM BHATTUMURTI'S TELUGU *VASU'S LIFE*

1. David Shulman, "Empirical Observation and Embodied Nature in Sixteenth-Century South India" in *What Reason Promises: Essays on Reason, Nature, and History*, ed. Wendy Doniger, Peter Galison, and Susan Neiman (Berlin: De Gruyter, 2016), 95.

2. See the earlier passage from Kamban's *Ramayana* in this unit.

UNIT V. LOVE'S INTERIOR LANDSCAPES

1. A.K. Ramanujan, "Afterword," *The Interior Landscape: Love Poems from a Classical Tamil Anthology*, trans. A.K. Ramanujan (Bloomington: Indiana University Press, 1975), 115.

2. E.M. Forster, *Howard's End* (New York: Penguin, 2000), 159.

12. "TEN ON THE WILD BOAR"

1. Carissa, *kaḷā*—dark as a plum. The unripe fruit is poisonous; the ripe fruit is tart and nutritious.

2. Martha Ann Selby, *Tamil Love Poetry: The Five Hundred Short Poems of the Aiṅkuṟunūṟu* (New York: Columbia University Press, 2011), 13.

13. THREE POEMS ABOUT LOVE'S INNER MODES

1. The unbaked clay pot dissolves in water.

2. R. Cheran, *Thinai Mayakkam* (Nagercoil: Kalachuvadu, 2019), 47.

3. Perundevi, "Ethirk kavithai munnodi Nicanor Parra," *Kalkuthirai* 28 (2017): 132–36.

4. This is one of several popular battlefield songs by Putuvai Ratnathurai, the official LTTE bard. It was sung by the late S.G. Santhan.

5. *Kurontokai* 40. A.K. Ramanujan, trans., *Poems of Love and War* (New York: Columbia University Press, 1985), xi.

6. Ibid., 162.

7. Ibid., 145.

8. A. Daksinamurthy, trans., *Ancient Tamil Classic Pattuppattu in English (The Ten Tamil Idylls)* (Chennai: Tamizh Academy [SRM University], 2012), 266. See also the *Mathuraikanji* verses (160–176) in that same volume.

9. *Puṟanāṉūṟu* 46. A.K. Ramanujan, *Poems of Love and War* (New York: Columbia University Press, 1985), 122.

10. Both are published by Kalachuvadu (2018).

11. R. Cheran, "Theorizing diasporiCity," in *History and Imagination: Tamil Culture in the Global context*," ed. R. Cheran, Chelva Kanaganayakam, and Darshan Ambalavanar (Toronto: Mawenzi, 2008), 150–68.

12. Amrit Lal, "Today's Sangam Explores Grief, Trauma, and Exile," *Times of India*. https://timesofindia.indiatimes.com/city/chennai/Todays-Sangam-explores-grief-trauma-and-exile/articleshow/39691511.cms.

13. Personal communication with a parent in Switzerland, Nov. 21, 2018. This communication was part of an exchange on caste and second- and third-generation diaspora Tamils

on Instagram. For caste in Tamil diaspora, see Paramsothy Thanges, "Caste within the Sri Lankan Diaspora: Ur Associations and Territorial Belongings," *Anthropology Matters* 18, no. 1 (2018): 52–82.

14. NAMMALVAR'S TAMIL *A HUNDRED MEASURES OF TIME*

1. Nappinnai, the god's local Tamil wife.
2. Hans-Georg Gadamer, *Truth and Method* (London: Continuum 2006 [1975]), 305.
3. Arthur C. Danto, "Narrative Sentences," *History and Theory* 2, no. 2 (1962): 146–79.
4. Andrew Ollett, *Lilavai* (Cambridge, MA: Harvard University Press, 2021), 249, verse 1011.
5. Ellen Prince, "Toward a Taxonomy of Given–New Information," in *Radical Pragmatics*, ed. Peter Cole (New York: Academic Press, 1981), 223–54.
6. The distinction between primary and secondary qualities (not exactly in the terms invoked here) comes from John Locke, *An Essay Concerning Human Understanding* (London: Thomas Tegg, 1825 [1689]): 174–75.

15. A PERSIAN GHAZAL BY HAFEZ AND AN URDU GHAZAL BY GHALIB

1. This poem was translated in collaboration with Sergio La Porta.
2. Hence, the frequent references to the *ma'shūq* as a *but* or *ṣanam*—literally, an "idol."

CONTRIBUTORS

MUZAFFAR ALAM is a historian with field specialties in Mughal religious and literary cultures, and the South Asian world of Islam more generally. He teaches in the Department of South Asian Languages and Civilizations at the University of Chicago.

TALIA ARIAV is a researcher of premodern south India, interested in Sanskrit and Tamil literatures and in the cultural, historical, and religious worlds in which they were written and received. She is currently writing her doctoral dissertation in the Department of South Asian Languages and Civilizations at the University of Chicago.

YIGAL BRONNER is a Sanskritist whose areas of interest include literature, literary theory, and South Asian intellectual history more generally. He teaches in the Department of Asian Studies at the Hebrew University of Jerusalem.

R. CHERAN (CHERAN RUDHRAMOORTHY) is a Tamil poet whose poems have been translated in twenty-one languages. His areas of teaching and research include genocide, literatures of mass atrocity, and Tamil studies. He is a professor in the Department of Sociology, Anthropology, and Criminology at the University of Windsor.

JENNIFER CLARE is a writer, teacher, and translator. Her interests include comparative literature, literary theory, and Tamil, but mostly she is interested in people and how they make sense of the world. She lives in San Francisco with her family.

Poet and translator PETER COLE divides his time between Jerusalem and New Haven, where he teaches each spring at Yale University.

WHITNEY COX's primary languages of research are Sanskrit and Tamil, especially poetry and literary theory; his other interests include medieval political and cultural history and premodern Shaivism. He teaches in the Department of South Asian Languages and Civilizations at the University of Chicago.

TAWFIQ DA'ADLI is an archeologist and art historian, specializing in Islamic material culture throughout the medieval period. He teaches in the Department of Islam and Middle Eastern Studies and the Department of Art History at the Hebrew University of Jerusalem.

DONALD R. DAVIS, JR., studies the history of religion and law in medieval India, especially the Hindu law tradition. He teaches in the Department of Asian Studies at the University of Texas at Austin.

WENDY DONIGER'S main claim to fame is that David Shulman was her first PhD student when she was a lecturer at the School of Oriental and African Studies in London in the early 1970s. She is now the Mircea Eliade Professor Emerita of the History of Religions at the University of Chicago.

SIVAN GOREN-ARZONY studies Kerala's literary traditions, in particular Sanskrit and Maṇipravāḷam. Her areas of interest include literary theory, vernacular poetics, Kerala's social history, and the study of women in premodern South Asia. She is a junior fellow at the Harvard Society of Fellows.

N. GOVINDARAJAN teaches Tamil Language and Literature at the American College, Madurai, Tamil Nadu, India. His areas of interest include Tamil classical and devotional literatures, Tamil literary theories, and colonial Tamil studies.

YEHOSHUA GRANAT'S scholarly work is focused on Hebrew poetry of late antiquity, the Middle Ages, and the early modern period. He teaches in the Department of Hebrew Literature at the Hebrew University of Jerusalem.

CHARLES HALLISEY is a student of Buddhist literatures whose areas of interest also include Buddhist ethics, Buddhist scriptures, and the cultural history of Theravada Buddhism more generally. He teaches at Harvard Divinity School.

THIBAUT D'HUBERT works on Middle Bengali and Indo-Persian literature. His research focuses on poetics, the history of literacy, and textual criticism. He teaches Bengali in the Department of South Asian Languages and Civilizations at the University of Chicago.

JAMAL A. JONES studies Sanskrit and Telugu with interests in poetics, literary history, and the wider social and religious history of South Asia. He teaches in the Department of Asian Languages and Cultures at the University of Wisconsin-Madison.

SONAM KACHRU is a student of the history of philosophy. His work centers on the history of Buddhist thought and literature in South Asia. He teaches in the Department of Religious Studies at the University of Virginia.

RAJEEV KINRA is a scholar of South Asian and global history and comparative literature, specializing in early modern Indo-Persian literary and political culture. He teaches in the Department of History and the Comparative Literary Studies Program at Northwestern University.

T.M. KRISHNA is a musician, author, and public intellectual. Uncommon in his rendition and original in his interpretation of music, Krishna speaks and writes about issues affecting the human condition. He is the author of multiple critically acclaimed books that traverse the intersection of music, culture, and politics.

GABRIEL LEVIN, a poet and an essayist, lives in Jerusalem. His own vagabonding has been limited to the Levant, but he does hope one day to extend his wanderings to south India.

ILANIT LOEWY SHACHAM is a scholar of South Asian literature, focusing on texts in classical Telugu and Sanskrit. She teaches in the Department of East Asian Studies at Tel Aviv University.

AFSAR MOHAMMAD teaches in the Department of South Asian Studies at the University of Pennsylvania. His areas of interest include South Asian Islam, Muslim writing, Hindu-Muslim shared practices, and Telugu studies.

ANDREW OLLETT studies the intellectual and cultural traditions of premodern South Asia, especially literature, literary theory, and the philosophy of language. He teaches in the Department of South Asian Languages and Civilizations at the University of Chicago.

DEVEN M. PATEL is a Sanskritist whose research interests include literature, literary theory, and philosophy. He teaches in the Department of South Asia Studies at the University of Pennsylvania.

SHELDON POLLOCK is general editor of the Murty Classical Library of India. He taught Sanskrit and classical Indian studies at Columbia University until his retirement in 2021.

GAUTHAM REDDY is a historian of colonial India. His areas of interest include Telugu literature, book history, and the intellectual and cultural history of southern India. He serves as research librarian for South Asian Studies and Religion at Emory University.

ANNA LISE SEASTRAND is an art historian whose interests intersect in the embodied experience of art, literature, and history of southeastern India. She teaches at the University of Minnesota.

MEIR SHAHAR teaches at Tel Aviv University. His research interests cover the fields of Chinese religion and literature, Chinese martial arts history, the impact of Indian mythology upon Chinese culture, and, most recently, Chinese animal studies.

SANJAY SUBRAHMANYAM works on South Asian, Indian Ocean, and other histories, usually of the early modern period. He teaches history at UCLA.

GARY TUBB is a Sanskritist whose interests include poetry and poetics, grammatical and commentarial traditions, and connections between philosophy, religion, and literature. He teaches in the Department of South Asian Languages and Civilizations at the University of Chicago.

KESAVAN VELUTHAT is a historian with a special interest in the earlier periods of India's past. A trained epigraphist, he is also at home with Tamil, Kannada, and Sanskrit. He is currently director of the Institute for Studies in the Heritage of Coastal Kerala, India.

ARCHANA VENKATESAN is a translator of Tamil bhakti texts with an allied interest in Tamil temple festivals. She holds a joint appointment in Religious Studies and Comparative Literature at the University of California, Davis.

ANAND VENKATKRISHNAN studies the lives of scholars in early modern and modern South Asia. He teaches at the University of Chicago Divinity School.

Founded in 1893,
UNIVERSITY OF CALIFORNIA PRESS
publishes bold, progressive books and journals
on topics in the arts, humanities, social sciences,
and natural sciences—with a focus on social
justice issues—that inspire thought and action
among readers worldwide.

The UC PRESS FOUNDATION
raises funds to uphold the press's vital role
as an independent, nonprofit publisher, and
receives philanthropic support from a wide
range of individuals and institutions—and from
committed readers like you. To learn more, visit
ucpress.edu/supportus.